Dog Grooming For Dummies

Cheat Sheet

Keeping Basic Equipment and Supplies on Hand

These items will get you grooming fast, but be sure to check out Chapter 3 for a more complete list of tools that you need to invest in over time or when your dog has special grooming needs.

- **Comb.** A medium-toothed comb is a good all-around comb, but get a fine-toothed comb if your dog has thin hair or a wide-toothed comb if her hair is thick. And get a flea comb for both removing fleas and tangles.

- **Brush.** A slicker brush is a good all-purpose brush, but get a curry brush if your dog has short hair or a pin brush if your dog has a long single coat.

- **pH-balanced shampoo and conditioner made for dogs.** Keep plenty of towels on hand for drying.

- **A toothbrush and toothpaste made for dogs.**

- **Dog toenail clippers and styptic powder.** The powder helps stop bleeding in case you clip too close to the quick (Chapter 6 helps you avoid doing that).

- **Otic solution, forceps, and gauze.** Use these tools to clean your dog's ears.

- **Electric clipper.** If your dog's coat needs to be clipped, you need a good electric clipper and blades including a No. 10 general use blade.

Following an Efficient Grooming Routine

These basic steps form a great grooming routine you should perform at least once a month, more often depending on the type of hair your dog has (check out Parts II and III for more detailed guidance). Many of these tasks (such as brushing your dog's teeth) should be done a minimum of once a week, but others such as bathing and clipping need to be done less frequently.

1. Brush out your dog, thoroughly removing any tangles or mats (see Chapter 5).
2. Do a prebath clip or strip if your dog's coat needs it (see Chapters 7 and 12).
3. Express anal sacs if needed (see Chapter 5).
4. Bathe and rinse thoroughly (see Chapter 5).
5. Dry using towels, a dog hair dryer, or human hair dryer set to no heat (see Chapter 5).
6. Clean ears with otic solution; dry thoroughly (see Chapter 6).
7. Clean eye tear stains if there are any (see Chapter 6).
8. Trim toenails (see Chapter 6).
9. Brush teeth (see Chapter 6).
10. Brush out again and apply any leave-in coat conditioner (see Chapter 5).
11. Clip hair if necessary (see Chapter 7).

For Dummies: Bestselling Book Series for Beginners

Dog Grooming For Dummies®

Cheat
Sheet

Easy Steps to Grooming Nails, Teeth, and Ears

These tasks may seem frivolous, but they're as important to your dog's good health as heartworm preventative and pest protection, so perform these tasks at least every week (see Chapter 6 for more details).

Nail trimming

1. Hold the foot steady.
2. Snip off a small bit of the end of each toenail below the quick.
3. Repeat Steps 1 and 2 on each foot, and don't forget to clip the dewclaws.

Ear cleaning

1. Gently hold your dog's head so that the open ear is exposed.
2. Apply otic solution.
3. Using a sterile gauze pad or sponge, gently wipe out the excess solution.

Teeth brushing

1. Squeeze some doggie toothpaste onto the brush and allow your dog to lick it off.
2. Flip up your dog's lips and gently rub the toothbrush and toothpaste against your dog's teeth and gums for a few seconds.
3. Give your dog a treat, even if he allows you to work on his teeth for only a few seconds.

Quick Fix for Stinky Stuff

Keep this recipe on hand for when your dog comes home smelling like a skunk rather than a rose.

1. Combine ½ quart hydrogen peroxide, ⅛ cup of baking soda, and 1 teaspoon hand dishwashing soap in an open container.
2. Draw a tepid bath and put your dog in it.
3. Apply the solution liberally throughout your dog's coat and suds him up well (to the skin). Avoid getting any solution in his eyes.
4. Rinse your dog well, drain the tub, and rinse well again.
5. Smell for any spots you've missed, and repeat Steps 1 through 4 if necessary.
6. Follow up with a pH-balanced shampoo and conditioner for dogs; rinse well to remove all residues.

Mat Removing Tips

- If the mat isn't too bad, spray it with detangler solution and use a comb to slowly work the mat free. Work from the outside of the mat (where the hair isn't tangled) and slowly untangle the hair without pulling.
- If the mat won't come out with a comb, try cutting through the mat with a mat rake.
- If the mat rake isn't cutting it (so to speak), try using a mat splitter. Start by splitting the mat in horizontal or vertical strips and then use either a mat rake or a comb to tackle the smaller pieces individually.
- In the worst conditions, use electric clippers to slowly shave away the mat.

Wiley, the Wiley Publishing logo, For Dummies, the Dummies Man logo, the For Dummies Bestselling Book Series logo and all related trade dress are trademarks or registered trademarks of John Wiley & Sons, Inc. and/or its affiliates. All other trademarks are property of their respective owners.

Copyright © 2006 Wiley Publishing, Inc. All rights reserved. Item 7390-5. For more information about Wiley Publishing, call 1-800-762-2974.

For Dummies: Bestselling Book Series for Beginners

Dog Grooming

FOR

DUMMIES®

Dog Grooming

FOR

DUMMIES®

by Margaret H. Bonham

WILEY

Wiley Publishing, Inc.

Dog Grooming For Dummies®

Published by
Wiley Publishing, Inc.
111 River St.
Hoboken, NJ 07030-5774
www.wiley.com

Copyright © 2006 by Wiley Publishing, Inc., Indianapolis, Indiana

Published by Wiley Publishing, Inc., Indianapolis, Indiana

Published simultaneously in Canada

WILEY

About the Author

Margaret H. "Maggie" Bonham is a four-time award-winning professional dog, cat, and science fiction and fantasy author who lives in Colorado. She has worked as a vet tech, grooming dogs for clients. She also has groomed various dogs as pets and for show. She has trained more than 50 dogs in sledding, agility, packing, obedience, weight pulling, and conformation, earning multiple titles on several of her own dogs. She has written educational coursework (dog agility and activities) for dog trainers with Thomson Education Direct. She also is a professional member of Association of Pet Dog Trainers (APDT).

Maggie has been a professional writer since 1995, writing novels, nonfiction books, short stories, courses, educational materials, and articles. Her books include *Having Fun with Agility; A Dog's Wisdom: A Heartwarming View of Life; The Complete Guide to Mutts: Selection, Care and Celebration from Puppyhood to Senior; Bring Me Home: Dogs Make Great Pets; Bring Me Home: Cats Make Great Pets; The Complete Idiot's Guide to Labrador Retrievers; The Complete Idiot's Guide to Dog Health and Nutrition; The Complete Idiot's Guide to Designer Dogs; The Complete Idiot's Guide to Golden Retrievers; Soft Coated Wheaten Terriers; An Introduction to Dog Agility; Northern Breeds: The Simple Guide to Getting Active with Your Dog; Cancer and Your Pet: The Complete Guide to the Latest Research, Treatments, and Options; Your Siberian Husky's Life: Your Complete Guide to Raising Your Pet from Puppy to Companion;* and *Prophecy of Swords.* Her work has appeared in various national publications including *Dog Fancy, Dog World, Dog and Kennel, Pet Life, Pet View, The Dog Daily, The Daily Cat, Catnip, Natural Pet, Contract Professional,* and *Mushing* magazine. She has been a columnist and contributing editor for *Dog and Kennel* and *PetView* magazines, and she was a frequent contributor to Pets.com and Vetmedcenter.com Internet sites. She is editor of *Merial PawPrints,* a newsletter that covers topics about dogs and cats and is distributed to veterinarians for their clients.

Maggie currently trains various breeds for agility, sled-dog racing, obedience, and conformation. She lives with many purebred and mixed breed dogs, and one cat.

Dedication

To Larry and the Malamutes. And to Hailey, who is pretty much self-grooming.

Author's Acknowledgments

I'd like to thank the following people who made this book possible:

- Jessica Faust of Bookends
- Stacy Kennedy, acquisitions editor at Wiley
- Alissa Schwipps, senior project editor at Wiley
- Larry Bonham, my husband, who puts up with my crazy schedules
- Kodiak, Kira, Haegl, Hailey, and Mishka, who constantly amuse me
- Sue Johnson, who taught me how to groom for show

Publisher's Acknowledgments

We're proud of this book; please send us your comments through our Dummies online registration form located at www.dummies.com/register/.

Some of the people who helped bring this book to market include the following:

Acquisitions, Editorial, and Media Development

Senior Project Editor: Alissa Schwipps

Acquisitions Editor: Stacy Kennedy

Copy Editor: E. Neil Johnson

Editorial Program Coordinator: Hanna K. Scott

Technical Editor: Janice Fehn

Senior Editorial Manager: Jennifer Ehrlich

Editorial Assistants: Erin Calligan, Nadine Bell, David Lutton

Cover Photos: © Seth Richardson/ Wiley Publishing, Inc

Cartoons: Rich Tennant (www.the5thwave.com)

Composition Services

Project Coordinator: Jennifer Theriot

Layout and Graphics: Denny Hager, Stephanie D. Jumper, Clint Lahnen, Lynsey Osborn, Alicia B. South, Julie Trippetti

Special Art: Illustrations by Barbara Frake. Photographs by Todd Adamson.

Proofreaders: Techbooks

Indexer: Techbooks

Special Help
Danielle Voirol

Publishing and Editorial for Consumer Dummies

Diane Graves Steele, Vice President and Publisher, Consumer Dummies

Joyce Pepple, Acquisitions Director, Consumer Dummies

Kristin A. Cocks, Product Development Director, Consumer Dummies

Michael Spring, Vice President and Publisher, Travel

Kelly Regan, Editorial Director, Travel

Publishing for Technology Dummies

Andy Cummings, Vice President and Publisher, Dummies Technology/General User

Composition Services

Gerry Fahey, Vice President of Production Services

Debbie Stailey, Director of Composition Services

Contents at a Glance

Table of Contents

Introduction

· ·

Do you consider your dog a family member? Chances are you said yes before you finished reading the sentence. You're in good company. Most pet owners consider their dogs as important as other family members or even a child. According to the Association of Pet Products Manufacturers, every day some 44 million households wake up to the loving licks of humankind's oldest and dearest friend.

Dogs have served people as protectors, workers, friends, and partners throughout thousands of years. And yet the role of the dog is changing. A few hundred years ago, not many people would be reading a book about grooming their dogs. Back then, dogs for the most part were outdoor animals that were kept in a doghouse or kennel and treated perhaps a little better than a tool or at best a type of livestock. With the exception of the pampered lap dogs and the few working dogs that shared the master's home, most dogs had a pretty tough life, usually hanging out in the backyard (if there was one) or running around on the farm.

How times have changed! Dogs have moved from outside to inside and wiggled their way into the hearts (and even onto the couches and beds) of their owners. But now that they've arrived — so to speak — pet owners want their dogs to be presentable. A dirty dog is no joy; a clean dog is pure happiness.

And that's what this book is all about. You're no dummy for wanting a clean and presentable dog. A well-groomed dog usually is one that goes places and is better socialized than one who isn't. You don't mind having a well-groomed dog around, and you're friends and neighbors are likely to think how wonderful your dog is because he's well-groomed.

About This Book

Many books about grooming dogs are on the shelves of libraries and bookstores, so you may be wondering what makes this one different than the others. Well, first of all, you don't have to be a grooming expert (or an expert with dogs) to read and understand this book. I explain everything in easy-to-understand language that someone who's never groomed a dog can understand.

And you can read this book any way you'd like. I'd prefer that you read it cover-to-cover, but quite frankly that isn't what this book is about. This book is set up in a modular fashion where you can pick your topic and start reading about it right away. You don't need to wade through text to find out what the best remedy is for de-skunking a dog (and trust me, you don't want to when your dog is skunked) — just flip through the table of contents or the index to find the section you're looking for and then read it.

Although I talk about aspects of dog grooming that you may never use with a pet dog — preparing for a dog show is one — I have plenty of information about how to groom the everyday pet. Who knows? The next dog you get may be a purebred you'll want to show. I go into different coat types and what you need to do with them, even if your dog is a mixed breed, all so you can figure out which section applies to your dog and get useful information.

You'll love being able to go to the section that's most appropriate to you and your dog. Whether it's simple weekly grooming, choosing a professional groomer, clipping a dog, or getting rid of fleas, this book is for you.

Conventions Used in This Book

To help you navigate through this book, I've set up a few conventions:

- *Italic* is used for emphasis and to highlight new words or terms that are defined.

- **Boldfaced** text is used to indicate the action part of numbered steps and to highlight key words in bulleted lists.

- All Web addresses appear in `monofont` for easy identification.

Many different books treat dogs as objects rather than as beings. I consider dogs to be "he"or "she," not "it," so you'll see me refer to dogs in this manner. Dogs aren't objects, they're companions, and I know they'd be offended if they knew I referred to them as "its" in a book.

Likewise, many books don't capitalize dog breeds, which I think is very wrong, so I do and so do my contemporaries — and with good reason! The American Kennel Club and the United Kennel Club both capitalize dog breeds. What's more is that many of the breed names actually come from names of ancient peoples and countries. For example, the word, "Malamute" is an Anglicized name of a tribe of Inuit people in Alaska. So a dog isn't an Alaskan malamute, a golden retriever, or a komondor. The dog is an Alaskan Malamute, a Golden Retriever, or a Komondor.

I also lean toward colloquial words to describe things. Dogs have legs not limbs (isn't a limb on a tree?), and they pee and they poop, rather than urinate and defecate. I use the words paws and nails and puppy dog tails. Because that's what I use and that's what I'm comfortable with. I hope that's okay by you.

What You're Not to Read

You don't absolutely, positively have to read every thing in this book, but that doesn't mean that you shouldn't read it all. Instead, it means that if you're in a hurry, you can skip some topics and still not miss the important stuff you need. The skipable text includes:

- **Text in sidebars:** Sidebars are shaded boxes of text that appear throughout the book. They're crammed full of interesting information and personal insight that you may find useful, but they're more in-depth and more technical than the regular text.
- **Anything with the "Technical Stuff" icon attached:** This icon (see the "Icons used in the Book" section later in the Introduction) gives you a more in-depth explanation of what I'm talking about, but it isn't really necessary to read these paragraphs.
- **The copyright page, the acknowledgments, and the dedication:** You really don't have to read these pages unless you're bored or you're looking for a cure for insomnia.

Foolish Assumptions

I thought a lot about you, dear reader, while writing this book, and here's what I assumed about you:

- You own a dog and you're wondering how to keep him clean, nice looking, and sweet smelling.
- You want to groom your dog at home to save the expense of professional grooming, but you don't have much time to wade through pages of grooming texts to figure out how to get your dog looking his best.
- You may have a dog that has a coat that requires a little more time-consuming grooming and care than you expected, and you want some time- and hassle-saving tips to keep your dog's coat in great shape.

   ✔ You want to know whether you can really groom your dog or if you per-haps need to take him to a professional groomer.

   ✔ Maybe you know quite a bit about dog grooming, and you're considering grooming for show or professionally.

How This Book Is Organized

To make this book easy to read and understand, I've grouped *Dog Grooming For Dummies* into five easy-to-manage parts. Each part covers a different aspect of grooming.

Part I: Getting Started

In this part, you discover the basics of why grooming is important and how to get ready to groom your dog. I cover why you need to groom your dog (some reasons may surprise you!) and whether you need perhaps to hire a professional groomer to help get you started (or do the job instead). I cover the basics when it comes to coat types and anatomy — the stuff you need to know before breaking out the brushes and combs. I also cover how you can train your dog for grooming. As odd as that may sound, if you can't get your dog to stand still for a brushing, it's tough to keep him clean. Lastly, I talk about buying quality equipment and supplies for grooming your dog — including what works and what doesn't.

Part II: Making Your Dog Look Good: The Basics

In this part, you get all the basics for grooming a dog. I cover everyday groom-ing techniques and basic clipping — stuff you need to know for every dog.

Part III: Grooming by Coat Type: Beyond the Basics

In this part, I give you the scoop on the basic coat types — what breeds have them and how to go about grooming each particular coat. I also provide you more-advanced coat-specific tips for grooming for the show ring.

Part IV: Grooming Specialties

In this part, you discover the intricacies of grooming a dog — from dealing with skin and hair problems to turning professional and opening your own business. Whether it's handling serious hair disasters (like sticky gum in the fur) or recognizing a hereditary or congenital problem with your dog's coat, I cover it. I also cover emergencies that I hope you never run into while grooming your dog, and I tell you about the dog show scene — what's it all about and how important grooming is when showing your dog.

Part V: The Part of Tens

In this part, I cover some interesting facts that can help make you a more knowledgeable groomer and take some of the hassle out of the grooming experience for you and your dog.

But wait — there's more! Turn to the handy dandy Appendix at the end of the book to find dog grooming Web sites, the names of grooming magazines, and other stuff that helps you discover even more about grooming and get the equipment and supplies you need.

Icons Used in This Book

The icons used in this book help steer you to particular kinds of information that may be useful to you:

You see this icon any time I suggest time- or hassle-saving advice that makes grooming your dog easier or more comfortable.

This icon appears when I explain important information that you shouldn't overlook and that sometimes bears repeating.

This icon appears when I'm explaining topics that include the potential for harming you or your dog. Don't ignore this icon!

I'm a geek at heart, so you'll see several of these icons with interesting information that may be a little more technical than most people want to know, but it's helpful if you want a fuller picture.

Where to Go from Here

Where do you want to start reading? Well, it depends on what you're looking for. Try these hints:

- ✔ If you want to know what tools you need to buy for grooming, look in Chapter 3.

- ✔ If you want to know how to do basic grooming on your dog, check out Chapters 5 and 6 for starters.

- ✔ Need to get rid of a mat in a dog's coat? Chapter 5 can help you.

- ✔ You can find out how to get rid of really nasty stuff in a dog's coat (including skunk spray) by perusing Chapter 15.

- ✔ Check out Chapter 16, so you can recognize possible health problems associated with the appearance of your dog's coat.

- ✔ If you want to show your dog, Chapter 18 explains dog shows and helps you prepare your dog for the show ring. Then you choose a chapter in Part III that pertains to your specific dog's coat.

If you're looking for something that I haven't mentioned here, check out the table of contents or index or peruse the Appendix for other resources.

So now you're ready to begin grooming your dog. I know you'll enjoy it as much as I do, and I know you'll find this book a helpful guide.

Part I
Getting Started

The 5th Wave   By Rich Tennant

"We're very careful about grooming. First I'll check his teeth and nails, then trim any excess hair from his ears, nose, and around the eyes. After checking for fleas and parasites I'll let Roger go off to work so I can begin grooming the dog."

In this part . . .

Grooming your dog is an important part of dog ownership. In this part, I cover why you need to groom your dog, or whether perhaps you need to hire a professional groomer instead. Part I also covers the basics when it comes to coat types and anatomy and how easy or difficult it is to groom dogs with various characteristics. I also explain how you can train your dog to be groomed, and I provide insight on what grooming equipment and supplies work best.

Chapter 1

What Good Grooming Is All About

In This Chapter

▶ Understanding why grooming is important to your dog's health

▶ Tallying up the costs of grooming

▶ Determining which dogs (and coat types) need the most and least grooming

▶ Figuring out when to do it yourself and when to hire a pro

I know that when I think of grooming, the vision of the froufrou doggie beauty parlor springs to mind, complete with bows, silly hairstyles, and nail polish. I've got news for you: I've never put a bow in my dogs' hair, and my dogs would protest mightily if I even suggested painting their nails.

But grooming's important. No one likes a bad hair day. Your dog certainly doesn't; he feels just as uncomfortable as you do when his hair is all ratty and snarled. But grooming is more than just having him look and feel good; it's vital for his health. And it's more than just a bath — it includes brushing, combing, keeping his teeth and ears clean, clipping his nails, and keeping him in top shape.

In this chapter, you get an overview of dog grooming and why it's so important for your dog's health and well-being. You also find out how much time and money it takes to keep your dog well-groomed and when a little help from the pros is more than just greatly appreciated — when it's a necessity.

Big Hairy Deal: Discovering Why Grooming Is Important

Your dog isn't healthy if she doesn't look good outside. A lackluster coat or one that's plagued with external parasites and sores is just the tip of the iceberg. If she looks icky outside, she probably feels icky inside, too. That's because her coat mirrors her health. Her outward appearance can be a signal of internal problems that no amount of brushing can fix. Look at the following sections for some of the various reasons grooming is important to your dog's overall health.

Sociability

When your dog is clean, you want him around more so you can bond and enjoy each other's company. Sure, he likes to play in the dirt and roll in stinky stuff, but he also likes how it feels to be clean, just like you do. And although he doesn't care how he smells (except when he's had the misfortune of meeting up with a skunk — check out Chapter 15 for more about deskunking a skunked pooch.), you do! You're less likely to enjoy having a dirty, smelly dog around, but a clean, refreshing one is definitely a more enjoyable companion.

Presenting a positive public image

Keeping your dog clean says something about you; it says that you're a responsible dog owner and that you care for your dog. You may be able to take your dog places where dogs aren't usually allowed. When practical, I've actually taken dogs to book signings and shopping malls — where dogs aren't usually permitted. One look at my dogs told the people in charge that I take care of my dogs and that they're well-mannered.

Your dog no doubt will join you on walks outside your home, but you may have occasion to do other things with your dog, such as go to special events or even compete in various dog sports and activities. Maybe you'd like to do some social work like visiting the sick or elderly. Your dog can become a therapy dog, but being clean and friendly is vitally important for your dog under those circumstances (see Chapter 5 for more about brushing and bathing your dog). No one wants to pet a dirty dog, no matter how lovable.

Dogs aren't always allowed everywhere you'd like to take them, no matter how well-behaved and well-groomed they are. The reason some places are off limits has to do with health department regulations, so make sure that you always get permission before taking a dog to a place that doesn't normally accept them.

Eliminating the spread of dirt and disease

Dirty dogs track dirt into your home and get dirt on your clothing, furniture, and carpet.

Ungroomed dogs are more likely to be infected by internal and external parasites, and external parasites — fleas and ticks — can harbor dangerous diseases, such as bubonic plague, typhus, Lyme disease, and Rocky Mountain spotted fever, which can make you and your family sick. If your dog is ungroomed, she may be carrying funguses such as ringworm that young kids and the elderly can pick up from her. Keeping your dog clean and free from these problems through good grooming eliminates many potential health problems.

Determining whether something's really wrong with your dog internally

Plenty of good reasons exist for grooming your dog. One such reason is finding out the difference between a coat that looks bad because it's dirty and one that looks bad because something is wrong with your dog. Grooming also eliminates various problems associated with an ill-kept dog, such as external parasites or open sores caused by a matted and dirty coat that traps bacteria.

A lackluster coat can be a sign that one or more things are seriously wrong with him, including

- ✔ Poor nutrition
- ✔ Allergies
- ✔ Internal parasites
- ✔ Hormonal imbalances or diseases
- ✔ External parasites
- ✔ Cancer
- ✔ Other diseases

Any one of these problems can severely shorten your dog's life, or in extreme conditions, even kill your dog. Knowing how to groom your dog so that he looks the best he possibly can helps you separate potential health problems from problems caused by not properly caring for your dog.

Considering the Necessary Investment

Now that you know that good grooming is necessary for your dog's health and well-being, you may wonder just how much it costs to have a good-looking dog. You may have visited the local groomer and asked how much bathing and/or clipping your dog costs. If you've done the math, you know it can be a bit pricey, especially when money's in short supply.

The truth is that when you start grooming your dog, you can do things just to get by, all the while keeping an eye out for the many places where you can buy really good equipment and supplies for not a lot of money. (Be sure to check out Chapter 3 and the Appendix for some good sources for grooming supplies.)

Your investment, however, isn't gauged entirely in terms of money. Your time is worth something, and grooming requires some of that, too.

You may find that grooming is expensive in time *and* money, or you may find it relatively inexpensive. Much of the cost of grooming depends on what kind of dog you have, what type of hair your dog has, and whether you're grooming your dog as a pet or for show. Regardless of cost, grooming is a part of dog ownership, and as a pet owner, you must take care of your dog for her health and well-being — not to mention how really spiffy she'll look.

Anyway, the sections that follow can help you figure out how much time and money you need to keep your pup well-groomed.

The cost in money

Most people think and talk about costs in terms of money. You know: How much in dollars is this or that going to cost? Well, the bad news is that getting stocked up with grooming equipment and supplies is fairly expensive (see Chapter 3 for more about the costs of supplies). The good news is that after you dole out the initial investment for your equipment, you probably won't encounter that expense again unless something breaks or wears out, and by comparison, the cost of buying your own supplies is relatively cheap.

How much does at-home grooming cost compared to a year's worth of grooming sessions from a pro? Well, if you're paying from $20 to $50 a month in grooming, you're paying $240 to $600 a year. You can buy some pretty nice grooming equipment for that amount of money, and doing it yourself pays off during the first year or two.

Some dogs need more grooming equipment and supplies than others. For example, a dog who needs daily brushing and regular clipping is going to need more equipment than a dog with a wash-and-wear coat. (See "Familiarizing Yourself with Your Dog's Coat" in this chapter for more on fur types.)

The cost in time

Although the old adage that time is money is true where dog grooming is concerned, you nevertheless need to think about the work and the fun you can have when you bathe or brush your dog. As you know, grooming your dog is as much a necessity as housetraining your dog or taking him to the vet for an annual exam.

When taking time into account, be aware that

- The shorter the natural coat of the dog, the less grooming he's going to need.
- The smaller the dog, the less grooming he's going to need.
- Dogs who need stripping (see Chapter 12) or clipping (see Chapter 11) usually take more time than dogs who don't.
- A dog with long hair (see Chapter 13) or a double coat (see Chapter 9) takes more time to groom than one with a medium- or short-haired coat (see Chapter 8).
- Different procedures take different amounts of time. A quick brushing with a well-maintained coat takes less time than a bath (see Chapter 5).
- The condition of your dog's coat dictates the amount of time grooming takes. Brushing out a clean dog with a well-maintained coat takes very little time when compared to one with a dirty and matted coat.
- Dogs with wash-and-wear coats can usually get away with once-a-week grooming.
- Dogs with average coats can usually get away with twice-a-week grooming.
- Dogs with high-maintenance coats need to be groomed three times or more per week.
- When some dogs are adolescents or when they're shedding, they require coat care *every day*.

When planning your initial grooming session, you need to set aside at least two hours, because you'll be going more slowly and your dog's coat may not be in the best condition. Later, you can whittle down your grooming sessions to an hour or even a half-hour as you get better at grooming and your dog's coat is better maintained.

If you don't have the time to groom your dog's coat into good shape, consider first taking him to a professional groomer and then maintaining the coat after the groomer works it into manageable shape. Doing so reduces the hassle of trying to groom your dog's coat into the proper condition without using too much of your valuable time.

The added investment: Grooming for show

Grooming your dog for show costs plenty more in terms of time and money over what you'd spend on grooming a pet dog. Special show clips (see Chapter 11) and stripped breeds (see Chapter 12) usually take a while to develop and maintain. Many coats need special leave-in coat conditioners, bodifiers, and coat dressings. See Chapter 18 for more information about grooming your dog for show.

Familiarizing Yourself with Your Dog's Coat

Dogs have some of the most amazing coats, ranging from curly to straight, puffy to wiry, bald to long. Their fur comes in short coats, long coats, and every variation in between. Some dogs even come equipped with dreadlocks!

It's truly hard to believe that the wolf produced descendants with such wide varieties of coats, but it did, and that means you're going to have to evaluate the type of coat your dog has and what that means in terms of the grooming equipment and supplies you're going to need. In the sections that follow, I fill you in about the differences in the basic types of coats.

Coat types: Single versus double

Dogs basically have two types of coats:

- Most dogs have a *double coat* (also referred to as a *two-ply coat*) that has a top coat and an undercoat. The *top coat* is composed of stiffer *guard hairs,* which tend to be naturally water-repellant. Top coats protect the dog's skin and undercoat, acting as a natural guard against the elements. The *undercoat* is a fleecy or downy type of fur that's a bit shorter than the top coat. The undercoat serves as insulation to keep the dog warm during cold or inhospitable weather. The dog sheds (or *blows out*) the undercoat twice a year — it's a seasonal thing.

- Some dogs have a *single coat,* in which only a top coat is present without an undercoat, often making dogs with this kind of coat shed less than their double-coated counterparts.

You can tell what kind of coat your dog has in two ways. The first way is easy: Read the American Kennel Club (AKC) breed standard for your breed and look under the *coat* listing. The second way is to part the hairs on your dog's coat to find out whether it's a longer, harsh coat combined with soft, downy fur. If so, your dog has a double coat. If the hair is more or less even and doesn't have an undercoat, then your dog has a single coat.

Both types of coats, however, have different issues when it comes to grooming, so be aware that one type isn't necessarily better than another. Knowing the type of coat your dog has helps you determine how to groom him properly. Knowing whether your dog is going to go through a seasonal shed, or blow his coat, is also important — no sense in being surprised when your dog leaves enough hair on the rug to knit three more dogs his size!

Defining coat terms

Many funny-sounding words are associated with dog coats. They're worth mentioning, because you may come across them when working on a particular breed or reading a particular breed standard (see Part II of this book). Here's a rundown of various coat textures and what they mean:

- **Blow coat:** Describes the yearly or biannual shedding that some dog breeds go through. The coat comes out in handfuls during a short period of time.

- **Bristle coat:** A wiry or broken coat, or can mean *bristly coat,* such as the one worn by the Chinese Shar-Pei.

- **Broken coat:** See *wire coat.*

- **Corded coat:** A coat that has dreadlocks.

- **Crinkly coat:** A wire coat found on the Wire (Haired) Fox Terrier.

- **Curly coat:** A coat with curls, like that of the Poodle or the Curly-Coated Retriever.

- **Double coat:** A coat with an undercoat and a top coat.

- **Guard hairs:** See *top coat.*

- **Linty coat:** A coat that has an unusual soft, downy texture. (Also what your light-colored dog gets when you carry her around while you're wearing black cashmere.)

- **Open coat:** A sparsely haired coat; usually a single coat.

- **Out of coat:** Describes a dog who has shed his undercoat and is waiting for his new coat to grow in. Out-of-coat dogs usually are not as pretty as when they're in full coat.

- **Pily coat:** A coat with a dense, harsh top coat with a soft, fur-like undercoat. Usually found in Dandie Dinmont Terriers.

- **Single coat:** A coat that lacks an undercoat.

- **Smooth coat:** A short coat that lays back against the dog's skin.

- **Stand-off coat:** A long coat that does not lay flat against the body but stands straight up. (Also the kind of coat your dog will have if the two of you can't come to terms about grooming.)

- **Top coat:** The outer coat that protects the dog's skin and undercoat. Usually harsh and weather resistant.

- **Two-ply coat:** See *double coat.*

- **Undercoat:** The downy second coat that lies beneath the top coat. It usually is shed once or twice a year.

- **Wire coat:** A type of harsh coat that may be single or double with stiff, wiry hairs.

Whenever I talk about double coats in this book, I talk about them in two ways. One is to describe dogs who have what can be considered a *natural coat* — that is, a coat with two layers. The second way is to describe longer-haired breeds that have those two-ply coats that obviously need more care than the standard medium coat.

Coat textures

In the same way there are different types of coats, different coats have different textures. Understanding the texture of your dog's coat is crucial for proper grooming. The following list describes different coat textures:

- **Smooth coats:** The smooth-coated or short-coated dog has very short hair that lays back against the dog's skin. A smooth coat can be either double-coated or single-coated, depending on the breed. These coats tend not to be much of a hassle when it comes to grooming — even though they do shed. Dalmatians and Bulldogs have his kind of hair.

- **Wire coats:** The wire coat (broken coat) is a type of coat that is wiry on the outside and often has a soft undercoat on the inside, but it can be a single coat. Wire coats are wavy looking, but when you pet them, the hair feels a bit coarse. Think Terrier when you think about wiry coats. These coats usually need to be stripped or clipped, which adds an extra step to the average grooming routine (see Chapters 11 and 12).

- **Curly coats:** The curly coats are few in number, but you'll recognize them. They're the Poodles, the Portuguese Water Dogs, and the Irish Water Spaniels. These dogs have curly coats that require extreme maintenance, including clipping and brushing (see Chapters 7, 11, and 14).

- **Corded coats:** Dogs with dreadlocks or corded coats have coats that are twisted into dreadlocks. These coats need a fair amount of work upfront to prevent the hair from tangling into mats. After the cords are twisted, keeping them well-maintained takes time (see Chapter 10). Dogs with corded coats include the Puli and the Komondor. Poodles can also be corded.

Coat length

Besides different textures and types, canine coats also come in different lengths. Don't forget that shorter coats in general are easier to groom than are longer coats. Check out the other differences in the list that follows:

- **Hairless dogs:** On one side of the spectrum is the hairless or near-hairless dog (see Chapter 8). These dogs are quite lacking when it comes to hair, although some breeds like the Chinese Crested actually have some hair on the head or legs (and the Powderpuff variety is a hairy dog!). But just because they're hairless dogs doesn't mean that you don't groom them. Although you may not be brushing their hair, their skin requires plenty of attention.

- **Short coats:** Dogs with short coats are pretty much the wash-and-wear dogs. Their coats don't offer them much protection against the elements, so they're more likely to have problems with cold climates than their furrier counterparts. They may be single- or double-coated. Examples include the Basenji and the Beagle.

- **Medium coats:** Dogs with medium coats tend to look pretty good. A medium coat is not so short that the hair doesn't give the dog protection; furthermore, it isn't so long that the hair tangles or mats terribly. Medium-coated dogs usually are double coated with both a top coat and under-coat, but unlike dogs with the long-haired double coats, they're usually a bit easier to groom (see Chapter 8). Border Collies and Cardigan Welsh Corgis have medium coats.

- **Long coats:** Dogs with long coats often are the show stoppers of the dog world. Long and beautiful, they attract oohs and ahhs wherever they go. But all that beauty has a price. Long-coated dogs often are single coated and prone to mats and tangles if their hair isn't kept up. If your dog has a long coat, you can expect long grooming sessions or trips to the groom-ing parlor (see Chapter 13). Afghan Hounds and Irish Setters have long coats.

Coat color

Dogs come in a variety of colors — everything from black to white and every shade in between, or so it seems. And their colors come in many different patterns including bi-color, tri-color, and *brindle* (where the dog is mottled with brown and black — often looking like stripes). Colors and color combi-nations depend a great deal on the breed and whether they are acceptable as part of the breed standard.

Some shampoos and conditioners help bring out the best in your dog's coat. When buying supplies, you can look for the ones that make your white dog sparkling white, your black dog glossy black, or your brown dog look his very best.

Having the Proper Tools on Hand

Different coats require different grooming methods, and different grooming methods require different equipment and supplies. After you familiarize your-self with your dog's coat, you have a better idea of what tools and supplies you need to properly groom your dog. For example, depending on your dog's coat, you may be simply brushing and bathing, or you may be clipping or stripping it, too.

Good grooming requires more than brushing, bathing, and possibly clipping your dog. It also involves routinely trimming his toenails, brushing his teeth, cleaning his eyes and ears, and possibly expressing his anal sacks. Chapter 3 explains what equipment you need to tackle these jobs and where to find it, and Chapter 6 provides the instruction.

Coaching Your Canine to Be Groomed

Grooming your dog requires a bit of a partnership. Although you don't necessarily need your dog's full compliance when grooming, it sure makes things easier!

Good grooming starts when your dog is a puppy. Getting her used to routine tasks, like being brushed and combed and having her feet handled so you can clip her toenails, is all part of grooming. Otherwise, your dog may fight you, and you may end up with results neither of you will like (at worst, an injury; at best, a bad hair day).

Teaching your dog simple cues, such as Sit, Down, and Stay, is important to wise grooming. If you can't keep your dog in one place, it's very hard to do anything. Chapter 4 provides advice for training your dog to enjoy grooming (or at least tolerate it and cooperate).

Taking Note: Keeping a Grooming Diary

A grooming diary is an invaluable tool for grooming your dog. It doesn't have to be fancy — just something in which you can make notes to keep track of what you've done and how your dog looks and reacts.

Jot down the following list at the front of your diary and be sure to include this basic info about each grooming session:

- **Date:** This lets you know when your last session was.

- **Grooming procedure(s):** Did you simply trim your dog's nails and brush his teeth, or did you groom him from nose to tail?

- **Possible health concerns:** Note that the coat looks dull or is greasy, for example, or include other changes that may warrant a trip to the vet.

- **Behavioral changes:** Track how your dog responds. For example, if your dog is antsy when you put him on the table, was he antsy before, or is this something new you're working with?

- **Notes:** You may develop a new technique that you want to try again in the next grooming session — the notes can serve as a reminder.

Choosing a low- or high-maintenance pup

Grooming can arguably be a piece of cake or a nightmare, depending on your patience and the breed of dog you've chosen. Although I don't think you should choose your dog strictly on the basis of whether the dog needs little grooming, I think it is something that should factor into everyone's decision-making process when choosing a dog.

Which dogs are low maintenance when it comes to coats? Think short and medium coats that don't need clipping and don't need a lot of brushing and detangling (but they do shed). Here is a partial list of some dogs with low-maintenance coats:

- Basenji
- Beagle
- Boston Terrier
- Dalmatian
- Doberman Pinscher
- German Shorthaired Pointer
- Great Dane
- Labrador Retriever
- Pointer
- Rottweiler

Why would anyone want a dog with a high-maintenance coat? Well, as you've seen, they can be very beautiful. Owners and breeders like that certain look that you don't see with a short-coated dog. The dog's temperament figures in, too — many people like certain temperaments that come in a particular package. Here's a partial list of some dogs with high-maintenance coats:

- Afghan Hound
- American Cocker Spaniel
- Dandie Dinmont Terrier
- Keeshond
- Kerry Blue Terrier
- Poodle
- Portuguese Water Dog
- Puli
- Samoyed
- Soft Coated Wheaten Terrier

If you're in the market for a new dog, I suggest you do your research thoroughly and choose a dog not merely based on looks but also on temperament, health, activity level, and of course, how much grooming you're willing to do. Check out the following books to help you choose wisely:

- *Dogs For Dummies* by Gina Spadifori (Wiley, 2000)
- *Choosing a Dog For Dummies* by Chris Walkowicz (Wiley, 2001)
- *Bring Me Home: Dogs Make Great Pets* by Margaret H. Bonham (Howell Book House, 2005)

Writing down everything about your grooming session while it's still fresh in your mind is important. You can keep your grooming diary with your tack box (or whatever you use to carry your grooming gear) so that it's ready to go when you need to make notes.

Knowing When to Call a Pro

Although you're ready to invest your time and money in grooming your pooch, you may run into situations in which you need to rely on the skills and advice of an expert. Precious, your Bearded Collie, may tangle with a sticker bush, and you may not have time or patience to pick every last sticker out of her coat. Maybe Rex, your Great Dane, is easy to bathe and brush but a gigantic pain when you're trimming his nails and brushing his teeth. Perhaps you adopted a dog who's never been groomed before, and you need help getting his coat into shape so you can then maintain it. You may even love to keep Sissy, your Standard Poodle, in a New Yorker cut, but you can't trim your own bangs.

If you're an honest soul who has admitted to yourself that you have neither the time nor inclination to do it right, there's no shame in that. And why should there be? You call a plumber when your sink faucet is spraying water. You have a teacher teach your kids. You buy an airline ticket to fly across the country instead of going to flight school. You pay someone else to do plenty of tasks that you can't or won't do, so nothing's wrong with hiring a professional groomer for your dog.

Assigning children to groom the dog usually isn't a reliable alternative to routinely grooming the dog yourself. No matter how much your kids promise that they're going to take care of the dog (including grooming), don't believe them. This task ultimately falls on an adult in the household. Younger children are neither responsible enough to take care of a dog without adult supervision nor capable of tackling the grooming process. I say this from experience. I've seen many dogs given up to shelters or given away because they were originally "for the kids," but when it came down to it, the children weren't responsible enough to care for a living, breathing being.

Considering the cost

Most pet owners hesitate to look for a professional groomer because, quite frankly, it's costly. Yet that's all a matter of perspective. If you take three or four hours to groom your Standard Poodle, paying someone $45 to $65 to bathe, brush, and clip your dog is actually a deal.

The cost of having a professional groom your dog varies widely depending on where you live and what you want done. Time- and skill-intensive procedures like stripping or clipping coats cost more than a simple bath and brush out. Problem coats (matting and tangles) also add to the cost.

Keep these points in mind when considering the cost of grooming:

- ✔ Most groomers charge between $35 and $70 for complete grooming.

- ✔ Some groomers charge more or less depending on the breed, the location (New York City is more expensive than Great Falls, Montana), the size of the dog, and the type of work done.

- ✔ Dogs with matted or dirty fur cost more, and so do dogs who need a show trim.

- ✔ Groomers add from $8 to $12 for mats and add at least $40 for show cuts over the average cost of grooming.

 Most but not all groomers offer baths, brushing, clipping, stripping, ear cleaning, and nail cutting as part of their services. Ask what the full grooming price includes. Some groomers won't quote a price until they see your dog and can gauge how much work grooming your dog will be.

Most dog owners who use professional groomers have their pets groomed once a month and then maintain their coats with brushing and combing.

Looking for a professional groomer

Now that you've decided to use a professional groomer, you can look for one by simply opening the Yellow Pages to *Dog Groomers,* closing your eyes, and pointing to an entry. On the other hand, I have a better method.

Finding a professional groomer

Finding a groomer is pretty easy. You're likely to see a shop on the corner in your neighborhood, but you may not be sure whether that groomer is any good. Here are the steps you need to go through to find a good one:

1. **Ask your dog-owning friends whether they use a groomer for their dogs or know of one they'd recommend.**

   A good recommendation is worth its weight in gold. If your dog-owning friends praise a particular groomer, go with that one.

2. **Ask your veterinarian what groomer he or she recommends.**

   Sometimes your vet will employ a groomer onsite.

3. **Look for groomers near you in the Yellow Pages or online at**

   - **Find A Groomer Directory (www.findagroomer.com):** This groomer directory is the pet owner's side of PetGroomer.com (www.petgroomer.com). Groomers list themselves here. You can search by city and state or even by zip code.

- **BreederWeb.com (breederweb.com/services/dogGroomers.asp):** This resource is another good one to use in your search for a groomer.

- **DexOnline.com (dexonline.com):** Use this Internet Yellow Pages site to do a search on "dog grooming" in your city and state for a listing.

Certifications

Certifications are a mixed bag. Plenty of good groomers who have well-established businesses and do an exceptional job are not certified. Considering a groomer who is neither certified nor professionally trained depends on whether that groomer has a good reputation and references that check out. If so, that groomer probably is a good bet.

A certified groomer is someone who is professionally trained and certified to a certain standard. You don't know what level of expertise a groomer who hasn't been certified has achieved. An uncertified groomer may be better or worse than someone who is certified. With certification, you know the standard to which the groomer should be able to perform.

Certifications are offered through certain grooming schools and through the National Dog Groomers Association of America (NDGAA). You can find out more about NDGAA certification at www.nationaldoggroomers.com or check out Chapter 19 and the resources listed in the Appendix.

Screening the professional groomer

After you find a professional groomer you're interested in using, you need to determine whether that groomer is the right one for your dog. Not all groomers are comfortable with all dogs, and some groomers prefer to work only with certain breeds.

Some groomers may use tranquilizers, especially with difficult-to-handle or aggressive dogs. I don't recommend tranquilizers at all, except under extreme circumstances, such as a totally freaked out pooch. If you don't know whether a groomer uses tranquilizers, ask. Dogs prone to seizures can experience seizures when administered certain common tranquilizers. Tranquilizers also make dogs more susceptible to problems caused by changes in temperature, such as hypothermia and heatstroke.

Knowing the right questions to ask

Let your fingers do the walking here. You can prescreen most professional groomers over the phone to find out whether they're right for you and your dog. Here are some questions you'll want to ask:

✔ What hours are you open for business?

✔ Are you available for emergencies or after hours?

✔ How long have you been in business?

✔ What are your certifications? With what organization?

✔ How many clients do you see?

✔ What breeds do you see most of?

✔ How many <insert breed here> do you see?

✔ Are you comfortable with working on <insert breed here>?

✔ How much do you charge for a full grooming? What procedures does a full grooming include?

✔ How do you handle difficult dogs? Do you muzzle or tranquilize them?

✔ Do you use cage dryers? If so, how often do you check on dogs with cage dryers?

✔ What do you charge for just a bath and brushing? Nail clipping?

✔ How many staff members do you employ?

✔ What other services do you offer?

✔ Do you have an emergency on-call vet? Who is it?

✔ Do you have references?

Visiting a professional groomer

After you prescreen the professional groomer on the phone, it's time for a visit. Ask whether you can drop by and check out the groomer's facility some time. The grooming shop should be neat, clean, and organized. If the shop is especially busy, you may find hair and water on the floor, but overall the shop needs to leave you with a good impression.

Watch how the groomer and staff members handle dogs. Are they gentle and caring, or do they move the dogs around like they're just another commodity? Watch body language; from it you generally can tell whether the groomer is just going through the motions or sincerely likes what he or she is doing. Although everyone is entitled to a bad day, the groomer shouldn't take out any frustrations on the dogs.

After you're convinced that a particular groomer is the one for your dog, make an appointment. You may need one or two sessions to really decide whether the groomer is a good fit.

A dirty or terribly chaotic and disorganized grooming shop may be a sign that the groomer doesn't have enough staff and may not have time to care for and watch all the dogs, especially the ones in cage dryers. When that's the case, you may want to look for another groomer.

Becoming a Pro Yourself

You may enjoy grooming so much that you're thinking about becoming a professional groomer. After all, you like dogs and may have a knack for grooming pooches. However, before you hit the books and start working toward your certifications, remember that going pro means that you're going into business, and you have to be a savvy businessperson in addition to being a dog groomer.

Be sure to check out Chapter 19 for more information about becoming a professional groomer.

Chapter 2

Inside and Out: What Affects a Dog's Coat and Grooming

In This Chapter

▶ Understanding parts of the dog and how they relate to good grooming

▶ Exploring how diet and good care can affect your dog's health

▶ Discovering how haircoat, genetics, and other factors may affect your dog's grooming

So you're well acquainted with the importance of good grooming for your dog's health and well-being — if you read Chapter 1, you're well on your way — and you've grabbed your slicker brush and Greyhound comb and decided it's time to make your dog beautiful.

Before you get started here in Chapter 2, I'd like to let you know about the canine anatomy and how it affects the way you groom your dog. After all, it's more than heads and tails: It's croups, withers, and hocks. Likewise in this chapter, I tell you about the effects of good care — and bad care — on a dog's skin and coat and how you can use that information to make a difference when grooming your pooch. Lastly, you can find out about hereditary and congenital diseases that can affect your dog's good health.

Anatomy of the Dog: The Hipbone's Connected to the . . .

Through the years, the dog world has come up with names to describe the parts of the dog. Knowing what part of the dog you're working on is extremely important in grooming. After all, if you don't know what those pointy joints that jut out at the back of the rear legs are called, you won't know what I'm talking about when I (or other groomers) say "hock."

Okay, this isn't Anatomy 101, where I talk about fibulas and tibias. It's more about how you describe what you're seeing when you look at the outside of the dog. Tons of different descriptions are used when it comes to the dog's anatomy — so many so that books have been written on the subject. I try to standardize the terms a bit for you, but you may see different terminology used in the breed standards or in other books.

Some canine anatomical names may be familiar to you; others may be downright foreign. Many of the anatomical terms used to describe parts of a dog are similar to the ones used for horses, so if you're at all familiar with horse terminology, you'll probably be comfortable with them.

When looking at the anatomy of a dog (see Figure 2-1), you need to know the basic terms for the major parts: rump or croup, withers, head, hind legs, forelegs, and tail. You can pick up the finer points later, but for now, these are the important ones to know. In the sections that follow, I tell you about the major parts and the terminology surrounding each of them.

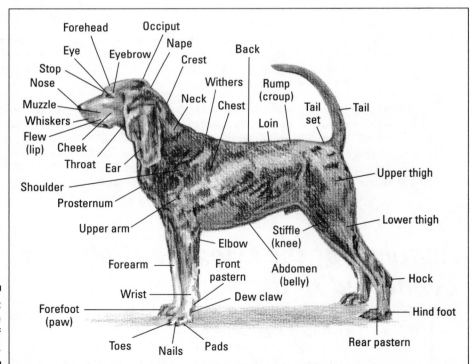

Figure 2-1:
The anatomy of the dog.

Head

The dog's head is probably the first thing you look at. And why not? After all, it's pretty expressive. When you want to groom a dog, you'll be cleaning ears, brushing teeth, and removing those gunky tear stains from beneath the eyes. And yes, you'll be washing your dog's face, too.

Different dog breeds have different types of heads that have a variety of names. Dogs basically have one of three head types:

- **Dolichocephalic:** This head type is the long and thin head seen in dog breeds like the Collie, Borzoi, and Saluki. Dogs with this type of head have really long muzzles and noses and usually have really good eyesight or a keen sense of smell.

- **Brachycephalic:** This head type is the exact opposite of dolichocephalic heads. Brachycephalic heads are short with muzzles that often have a pushed-in look. Some dog breeds with this type of head have problems breathing because of the closeness of their features, and some have wrinkles that must be cleaned frequently. Dogs with brachycephalic heads include the Bulldog, Pug, and Pekingese.

- **Mesaticephalic:** This head type is medium-sized, as seen in the Samoyed, Brittanies, and Alaskan Malamutes. These dogs need general grooming for their heads.

Depending on the type of head your dog has, you may have certain grooming issues. For example, dogs with brachycephalic heads may have eyes that bulge, and extreme care must be taken to avoid scratching them. Long noses of the dolichocephalic head type may be prone to getting things like grass awns (bristle-like tips) in them more easily, because, well, the dog's nose naturally arrives five minutes before the rest of the dog.

The head is comprised of the

- **Nose:** You're all familiar with your dog's nose. For one thing, dog noses are often cold and wet, and of course, they usually get stuck where they're not wanted. Plenty of terms associated with the dog's nose refer either to its shape (Ram's nose or Roman nose) or color (liver, snow nose, or Dudley nose).

- **Muzzle (foreface):** The *muzzle* or foreface is the part of the skull that's comprised of the upper and lower jaws. You'll pay close attention to the dog's muzzle while grooming.

   Muzzle also is a term for a device that keeps the dog's jaws shut and thus inhibits biting.

- **Stop:** The *stop* is an indentation (sometimes nonexistent) between the muzzle and the braincase or forehead (see next item).

- **Forehead (braincase):** The *forehead* is the portion of the head that's similar to your own forehead; it goes from the back point of the skull (occiput) to the stop and eyebrows.

- **Occiput (point of skull):** The *occiput* is simply the highest point of the skull at the back of the head and a prominent feature on some dogs.

- **Ears:** It's pretty obvious what these are, but different dogs have different types of ear carriage. Among the several types are

  - **Pricked:** Pricked ears are upright.

  - **Dropped:** Dropped ears hang down. Dogs with this kind of ears need more care for their ears because they're more prone to getting infections than dogs with pricked ears.

  - **Button:** Button ears have a fold in them. Button ears, like dropped ears, may need more care because they're more prone to getting infections than pricked ears.

  - **Cropped:** Cropped ears are surgically altered.

  You need to clean your dog's ears and check for problems like ear mites. You likewise want to check frequently behind the ears for knots and tangles that form.

- **Eyes:** Again, the eyes are a pretty obvious part of the anatomy, but a multitude of descriptions deal with a dog's eye color and shape. Most are self-explanatory. You may be cleaning tear stains beneath the eyes if you have a breed that's prone to that condition.

- **Eyebrows:** Like humans, dogs have eyebrows, or simply brows.

- **Whiskers:** Dogs have whiskers that provide some sensory feeling. They sometimes are trimmed to provide a clean look for the muzzle.

- **Flews (lips):** *Flews* is just a fancy word for a dog's lips. You'll be touching them a lot when you brush your dog's teeth.

- **Cheek:** The skin along the sides of the muzzle is what cheeks are to a dog. Dog cheeks are in a position similar to where your own cheeks are.

Neck and shoulders

The neck and shoulders are the next parts of the canine anatomy that I cover. Parts of the neck and shoulders include the

✔ **Nape:** The *nape* of the neck is where the neck joins the base of the skull in the back of the head. If you're clipping around the neck, you'll quite often need to locate the nape.

✔ **Throat:** Like your own throat, the dog's throat is beneath the jaws. It's tender, and many dogs don't like their throats handled roughly. Be mindful when brushing or clipping.

✔ **Crest:** The *crest* starts at the nape and ends at the withers (see the last item in this list).

✔ **Neck:** The neck is pretty self-explanatory; in dogs, it runs from the head to the shoulders.

✔ **Shoulder:** The shoulder is the top section of the foreleg from the withers to the elbow.

✔ **Withers:** One of those horse terms I mentioned earlier in the "Anatomy of the Dog: The Hipbone's Connected to the . . ." section, the *withers* are the top point of the shoulders, making them the highest point along the dog's back.

Back and chest

I include the back and the chest together here, because they're part of the dog's torso, which includes the

✔ **Prosternum:** The *prosternum* is the top of the *sternum,* a bone that ties the rib cage together.

✔ **Chest:** The chest is the entire rib cage of the dog.

✔ **Back:** The back runs from the withers to the loins, or from the point of the shoulders to the end of the rib cage. The term *back* is sometimes used to describe the back and the loin.

✔ **Flank:** The *flank* refers to the side portion of the dog between the end of the chest and the rear leg.

✔ **Abdomen (belly):** The belly portion of the dog is notably the underside of the dog from the end of its rib cage to its tail. If your dog's belly is low to the ground, you probably have to take a little extra care in making sure it stays clean.

✔ **Loin:** The loin is the portion of the back between the end of the rib cage and the beginning of the pelvic bone.

Forelegs and hind legs

You'd think that the forelegs and hind legs of a dog would be similar, but they're about as different as your own arms and legs. The parts of the forelegs and hind legs include the

- **Upper arm:** The upper arm on the foreleg is right below the shoulder and is comprised of the humerus bone, which is similar (in name anyway) to the one found in your own upper arm. It ends at the elbow.

- **Elbow:** The elbow is the first joint in the dog's leg that's located just below the chest on the back of the foreleg. It's like your elbow.

- **Forearm:** The long bone that runs after the elbow on the foreleg is the forearm. Like your arms, it's comprised of the ulna and radius. The forearm may have feathering on the back of the arm that tends to pick up burrs and other foreign objects; it can also mat and tangle.

- **Wrist:** The wrist is the lower joint below the elbow on the foreleg. This joint bears as much as 90 percent of the dog's weight when he's jumping or doing other athletic feats.

- **Pastern (front and rear):** Sometimes called the carpals, pasterns are equivalent to the bones in your hands and feet — not counting fingers and toes. Like the wrists, pasterns are weight-bearing bones (especially the front ones) that are subject to many of the injuries suffered by sports dogs.

- **Foot or paw (forefoot or hind foot):** Try just standing on your toes or fingers, and you get an idea of what dogs do their entire lives. The foot or paw has nails (sometimes called claws), paw pads, and usually dewclaws. Most dogs have larger forefeet than hind feet. Among the many descriptions for the shape of the dog's foot are

  - **Splayed:** A dog with splayed feet has toes that are in a splayed or wide position when the dog steps down.

  - **Hare:** Hare feet have middle two toes jutting out farther than the outer two toes, making the dog's foot look like a rabbit's foot.

  - **Snowshoe:** Snowshoe feet are round and compact with heavy webbing between the toes and plenty of fur. Snowshoe feet are often seen in northern breeds like Samoyeds and Siberian Huskies.

- **Toes:** The toes of a dog are the equivalent of fingers and toes of your hands and feet. Although a dog's toes don't wiggle too much, dogs can move them in a stretch motion or even curl them up. You occasionally have to trim the hair between the pads of the toes.

- **Dewclaws:** Dewclaws are vestiges of thumbs on your dog. Because dogs never figured out the opposable thumbs concept (thank goodness, too — can you imagine what mischief they'd get into with them?), their thumbs, if you will, have become more or less useless appendages. Some dogs are not even born with them, and many are born with only front dewclaws. Some breeders elect to remove dewclaws when their puppies are a few days old, but some standards require intact dewclaws or even double dewclaws (two dewclaws on each foot — as if you had two thumbs). Dewclaws, like the other toenails, grow. Some dog owners swear they grow faster than the other nails. Because they get no wear from walking, they need to be clipped to prevent them from growing into the pad or breaking off.

- **Nails:** The toenails or claws on the end of each toe are actually incorporated with part of the last bone of the toes. You need to clip toenails about once a week.

- **Pads:** On the underside of the foot are several pads, including one main pad (communal pad) and a pad under each toe, for a total of five pads. If you look at the back of the foreleg, you can find stopper pads behind the wrist. Six pads are found on the forelegs and five on the back — unless your dog has more than one dewclaw per front leg, and then there may be pads associated with them.

- **Upper thigh:** The part of the dog's leg situated above the knee, or stifle, on the hind leg is the upper thigh. It corresponds to that portion of the leg where the femur is in humans.

- **Stifle (knee):** The stifle is the joint that corresponds to the knee in humans. It sits on the front of the hind leg in line with abdomen.

- **Lower thigh:** The lower thigh is the portion of hind leg situated beneath the stifle (knee); it extends to the hock joint (see next bullet). It runs along the fibula and tibia bones in the dog's leg. Some dogs have feathering along the back of their lower thighs and hocks, so it's important to make sure the feathering is groomed properly and kept free of mats.

- **Hock:** This oddly shaped joint makes a sharp angle at the back of the dog's legs. It corresponds with your ankle.

Rear and tail

At long last (especially with Dachshunds and Basset Hounds) you come to the tail end of the dog. The parts that make up your dog's rear end include the

- **Rump (or croup):** This part of the dog is the proverbial rear end; it's where the pelvis bone is. You need to use care in grooming this section because it's tender. Fluffy hairs often found behind the rump under the tail tend to attract plenty of knots, tangles, and other nasties.

- **Tail set:** The tail set is where the tail attaches to the rump. Some dogs have high tail sets, others have low ones.

✔ **Tail:** Everyone recognizes the dog's tail (or its absence). It's usually wagging at you. The tail is a great place for picking up burrs, prickly stuff, mats, and tangles, especially if the tail fur is long. Special care is needed to keep the tail looking great.

Considering Factors That Influence a Dog's Appearance

Now that you know all the parts of the dog and how important it is to groom them, I'll tell you about what affects the appearance of those parts. Of course, you already know that not all beauty is skin-deep. Although much of how your dog looks has to do with genetics, you can do plenty to make your dog look her best. Beauty works two ways — from the outside in and from the inside out.

The sections that follow deal with factors that influence your dog's appearance that you won't be able to change.

Genetics

Your dog's genetic makeup is something you really can't do much about, so unless you're buying a new dog — and even then dog genes will be dog genes — you're pretty much stuck with whatever genetics he has. If your dog has a wavy or kinky haircoat, that's something his genes says he has, and you have to deal with grooming it.

An unfortunate side to genetics is that your dog can have some hereditary diseases lurking in his genes. He may have problems, like sebaceous adenitis or hypothyroidism, that can affect the way he looks and feels. Similarly, dogs can suffer from congenital problems that can greatly affect the way they look. Neither hereditary nor congenital anomalies are problems you can prevent, because the dog is born with them. I discuss these diseases and conditions in more detail in Chapter 16.

If you're planning to buy a new dog in the future, you need to look for a reputable breeder (check out the nearby "Looking for a reputable breeder" sidebar) who does health screening and testing. Although screening can't guarantee a 100 percent healthy dog, it does reduce your risk of buying a sick dog. Dogs from reputable breeders generally cost no more than those from disreputable sources — so buyer beware.

Looking for a reputable breeder

If you've ever bought a dog who ended up with a hereditary disease, you're probably wondering whether you can do anything to minimize the risk of buying a sick dog. Actually, you can do just that by purchasing your dog from a reputable breeder.

Unlike backyard breeders — people who breed dogs for the money, because they think it's fun, or because they want another dog just like Fluffy — or puppy mills that breed dogs solely for profit and not for health or quality, reputable breeders try to improve the breed and want to breed healthy dogs. Instead of breeding multiple litters every year, they settle for just one or two litters. Puppies aren't always available, and reputable breeders usually have waiting lists for their puppies.

You can discover more about finding a reputable breeder in my book, *Bring Me Home: Dogs Make Great Pets* (Howell Book House, 2005), but here's a basic rundown of what reputable breeders do. They

- Screen for hereditary diseases though the Orthopedic Foundation for Animals (OFA) or PennHip and Canine Eye Registry Foundation (CERF). Optigen and Vetgen are two other registries that provide screening services.

- Breed no more than three litters a year.

- Offer health guarantees.

- Take the dog back any time in his life.

- Show dogs actively in conformation or obedience competitions.

- Register dogs through the American Kennel Club (AKC), United Kennel Club (UKC), or a legitimate international kennel club.

- Keep puppies with their mothers for at least eight weeks.

- Talk directly to you and allow you to meet other dogs in their kennels (or homes).

- Work the dogs toward breed titles.

- Breed no more than two breeds.

- Provide health records for puppies that show vaccinations, dewormings, and other veterinary care.

- Require a written contract.

Puppies aren't always available from reputable breeders; you can nevertheless begin your search for the right dog at the AKC's Web site at www.akc.org.

Here is a partial list of the kinds of conditions that can affect a dog's appearance:

- **Allergies:** Allergies often manifest themselves in a poor-looking coat.
- **Addison's disease:** This disease is caused by a lack of or deficiency in hormones produced by the pituitary or adrenal glands and can result in hair and skin problems.
- **Cushing's disease:** This disease is the opposite of Addison's in that it's an overproduction of hormones; it causes hair loss and poor skin.

- ✔ **Hyperthyroidism:** This condition is an overabundance of the thyroid hormone. Although rare in dogs, it's usually associated with cancer.

- ✔ **Hypothyroidism:** This condition is a lack of thyroid hormone in dogs. It causes brittle coats and hair loss.

- ✔ **Sebaceous adenitis:** This hereditary skin condition is a disease that destroys the oil-producing sebaceous glands and causes hair loss.

- ✔ **Autoimmune disorders:** These disorders are varied and can cause hair loss and scaly skin.

- ✔ **Zinc-responsive dermatosis:** This condition, which may be hereditary, is one in which the dog fails to absorb enough zinc from his diet. Scaly skin and hair loss result.

- ✔ **Coat funk:** This condition is at least congenital if not hereditary. The outer coat breaks off, leaving the woolly undercoat exposed.

Haircoat

Although you can lump your dog's fur in with genetics, I talk about haircoat separately. The *haircoat* (or fur or whatever you'd like to call your dog's skin and hair) greatly influences the appearance and grooming of your dog. How your dog arrives at your grooming table is partly genetics, but more importantly, it's also

- ✔ How well you feed your dog
- ✔ How well you take care of your dog
- ✔ How often you take care of the haircoat

These three factors are crucial to how your dog looks after being groomed.

Your dog is born with a certain hair type. There's no denying it: Your dog can be wild and woolly, curly, straight and sexy, or bald and beautiful. The different textures of dogs' hair are far-ranging, from the Puli's usually tangled nightmare (until the dreadlocks form) to the Siberian Husky's heavy coat that can look ratty when she's shedding profusely (see Chapter 9 for more on blowing coat).

How you care for a dog's haircoat affects her appearance. Is your dog the rough and ready type that's always outdoors? Does your dog go for a dip without a shower afterward? Or do you always primp your dog with a bath and a mousse every week? Remember that a brushed-out dog naturally looks better than one that hasn't been brushed and combed in a while.

Additionally, your dog's haircoat changes over time. As a puppy, your dog is likely to have a downy puppy coat that looks oh-so-cute. That often gives way to an adolescent coat that may be harder to handle than an adult coat. Likewise, a senior coat is different than the adult coat.

Although I have only anecdotal evidence, I've noticed that spayed and neutered dogs tend to have more lush and more beautiful coats than their intact counterparts. One Alaskan Malamute I owned never really had a beautiful coat until I had her spayed, and then she was a beautiful dog. Go figure.

Health

Your dog's health greatly influences his appearance. Like humans, dogs never look their best when they're sick. In fact, your dog's coat can look downright awful when he isn't feeling well. No amount of grooming is going to make a sick dog look good, so you need to pay attention to his health.

Check your dog's haircoat. Is it healthy and shiny, dry and dull, or does it have too much dander in it? Some conditions like cancer or glandular (thyroid) problems greatly affect the consistency and the quality of a dog's haircoat.

When your dog is sick, the haircoat isn't the only part that's affected. Check out his ears and eyes for signs of goopy infections, and find out whether his nose is runny or clogged up. Sore, painful teeth likewise equal not only bad breath and a not-so-kissable smile but also underlying health concerns that also can change your dog's appearance (not to mention cause deadly heart conditions).

 Your dog's appearance is a good indication of what's going on inside. If the coat looks dry and icky or oily or if the hair is thinning, that may be a sign that something more serious is wrong with your dog. When that's the case, your dog needs to be examined by a veterinarian so the problem can be diagnosed and fixed. Your dog will thank you.

Exercise

Exercise doesn't mean going to the doggie gym; it simply means keeping your dog (and you for that matter) fit and trim by having a little fun doing the activities that you and your dog already enjoy, such as walking, hiking, playing fetch, swimming, or playing some dog sports. Exercise is important to your dog's overall health and appearance (and that's what you're trying to improve when you groom, isn't it?). A dog that looks lousy because he's fat and flabby isn't going to look nice when you're grooming him.

Starting an exercise regimen

So you've decided you have a pudgy pooch. Before you strap on your Nikes for a ten-mile run with Fido, stop and think. If you're in shape, you didn't get into shape by running a marathon right off the bat . . . so don't expect your dog to do it. Overstressing your dog can be just as hazardous as overstressing an obese person. Be sensible; start out easy, but definitely start.

Here are some pointers for beginning an exercise regimen with your dog:

- Have your vet check your dog to be sure no underlying health problems exist.

- Ask your vet about what makes up a sensible and healthy diet and exercise program for your dog.

- Talk to your doctor about diet and exercise for yourself before starting an exercise program with your dog. Remember, you both can overdo it.

- Watch the temperature and humidity. Excessive heat and humidity can cause heatstroke in dogs (and humans!). When the weather's hot outside, try exercising during the coolest part of the day or in an air-conditioned area.

- Start slow and easy. You're not in a contest to see how fast you and your dog can go.

- Warm up. Start by walking to enable your dog's muscles to warm up. Doing so prevents injuries.

- Don't push too hard. Laying off the hard stuff is best until your dog is more fit. Like many weekend warriors, your dog won't know he's hurt until after a hard workout, and then you have another problem — an injured (and unhappy) dog.

- If your dog is reluctant to run or refuses to exercise, make note of what he won't do, and have a vet check it out. It isn't laziness; your dog probably can't do it for a reason.

- Discover the various activities you can do with your pet, including dog sports. Check out my books, *The Simple Guide to Getting Active with Your Dog* (TFH, 2002) and *Having Fun with Agility* (Howell Book House, 2004), or D. Caroline Coile's *Beyond Fetch: Fun, Interactive Activities for You and Your Dog* (Howell Book House, 2003). These books offer good ideas for fun activities to do with your dog.

Although exercise won't do much initially in terms of making a dog prettier, it nevertheless is a great way to make a flabby dog look simply spectacular over the long haul. The difference between a fit dog and a flabby one is astonishing. Fit dogs are sleek; they're the epitome of the canine ideal. A fat dog is, well, a fat dog.

Exercise is as good for your dog as it is for you, and it helps your dog live a longer and healthier life than his sedentary couch-potato counterparts. Don't you want your dog to be the canine version of a Greek god (or goddess) compared to other dogs?

Diet

If you consumed nothing but cupcakes and soda pop, how healthy do you think you'd look? Not very good; that's for sure. The same is true for your dog. Although you may not feed your dog candy and bubble gum (you'd better not; they're unhealthy), you may as well be if you're not providing your dog a healthy diet.

Diet is one area of your dog's care that you can do something about. By providing a proper diet, your dog can actually have a healthier looking coat.

One of the first places good or bad diets show up in is your dog's haircoat. If he has a dull, brittle, sparse, greasy, or dry coat that's shedding excessively, he may have a lousy diet. (These conditions show up for other reasons too, but feeding him a lousy diet can't help.) But if you feed your dog a healthy and nutritious diet (see the next section), he's bound to look and feel better. Abrupt changes in the haircoat call for investigation and consultation with your veterinarian.

Exploring the Importance of Nutrition

Nutrition can be a controversial topic for pet owners. In recent years, various groups have formed specifically to tell you what diet's right for your pet. One group figures that as long as the food meets government regulations, it's okay. Another group believes that feeding your dog premium dog foods is the way to go. Another group thinks you need to make your dog food at home. And other groups adhere to the idea that premium, certified, organic dog food is best.

If you're undecided about a proper dog diet, you probably get my drift that determining just which diet is right for your dog is extremely difficult. Maybe you're already in one of those camps. In that case, my thoughts and opinions probably aren't going to change the way you think, especially if your dog's coat looks good and she doesn't have any nutritional deficiencies. That's terrific! Keep doing what you're doing. But I encourage you to read on and also discuss your options with a vet, who can help you determine what diet is right for your dog.

Different opinions and myths about the proper way to feed a dog abound. Many dog owners hold fast to feeding methods regardless of their validity, so I sift the fact from fiction in this section to give you some good guidelines on how feeding your dog the right diet can perk up his appearance and make grooming him easier.

Providing a balanced diet

Regardless of what you feed your dog, you probably agree that good nutrition is vitally and inevitably important for your dog's appearance.

If you're not aware of the importance of canine nutrition, I can explain. You already know that you don't look or feel good when you're constantly eating junk food. Okay, I grant you that maybe you feel good eating junk food when you eat it, but that's a totally different story. Dogs are like people in this respect — garbage in, garbage out. If your dog isn't getting the proper nutrition for his health, he just isn't going to look or feel good. Makes sense, doesn't it?

Although a bit of an argument exists about what exactly makes a healthy dog diet, most people agree that the guidelines of the Association of Animal Feed Control Officials (AAFCO) are a good place to start. This association of government officials, veterinarians, and pet food manufacturers establishes guidelines for just what vitamins, minerals, protein, and fat are needed in a dog's food. These individuals and corporations conduct a considerable amount of research and testing on which foods work, and they apply what they discover toward improving dog foods and AAFCO guidelines. You can find out more about AAFCO at its Web site: www.aafco.org.

Regardless of whether you're getting your dog food from the supermarket, buying specialty pet food, or preparing a home-cooked or raw diet for your dog, you should always adhere to the AAFCO standards.

Feeding a diet that isn't balanced and strays too far from the guidelines can seriously ruin your dog's health. For example, too much or too little calcium can cause bone problems (thinning in the latter case) and can lead to deadly fractures. Overfeeding certain vitamins can actually cause deadly heart problems. Messing around with nutrition isn't usually a good idea, so unless you know what you're doing when it comes to formulating a dog's diet, steer clear of homemade and raw diets until you've at least talked to a veterinary nutritionist about how to formulate a balanced diet for your dog.

Changing your dog's food

Whenever you change your dog's food, you need to do it gradually to avoid stomach upsets. Start with 10 percent of the new food and 90 percent of the old food on the first day. Each subsequent day, increase the new food by 10 percent and decrease the old food by 10 percent.

After your dog is weaned onto the new dog food, don't expect to see any changes in your dog's appearance for at least six to eight weeks. This amount of time is the shortest in which research has shown verifiable physical changes in dogs.

Feeding for a beautiful coat

A dog must eat a complete and balanced diet, whether homemade or commercial, to have a beautiful coat. Your dog needs basic nutrients, but the quality and digestibility of the ingredients are just as important.

Not all dog food is the same — the same way that not all the food that you eat is the same. If you choose cheap, bargain-brand, $10-for-50 pounds, no-name dog food that you can buy at the local gas station, chances are, it isn't a good dog food. What you're likely to find is that it's mostly grain-based and is chock-full of fillers that your dog doesn't need. Your dog doesn't digest those fillers but instead poops them out as waste. So what you're paying for is pretty much crap — literally!

Not all commercial dog foods are formulated to meet AAFCO guidelines. Always look on the dog food package for a statement of nutritional adequacy that the dog food meets or exceeds AAFCO guidelines.

If you feed your dog a commercial dog food, look for a premium dog food that has a meat source listed as its first ingredient. The next ingredient may be a grain ingredient, but premium foods don't have one grain after another listed as ingredients. For example, a dog food may have poultry listed as the first ingredient (that's good!), but it shouldn't be followed by corn, wheat middlings, and crackled corn. A good dog food may have poultry, rice, poultry fat (preserved with tocopherols) and beef byproducts — see the difference?

Why are meat sources so important? Simple: Fillers and grains don't make beautiful coats, but proteins and fats do. Dogs are carnivores. They don't digest plant protein sources as well as they do meat sources, and they do best on animal fats and proteins.

Although dogs can and do live on vegetarian diets, that's largely the result of owners who feel the need to impose their values on their dogs. Unless your dog is truly allergic to animal products, there's absolutely no reason for your dog to be on a vegetarian diet.

Most premium foods are easy for dogs to digest and are high in protein and fats, which means that you need to feed the dog less of the premium than you would K9 Kibble Krunchies from the local grocery or big box bargain store. The cost of premium dog food usually is $30 to $50 per 40-pound bag, but because you don't need to feed your dog as much of it, you may actually *save* money.

Most dog owners overfeed their dogs, and as a result, obesity is as serious a problem among pets as it is among pet owners. Limiting your dog's food to sensible portions and exercising your dog daily can help get rid of those unwanted pounds.

Supplementing your dog's diet for a healthy coat

If you feed your dog a premium diet, chances are you won't need to provide any supplements to get a healthy coat. After all, you believe the statement on the label that says the dog food is complete and balanced, don't you? Well in the event that food alone doesn't perk up your pup's haircoat, plenty of supplements seem to be formulated for beautiful coats, including:

- ✔ **Omega-3 fatty acids:** These substances usually come from fish oils or flaxseed. They appear to have a positive effect on the coat, but too much of them is not a good thing. In extreme cases, they can reduce the ability of your dog's blood to form clots. Keep these fats below 5 percent of your dog's dietary intake of fat.

- ✔ **Omega-6 fatty acids:** These substances are normally found in meat and vegetable fats. Several types are available, but all are good for coats.

- ✔ **Linatone, Mirra-coat, Missing Link and similar supplements:** These supplements are blends of fats, fatty acids, vitamins, and minerals that are supposed to make your dog's coat more beautiful. I've never used them, but I've heard pet owners and breeders swear by many of them, so they're worth a try if your dog's coat is looking icky.

- ✔ **Raw egg (or cooked egg):** A daily dose of an egg is said to improve your dog's coat.

  I don't recommend using raw eggs because of the chance of exposing your dog to salmonella; however, a cooked egg doesn't hurt — unless your dog's allergic to them.

- ✔ **Vegetable or meat oils:** Giving your medium-sized dog a teaspoon of vegetable oil (oil from meat works too) every day is a simple and cheap way to add Omega-6 fatty acids to his diet. Reduce the amount for smaller dogs; increase it for larger ones.

All supplements add calories to your dog's diet. Fat is the most nutrient-dense at 9 kilocalories (standard calories) per gram. Protein and carbohydrates have 4 kilocalories per gram by comparison. So take these calories into account in your dog's diet to avoid having a roly-poly pup with a great haircoat.

Adding extras to your dog's diet can cause dietary imbalances that can actually do more harm than good. Some additives can even be toxic in excessive amounts. However, the amounts that I recommend won't cause any problems.

Don't expect the change in your dog's coat to happen overnight. Give the supplement at least six weeks to determine whether it's going to help.

Chapter 3

Prepping for the Prettying

*Y*our own doggie beauty parlor doesn't have to be fancy or extravagant, but it does have to be right. Otherwise, you're just wasting your time with odds and ends that really don't work when you need them.

In this chapter, I cover the basics of what you need to groom your dog properly. Some equipment and supplies may seem a bit extravagant, but when you add up the time it takes to do the job without them, you'll wonder how you ever managed. I also cover the costs and a proper setup so you can clean your pup in no time.

And I cover where to get these supplies and where the best deals really are. You may be surprised to discover that getting the right stuff is often no more expensive than buying the wrong stuff at a convenience place.

Gearing Up

If you read Chapter 2, you know how important grooming is for your dog's health, but now you're probably wondering where to begin. After all, you may have a brush or comb or maybe some shampoo that you bought at the local grocery or pet supply store, but is that what you need to make your dog pretty? Will the stuff you already have work in a pinch when you have virtually nothing besides a slicker brush and a garden hose? And will the basket of dog things that Uncle Ed gave to you after Missy the Coonhound died at 15 work for you and your dog?

Maybe, but then again, maybe not.

Taking stock in what you have

The first thing you need to do is take an inventory of all the equipment you already have. That includes the grocery-store nail cutters, the combs, the slicker brushes, the soft brushes, and — whatever the heck that thing is that you suspect has something to do with grooming but have no clue what it is.

In the sections that follow, you can match what you already have to what you need. There's really no need to go out and buy a brand new set of nail clippers if the one you have is adequate for the job at the moment. So if Uncle Ed gave you Missy's old comb and it looks sturdy and serviceable enough, you don't have to rush out and buy another one just yet. However, you probably will need to replace that old comb after it sees a bit of use, so be prepared to do that down the road.

With all due respect to Uncle Ed and Missy, unless your uncle is a vet or into showing or grooming dogs, he probably purchased the comb at a big-box or department store along with his camping supplies, dog food, big-screen TV, and tube socks. If he was conscientious, he may have bought the items at a local pet supply shop, so the items in question may be good bargains, or they may be junk. Plenty of good pieces of equipment are out there, but so are plenty of bad ones. Don't discount anything Uncle Ed gives you; just be aware it may not hold up to serious grooming chores, and you may have to replace it.

Say, for example, that you have some combs and brushes and an odd looking grooming thingy. Match them up the best you can with what you need and make sure that they won't do more damage than good. Nail trimmers can get dull over time, so you'll need to replace the blade (if the clippers are guillotine style) or have it sharpened (if they're scissors style). Otherwise, trying to trim your dog's nails can be a big headache.

Throw away any tools that appear damaged or rusted, including combs with bent teeth and rakes with wobbly handles. Throw out nail cutters if lubricating them doesn't fix the hitch in the action. You can try lubricating them with light machine-tool oil. But remember that you don't need anything that will cause problems; it's cheaper and safer to buy new ones at this point than it is to try to fix a problem or risk an injury to you or your dog.

After matching up your supplies with what you truly need, you may find that some of your equipment amounts to the wrong tools for the type of dog you have. Again, Missy was a short-coated breed who needed a grooming mitt, but your Sasha is an Alaskan Malamute, a double-coated breed who'll never need some pieces of Missy's equipment. Don't throw those tools out, though. Instead, donate them to your local humane society, where they can be either put to good use or sold to someone who can use them.

Be sure to disinfect all used grooming supplies with a disinfectant made for use on grooming tools. Otherwise, your dog risks infection from them.

What about the supplies you already have, such as the dog shampoo and flea stuff and the (whew — what is that stinky stuff?) doggie deodorant? Go through them and see what you can do with them:

✔ If the supplies are flea-and-tick powder or an insecticide-type treatment, throw them out. You have three reasons for doing so:

- You don't know how old the stuff is.

- You don't know whether it's safe for your dog.

- Better methods for controlling fleas and ticks are usually available from your veterinarian.

✔ If the supplies are not insecticides and are fresh, check the labels for expiration dates and to find out whether the products are pH-balanced for dogs. If they are, then you can use them if the scents aren't too obnoxious. Remember, *you* have to smell your dog. (***Note:*** Some dog shampoos and conditioners don't carry a pH-balanced label even though they are. When in doubt, show the bottle to your vet or simply replace it with a quality name-brand product.)

✔ If you're really not sure about what you have, toss them out and buy the right stuff. Just don't tell Uncle Ed you did, okay?

After you have the pile of equipment and grooming products sorted, I bet you don't have as much as you thought you did. So take a look at what equipment and supplies you need, which I discuss in the next section.

Gathering the essential equipment

You may need to spend some money upfront to keep your dog's coat clean and beautiful, but a well-groomed dog is worth that expense.

Good equipment is necessary for doing the job right. You don't, however, need to buy the most expensive equipment. In fact, some of the best equipment can be made or purchased without spending too much money. For example, I have a wonderful grooming table that a friend's son made for me. I tell you where to find quality grooming supplies at bargain prices in the "Purchasing Your Supplies" section later in this chapter.

So what equipment must you have? Much depends on your dog's breed. For example, an Alaskan Malamute is going to have different needs than a Poodle, and both are going to have different needs than a Bluetick Coonhound. So some of the equipment may not be optional if you have a particular type of dog. Another consideration is the type of grooming you're doing — whether it's for home or for show.

The following lists describe the equipment you need for basic grooming of all dogs. Yes, although these lists are quite lengthy, you probably can find ways to save money here and there. The big items (grooming table, clippers, and hair dryer) are probably your biggest investment, so buy the best that you can afford, and you won't be disappointed later on.

You may want to contact friends or groomers who own equipment to see whether they're willing to let you try it out on your dog. Recommendations aside, you also need to be happy with the equipment you're using, and the only way to know whether you will be is to try it out.

For brushing and bathing

Be sure to have these items on hand:

- **Brushes:** Cost $5 to $20.

  - **Slicker brush (see Figure 3-1a):** You need at least two types of slickers to handle brushing — one with soft bristles to use on faces and sensitive areas and another with harder bristles for more vigorous grooming. A slicker is a necessary brush, more or less, for all breeds except the hairless variety.

  - **Flexible or rubber curry brush (see Figure 3-1b):** These brushes (Zoom Groom is one) are great for long-haired and short-haired dogs. They're good for getting loose fur out of the coat quickly and easily, and most dogs seem to enjoy their touch.

  - **Grooming/polishing mitt (see Figure 3-1c):** This glove has little nubs or bristles that are good for giving a once-over to a short-coated breed. Also called a *hound glove*. They cost $10 to $20.

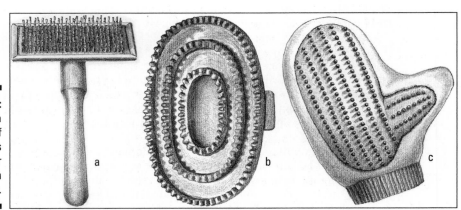

Figure 3-1:
Using a variety of brushes keeps your dog's coat in shape.

✔ **Combs:** Cost $5 to $30. All dog owners need fine- and medium-toothed combs regardless of the breeds of their respective dogs.

- **Fine-toothed comb (see Figure 3-2a):** This comb works best on dogs with fine hair.

- **Medium-toothed comb (see Figure 3-2b):** This comb is a good all-around basic comb.

- **Wide-toothed or coarse-toothed comb:** This comb is used on dogs with lots of hair or thick hair. Most groomers prefer Greyhound style combs (or combs without handles that have teeth running from end to end).

- **Flea comb (see Figure 3-2c):** You need at least one flea comb to help you check for fleas and to detangle, but because the low-end plastic flea combs are so cheap, buy a handful. Heavy-duty flea combs are a bit pricier but not by much. Costs range from under $1 to $10.

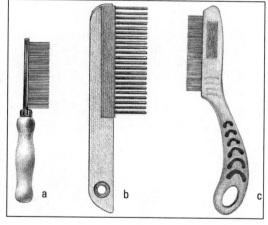

Figure 3-2:
An assortment of combs help you care for your dog's coat.

a   b   c

✔ **Grooming table:** I consider a grooming table essential even for home grooming because it keeps your dog secure and still. Grooming your dog while you're standing also saves your back! The table doesn't have to be fancy — just make sure it's big enough for your dog to stand on and for you to work around comfortably. It needs to be equipped with a nonskid surface and sturdy legs. You can build or buy one, depending on your inclination. Cost ranges from $50 to $200.

If you invest in a grooming table, I recommend adding a grooming arm and noose (as shown in Figure 3-3). The arm and noose keep your dog centered in one place on the grooming table while you work on him. Cost is about $20 to $40. **_Warning:_** Never leave a dog unattended in a grooming noose.

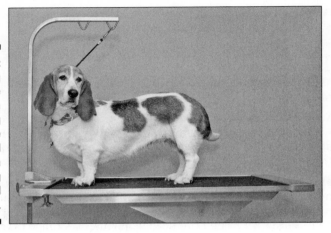

Figure 3-3: Your dog stays in one place on a grooming table equipped with a grooming arm and noose.

✔ **Mat rake (see Figure 3-4a):** This tool has sharp teeth that you use to rake through a mat. They occasionally need to be sharpened. Cost is $10 to $30.

✔ **Mat splitter (see Figure 3-4b):** A mat splitter is an essential piece of equipment for any dog with medium to long hair. Mat splitters come in different forms, but they work by cutting through the mat safely while you're combing the dog's coat. They occasionally need to be sharpened. Cost runs about $10 to $30.

If used improperly, mat splitters and rakes can cut into a dog's skin. See Chapter 9 for advice on how to use these tools properly.

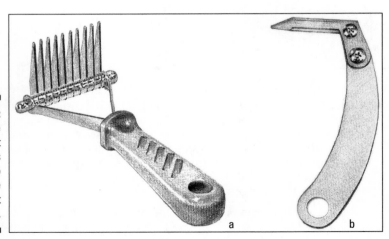

Figure 3-4: A mat rake (a) or mat splitter (b) is used to remove persistent mats.

a   b

✔ **Pet blow-dryer:** Pet dryers are made to blow off as much water as possible to dry your dog quickly. I recommend two styles: force dryers and stand dryers. *Force dryers* are used for drying a dog while she's loose; *stand dryers* are used for drying a dog on a table; they blow air on top of the dog. (I don't recommend cage dryers, which fasten to a dog's cage or crate, due to the number of overheating deaths associated with them.) Force dryers cost from $100 to $400, and stand dryers cost from $400 to $1,000, making these dryers less practical for most home groomers.

Luckily, you can use a blow-dryer for humans that's equipped with a no-heat setting to get the same effect; a dryer like that sets you back only $10 to $20.

✔ **Towels:** You can use your own towels or splurge for some that you use only for grooming your dog. If you decide to buy towels specifically for your dog, get white towels that you can easily toss in the washing machine with some detergent and bleach. Cost ranges from nothing to $20.

✔ **Tub:** You can bathe your dog for free in your home bathtub or sink (if you have a Toy breed), or you can go all out and splurge on a professional grooming tub (which I address in the "Adding optional equipment and supplies" section later in this chapter).

✔ **Undercoat rake:** This tool is for dogs who have thick undercoats or who shed quite a bit. Undercoat rakes have either two sets of teeth (see Figure 3-5) or a single set that's long enough to pull out the dense undercoat. To work properly, the rake teeth need to be as long as your dog's coat. Cost is $10 to $30.

Figure 3-5:
An undercoat rake is used on dogs with thick undercoats.

For clipping and neatening

Be sure to have these items on hand:

- **Electric clippers:** Electric clippers that are made for trimming dog hair are available in either rechargeable or plug-in styles. What you need depends largely on your dog and what kind of grooming you're doing. If your dog doesn't require a clipper-intensive grooming session — just a touchup here or there or the removal of a mat — then you can probably get away with a cheaper clipper (labeled for pet home use). If you plan to do several styles or show cuts or to work on more than one dog, you're probably looking at a more expensive clipper. Cost is about $40 to $300.

  Most clippers come with some type of blade, but you need other blades, depending on what type of clipping you're doing. See Chapter 7 for more about clipper blades. Cost of blades is $15 to $60 each.

  If your clippers don't come with lubricating oil, be sure to pick some up to keep your clipper blades well-lubricated and in tip-top working condition.

- **Forceps and clamps:** Not for surgery but rather for caring for the ears, these tools are the same as surgical instruments; they're sold through grooming shops and mail-order catalogs. Cost is $10 to $20.

- **Nail cutters:** These cutters can be either scissors-style (see Figure 3-6a) or guillotine-style (see Figure 3-6b), but they must be the appropriate size for your dog, and they need to be sharp. The guillotine-style has a guard and a blade that slides forward when you push down on the handle. The scissors-style operates much like a pair of scissors. Some scissors-style cutters have a safety gauge that helps keep you from trimming too much of the nail and *quicking* the dog (that is, cutting the pink part — see Chapter 6). You can replace the blades in guillotine-style cutters, but you can't do that with the scissors-style. Instead, you must have the scissors-style cutters sharpened. Either type of cutter works fine, and which one you use is pretty much a matter of personal preference.

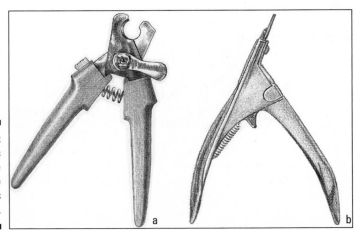

Figure 3-6:
Nail cutters
make
doggie
pedicures
simple.

✔ **Toothbrush for dogs:** I prefer the finger toothbrushes, which fit on your finger because they give you good control when brushing your pooch's teeth. They cost between $5 and $10. You can use a less expensive human toothbrush in a pinch.

Other important equipment to have on hand

Be sure to have these items on hand:

✔ **First-aid kit:** Just in case your dog gets injured, you need a first-aid kit. See Chapter 17 for more information about assembling the right kind of first-aid kit for dogs. Cost is $10 to $50.

✔ **Grooming diary:** You need a notebook or journal in which you can make notes on what you've done and how the grooming session went (see Chapter 1). Cost is $1 to $10.

✔ **Spray bottles and plastic bottles to hold supplies:** Cheap and easy, you can buy them just about anywhere for $1 to $5. Use them to hold liquids like doggie shampoo or detangler solution.

✔ **Tack box:** This storage box is where you put your equipment and supplies. You can get one that's fancy or one that's plain, depending on your budget and tastes. You can even use plastic storage containers to keep all your different kinds of equipment and supplies separate. Cost is $25 to $200.

Stocking up on important routine supplies

In this section, I talk about supplies you must have, stuff that you're probably going to purchase again and again, including shampoos, conditioners, and other items that you're going to use on your dog.

You need to purchase supplies that work for dogs, not people. Shampoos that work for people often are not intended for a dog's coat and can dry out or damage your dog's hair. Can they work in a pinch? Yes, of course, but they're not good over the long term. People toothpaste, however, should never be used on dogs, because it contains fluoride, which is quite toxic to dogs when swallowed.

The good news is that many professional-grade supplies are inexpensive when you know where to buy them. For example, a professional-grade shampoo can cost $10 to $30 a gallon, an amount good for dozens of washes.

Ask a dog-owner friend to share the expense of buying a gallon of doggie shampoo and conditioner. The amount that you both save on supplies is well worth the effort. Split the supplies up in plastic bottles and label them clearly.

The items in the following sections need to go in your tack box. For more about organizing your tack box check out the section on "Organizing Your Accoutrements" later in this chapter.

So check out the supplies that you really need.

For brushing and bathing

Be sure to have these items on hand:

- **Conditioner for dogs:** Sometimes called *cream rinse,* dog conditioner is used after the shampoo to help keep the coat shiny and to prevent tangles. The conditioner needs to be pH-balanced for dogs (in other words, don't use human hair conditioner). Choose one that you can rinse out (versus a leave-in coat conditioner, which I discussion later in the "Optional supplies" section). Cost ranges from $10 to $30 per gallon.

- **Detangler solution for dogs:** You spray this solution into snarls and mats in your dog's coat to make combing them out easier. It's generally intended for medium- or long-coated dogs. Cost is $10 to $20 per quart.

- **Shampoo for dogs:** This shampoo needs to be pH-balanced for dogs (shampooing your dog often with human shampoo can harm her coat and skin). Ask your vet to recommend a shampoo appropriate for your dog's coat, or look for a professional-grade grooming shampoo, which almost always works better than the grocery store varieties. You can get them in several varieties: scented (in all sorts of wonderful smells), hypoallergenic, antifungal, specifically for white or black coats, tearless (a great option for beginning groomers), waterless (for cleaning up your dog in between baths), and so on. Unless you have a specific problem that you're trying to address (ringworm, hot spots, and allergies), you're better off staying with a good dog shampoo that cleans the coat but isn't medicated. You can pick one that smells really nice, too. Cost is $10 to $60 per gallon.

For clipping and neatening

Be sure to have these items on hand:

- **Cotton swabs:** Not for ears, cotton swabs are used to clean around wrinkles. Cost is less than $5.

- **Eye topical ointment:** This ointment is used to protect your dog's eyes when bathing. Cost runs about $5 to $10.

- **Otic solution for dogs:** This solution is applied to your dog's ears to keep them clean. See Chapter 6. Cost is $5 to $10.

- **Sterile cotton balls:** You need cotton balls for cleaning ears and around your dog's eyes and to keep water out of ears while bathing your dog. Cost runs less than $5.

- ✔ **Sterile cotton gauze:** Sterile gauze is used for cleaning ears and around eyes. Cost is less than $5.

- ✔ **Styptic powder:** A powder with *styptic qualities,* or the ability to halt minor bleeding, this substance often is used on bleeding nails. Cost is less than $5.

- ✔ **Toothpaste for dogs:** Malt, chicken, or some other dog-pleasing flavor — what a great way to brush your dog's teeth! Cost is $5 to $10.

Other important supplies to have on hand

Be sure to have these items on hand:

- ✔ **Paper towels:** Cost is $1 to $2.

- ✔ **Plastic storage containers:** Tupperware, Glad, or Ziploc are good ones. They work for everyday use in grooming. You need them to hold stuff. Cost is $5 to $10.

- ✔ **Resealable plastic bags:** Ziploc or Glad zipper bags are good ones for everyday use in grooming. Use them to hold equipment or supplies. Cost runs less than $5.

Adding optional equipment and supplies

In this section, I focus on equipment and supplies that are optional. I use the term "optional" loosely, because you may find that you can't do without so-called optional items in certain circumstances, such as when preparing for the show ring or handling a specific type of (or even difficult) dog.

Without a doubt, other equipment and supplies that you may find useful or helpful are available. When considering them, use your best judgment on whether you think they'll work for you and your dog.

Optional equipment

Tools you may need but for the most part are considered optional include

- ✔ **Bathing noose:** This device usually affixes to the side of a tub with a suction cup. It fits around the dog's neck and holds him in one place while you bathe him. Cost runs $10 to $20. ***Warning:*** Even though a strong dog usually can pull free from this device, never leave a dog unattended in a grooming noose.

- ✔ **Bait pouch:** Used to hold treats while showing your dog (see Chapter 18). Cost is $1 to $10.

- ✔ **Bow, ribbons, and other "girlie" dog embellishments:** You know what I'm talking about. You'll pay $5 to $10.

- ✔ **Grooming apron:** Like any other apron, this one keeps hair and grooming stuff off your clothing. Cost ranges from $10 to $30.

- ✔ **Grooming harness for the grooming arm** (described in the "For brushing and bathing" section earlier in this chapter): This contraption keeps the dog standing while you groom. Cost is $10 to $25. ***Warning:*** Never leave a dog unattended in a grooming harness!

- ✔ **Nail cauterizer:** A high-tech version of styptic powder, this tool cauterizes the nail and stops the bleeding if you accidentally cut to your dog's nail to the quick. Groomers like to use this tool because it's fast and seals the cut right away. Cost runs $20 to $50.

- ✔ **Nail grinders:** Some dogs can't stand the nail clippers but can deal with a nail-grinding tool, similar to a rotary tool. Cost is $40 to $60.

- ✔ **Professional grooming tub:** This option is an expensive one, but if you can manage it, it's a wonderful way to bathe your dog without hurting your back. Cost is $200 to $2,000.

- ✔ **Pin and bristle brushes:** These brushes are two other types of brushes that can be helpful but aren't necessary if you have a slicker brush. Cost is $5 to $10.

- ✔ **Ramp or step stairs:** Stairs or a ramp is a good device for getting your dog either into/out of the tub or onto the grooming table without hurting your back or forcing a geriatric dog to jump. Cost is $50 to $200.

- ✔ **Scissors (or shears):** For styling and clipping (see Chapter 7). Cost ranges from $10 to $75 or more.

- ✔ **Shedding blade:** This grooming tool has small teeth like a serrated knife (but they're not sharp). Shedding blades are usually shaped like a loop attached to a handle, and they pull out a heavy undercoat quickly. Cost is $5 to $25.

- ✔ **Show slip collars:** Used when showing your dog (see Chapter 18). Cost runs $15 to $40.

- ✔ **Shower spray attachment:** A spray attachment makes water coming from a faucet into a more-showerlike spray, making dog bathing easier. Cost is $20 to $50.

- ✔ **Stripping knife:** This tool is used for stripping the coat to remove dead hair and is used only for stripped breeds (see Chapter 12). This tool is optional because it's specific for stripped breeds, and many stripped breeds can be clipped. Cost runs $10 to $20.

- ✔ **Thinning scissors (or shears):** For thinning the coat or blending one layer in with another. They cost $20 to $40 each.

- ✔ **Tub mats:** This antiskid protection helps your dog keep her footing in the tub. Cost runs $5 to $20.

Optional supplies

Supplies you may need but which are considered optional for the most part include

- ✔ **Bath wipes:** For in-between touchups. Cost is $5 to $10.

- ✔ **Chalk:** Used mainly to mask blemishes in color to give your dog's legs even appearance (mostly in show dogs, see Chapter 18). Cost is $5 to $10.

- ✔ **Cornstarch:** Used for chalking show dogs' legs (see Chapter 18), cornstarch provides a much more natural look than white chalk, and it isn't as abrasive or expensive as chalk. Cost runs less than $5.

- ✔ **Deodorant sprays:** Doggie deodorants give your canine a scent other than *Eau de Mutt*. Cost ranges from $5 to $10.

- ✔ **Doggie hair mousse:** For the stylin' dog. Cost is $5 to $15.

- ✔ **Ear powder:** Use this product if you pluck your dog's ear hair (see Chapter 6). Cost is $5 to $10.

- ✔ **Gel:** Yes, sparkle gel has hit the pets, too. Cost runs $5 to $10 for glittery glamour.

- ✔ **Hot spot spray:** Used for reducing itching and clearing up *hot spots,* or sore, itchy, inflamed skin. Cost is $5 to $15.

- ✔ **Leave-in coat conditioners:** These conditioners are useful for dogs with dry hair or dogs that are shown a lot. They usually give the coat the look and feel of a specific texture, depending on what you're trying to do with the coat. Cost is $10 to $30 each.

- ✔ **Medicated shampoo for skin conditions:** Cost is $20 to $100 per gallon.

- ✔ **Pet tear-stain remover:** Not all dogs get tear stains, so tear-stain remover isn't vital for all breeds. Cost: $5 to $15.

Where's the flea and tick stuff?

You may notice what appears to be a distinct oversight on my part when it comes to mentioning flea-and-tick items. The reason is a good one. Up until ten or so years ago, fleas and ticks usually were handled with grooming products like flea dips and sprays for the animal, flea bombs (or other such nasty devices) for the home, and insecticides for your yard and lawn.

All those items involve chemicals, rather poisonous ones at that. What's worse is that these insecticides react with each other, so the stuff you put on your dog is affected by the stuff in your house or on your lawn. What's more, dog flea products can be toxic to cats, so you have to be careful if you have feline friends.

In recent years, however, researchers figured out not only how to kill the bugs but also how to prevent them from growing up and reproducing on your dog. As a result, a number of new systemic flea-and-tick-control products are available from your veterinarian. These products can be administered either topically (spot-on) or orally, and not only do they kill the fleas and ticks, but they also stop them from reproducing, thereby ending the infestation permanently.

So if you have a flea-control problem, the first person you need to talk to is your veterinarian. He or she has the right systemics and can recommend control products that work together more safely than any of the ones you can choose on your own. See Chapter 16 for more info.

Purchasing Your Supplies

Okay, so now you have your list of equipment and supplies that you need to buy. Looking over the list of what you have versus what you need or want (doesn't that $2,000 grooming tub look cool?), you discover that you still have quite a bit to purchase. If you're like me, you're on limited funds and you've checked your bank account and decided that although you want to buy the best stuff, you don't want to take out a second mortgage to do it.

So where do you purchase your supplies? Do you go to the local big-box retailer and look for a grooming table? Do you look at the local pet boutique for ribbons and bows? Do you go pick it up at the local grocery store and ask the store manager which comb works best with your dog's undercoat?

I ask these questions in jest, because I'm sure you know by now that you're unlikely to get a lot of help from places that don't specialize in grooming equipment. That doesn't mean that these places won't have what you're looking for, but rather that you have to know what you're looking for and whether it's going to work for you. The sections that follow can help you discover where best to make your purchases.

From the grocery store

The grocery store isn't the first place that I'd look for pet supplies unless I was really in a pinch and had to pick something up right away. Grocery stores are great for getting groceries, but pet-related items are more of a convenience than a quality thing. Oh yes, they'll have doggie shampoo and combs and whatnot — and some may be of decent quality — but you can buy better-quality stuff elsewhere for the same price or less. It's kind of like using the cheap bargain-brand shampoo on your hair. Yes, it works. Yes, you'll live with it, but no, you won't always be 100 percent satisfied with the results.

The positive side is that when you have the grooming implement in your hand, you can actually see the quality of the item, feel it, and (when the store clerk isn't looking) try it out on your own hair. (Did I say that?) Seriously, if you need something now, the grocery may or may not have it. But if the store does have that item and you need it now, the grocery is a fine place to buy it.

From big-box retailers

Big-box retailers are kind of like super-duper discount department stores, and some of them even have grocery stores in them. They carry a wider variety of merchandise that usually includes more pet equipment and supplies. You know them as Wal-Mart, Target, and a number of other big-box stores that cater to people buying everything from pet supplies to breakfast cereal and prom dresses.

Big-box retailers usually have a pet section where you can purchase grooming equipment. They frequently have tools and supplies at a pretty deep discount because they buy in bulk and pass those savings along to consumers. You'll probably find a fair number of name-brand pet supplies and maybe some small distributor items too, but for the most part, you're not going to find much in the line of specialty equipment — so you may not find everything that you're looking for.

Like the grocery, one positive side to going to big-box stores is that you can touch and see the product you're going to buy, feel the instant gratification of checking something off your list when you buy it, and experience a fun shopping trip even if your bank account suffers, because big-box stores have so many different things on sale.

You can also buy generic supply items like cotton balls, towels, plastic containers, and the like from a big-box store. (You thought I was joking about the bank account thing, didn't you?)

One thing you need to keep in mind when going to the big-box stores is that although they usually have the best prices, that isn't always the case. Try shopping around if you can.

From big-box pet supply stores

If I'm going to talk about big-box discount department stores, I may as well talk about the big-box versions of pet supply stores like PETCO and PetSmart. These supply stores cater to guess who? You! Well, they cater to the pet owner. These stores offer you aisle upon aisle of pet stuff, including doggie grooming equipment and supplies. Why, you'll feel like you've gone to doggie nirvana.

The neat part of going to these stores is that you usually have more than one brand and more than one choice when it comes to the things you need to buy. You'll find plenty of doggie shampoos, conditioners, spritzes, sprays, deodorants, combs, brushes, and myriad assortment of other grooming products. You'll probably find a grooming table and maybe a doggie blow-dryer, but you may not have quite the choice you have when you look in catalogs or on the Internet.

However, you still have the ability to touch and handle the merchandise and actually have it in your possession after you leave the store. Most pet supply stores also have trained staff who at least try to assist you with your choices.

If groomers are on staff (and they usually are), you may be able to ask for advice about what equipment and products they like to use. Some of the store's own brand supplies are usually a bit less expensive than other name-brand or specialty items, and they're usually pretty good quality.

One downside to these mega–pet supply stores is that their prices can be very good or very bad, depending on the item and the demand. For example, you can save a bundle on shampoo but spend too much on clippers.

From très chic pet boutiques

The pet boutiques thrive even in places where the big mega–pet supply stores exist, simply because they're trendy and they serve a niche. No, they're not going to give you the cheapest price on your dog's kibble. In fact, pet boutiques probably aren't going to carry your dog's kibble, unless your dog eats a specialty brand that isn't carried by the big mega–pet supply stores.

Because these shops are so specialized, you're likely to walk into one, chat with the shop owner, and come out with some top-notch stuff — especially if she caters to show folks. You probably won't have a lot of money left, but you're bound to get some good advice and even suggestions for grooming your dog. If the shop doesn't have the supplies you're looking for, ask the shop owner. She probably can order it from her supplier within a few days.

The downside of pet boutiques is, of course, the price and in some cases, selection. If you have to special-order anything, getting it may take a few weeks. Nevertheless, getting to know someone who's knowledgeable about grooming items is kind of nice.

From groomer-supply stores and catalogs

My favorite way to shop is through groomer-supply mail-order catalogs. It's sort of like having a discount shop just a phone call away.

In most cases, you can find exactly what you're looking for as you peruse various groomer and pet-supply catalogs — and usually for much less than what you'd pay at a retail store or specialty shop.

One downside of buying from catalogs is that you don't necessarily have the ability to inspect the item firsthand to determine whether it's something you really want. However, if you've seen the item and can get it for a lower price, shopping by catalog is well worth the effort.

Another problem with buying through a catalog is that you must wait for it to be shipped to you. Depending on the shipping mode used, your order can take from a day to almost two weeks to be delivered.

Mail-order buying has two more major drawbacks. First, you need to be reasonably certain that the company is reputable and will replace an item or refund your money if you're not happy with it. Secondly, some catalog companies offer tremendous savings only to have that savings eaten up by shipping and handling fees. When shipping something big like a grooming table or a tub, companies can tack on some pretty hefty charges.

Whenever you can, make your mail-order purchases from a company that waives shipping charges on most orders.

From dog shows

A less-obvious place to shop for grooming supplies is at dog shows. Most major cities have dog shows at one time or another during the year, and on the East and West coasts, dog shows occur nearly every weekend.

You can find out what shows are in your area through the American Kennel Club Web site at www.akc.org or through the Dogpatch, which maintains a calendar of events on its Web site at www.dogpatch.org.

Dog shows are great because not only do you see people preparing their dogs for the ring, but you also receive some good grooming tips simply by watching handlers and owners and finding out what works for them. If you ever wanted to see the proper cut on a particular dog, a conformation dog show is the perfect place. Just be sure to stay out of the way as handlers rush their dogs to the ring. And be sure not to be a pest while someone's grooming, especially right before the ring time. Furthermore, never pet a show dog except with permission from the handler.

Most big dog shows have plenty of vendors with grooming supplies, and you can often buy some deeply discounted items on the last day of the show or when they run *show specials,* offering special prices during the show.

The downside to shopping at a dog show it that it can be hit or miss. You may find exactly what you're looking for, which is great, but although you may find plenty of good deals, you still may come home empty-handed. If you're attending a conformation show, you can use it as a resource. Otherwise, don't go completely out of your way just to attend, hoping that you'll get a really good bargain.

Online

Like catalogs, the Internet is quickly becoming a favorite place for pet owners (me included) to shop for pet supplies and equipment. So much so that catalog-based groomer and supply houses, mega–pet supply stores, and even trendy pet boutiques now offer products for sale online. Being online makes buying your grooming supplies easy, even at 2 a.m. when no bricks-and-mortar stores are open. You can also use online resources to make a list of what you need to pick up either directly from the (nearby) store or by calling in a phone order.

The good part about the Internet is that you can find some great bargains. However, just like mail-order companies, you can't examine the item instantaneously, so you have to guess whether the product will suit your needs. You also have to wait for the product to be delivered, and you may have to pay shipping and handling charges that eat up much of the savings you earn by shopping the Internet.

Always be careful when dealing with companies on the Internet. Make sure that you deal only with known reputable companies, because too many crooks are lurking online, trying to steal *your* credit-card numbers. If you do make purchases online, be sure that the company has SSL (secured socket layers) that keep the transaction safe from unscrupulous people. Lastly, if you're not sure about the company, you can use a transaction service like PayPal, which serves as an intermediary between buyer and seller, protecting the integrity of the transaction. You can learn more about PayPal, an eBay company, at its Web site: www.paypal.com.

Many companies offer Internet-only specials that reward you for ordering online. Take advantage of them whenever you can.

Setting Aside a Grooming Space

After you have all your equipment, you have to figure out not only where you're going to put it but also where you're going to groom your dog. Grooming requires enough room to brush and comb out your dog without getting in the way of cooking dinner, watching TV, or doing laundry. It takes a lot of room.

Your grooming area doesn't have to be elaborate, but it needs to be located where you can take your dog to work on him without many distractions. After all, you don't need kids underfoot while you're trying to trim your dog's coat, and you don't want your dog running around while you're trying to bathe him.

The basic needs for a grooming place are as follows:

- ✔ Enough room to set up your grooming table.

- ✔ Good lighting so you can see as you work on your dog.

- ✔ Adequate isolation that puts you far enough away from the beaten path in your household that you can work on your dog without any distractions.

- ✔ Enough power outlets for clippers and blow-dryers.

- ✔ Sufficient running water that you can use to bathe your dog (or close proximity to a bathroom).

- ✔ Adequate climate control. The area needs to be heated well enough to ward off drafts in the winter, and it needs to be cool enough in the summer to prevent overheating.

- ✔ Enough shelves and storage areas to keep grooming supplies stowed safely.

Plenty of possible areas exist. The sections that follow look at each of them.

A groom room of your own

The most ideal situation is having a separate room in which to groom your dog. A spare bedroom, a modified utility room, or even a basement can be made into a fabulous doggie beauty parlor. Just knock out the walls, add dog bathing tubs, wall-to-wall storage units, and you're all set.

But most people aren't made of money, and in some cases, space is at a premium. When that's the case, you can sometimes make do with a room doing double duty for grooming. A spare bedroom can quickly be made into a grooming area, and then after everything's put away, it becomes a spare bedroom again for your Aunt Emma when she visits with that yummy apple pie and homemade liver treats. Just be sure to clean the bedroom thoroughly, or she may not come back to visit.

Make sure that you check out unused or underused areas of your house. That nook under the stairwell, a small utility room, or that sunny alcove that doesn't have anything in it can be converted into a grooming area. Although the requirements for power and water may have you scrambling, having a place to set up your grooming table and tack boxes is all that you really need for most of your grooming procedures. And remember, your grooming table folds up so you can stow it in a closet whenever necessary.

You may have to invest in some space heaters during the wintertime if the area you choose is normally drafty.

The bathroom

If you're planning to bathe your dog, the bathroom tub is going to become important unless your dog is small enough to bathe in a sink or laundry tub. The bathroom tub doesn't have to be fancy; it just needs hot and cold running water, a nonslip mat, and a bathing noose to keep your dog in place while you're bathing him. You may want to use an extra hair trap to remove the hair from the water before it goes down the drain, blocks your pipes, and forces you to endure an expensive visit from the plumber.

The location of the bathroom in relation to the grooming area is important. Having your grooming bathroom near the grooming area is helpful, because you won't have to shuffle a wet dog through so much of the house. Just be sure that the bathroom is kept free of drafts in the winter and has proper air circulation through the summer.

The great outdoors

If you don't have enough space to do your grooming in the house, you can try setting up a grooming area outside. After all, you can give your dog a bath with a hose and then pop him up on the table for a brushing, right?

Well, maybe. First of all, grooming a dog outdoors isn't an ideal situation. For one thing, you can't control the temperature or weather. Grooming your dog during an electrical storm would be quite sporting to say the least, don't you think? So you can't control the temperature, the wind, the rain, or the snow, thus making outdoor grooming downright uncomfortable in most circumstances. What's more, windy conditions probably will get dust and dirt in your dog's clean hair.

Certainly bathing a dog outside has advantages. After all, after you bathe him, the dog can shake himself off without getting water everywhere. Many dogs tolerate outdoor baths, but I guarantee that your dog will detest being bathed in nothing but cold water, unless the air temperatures are higher than 90°F (32°C).

Dogs chill easily whenever the air temperature is below 80°F (27°C).

Lastly, the outdoors means many distractions for virtually any canine. Certain noises and activities can startle or frighten your dog, and squirrels, kids playing, other dogs, and other similar distractions can turn an otherwise routine grooming session into a disaster.

Dog washes: Options for grooming when you have no space

If you live in an apartment or have little or no space to groom your dog, don't despair — you still have options.

One recent innovation is the opening of grooming salons that enable you to groom your dog yourself. These do-it-yourself dog washes give you the best of both worlds. They provide really good facilities with dog tubs, grooming tables, and even doggie blow-dryers so you can groom your dog either with their equipment or yours. These salons may charge extra for shampoo, towels, and so on, but you conveniently bring your dog and use their facility without messing up your house.

Organizing Your Accoutrements

After you have your grooming area planned out and your equipment and supplies gathered, it's time to organize and put everything together. You want to organize and assemble your equipment according to the tasks you'll be performing. For example, you want to have all your bathing supplies in one area so that you have everything you need in one spot when bathing your dog. Organize your supplies as follows, using a separate plastic container for each supplies category:

✔ **Brushing supplies**

- Brushes
- Combs
- Mat splitter
- Mat rake
- Shedding blade
- Spray bottle of detangler solution
- Stripping knife

✔ **Bathing supplies**

- Conditioner
- Cotton balls
- pH-balanced shampoo
- Protective eye ointment
- Towels and a blow-dryer

- **Clipping supplies**
  - Electric clippers with clipper oil or lubricant
  - Extra clipper blades (as needed)
- **Toothbrushing supplies**
  - Doggie toothbrush
  - Doggie toothpaste
- **Ear-care supplies**
  - Cotton balls
  - Drying towels
  - Ear powder (optional)
  - Forceps
  - Otic solution
  - Sterile gauze
- **Face-care supplies**
  - Cotton swabs
  - No-rinse shampoo
  - Tear stain remover
  - Towels
  - Washcloth
- **Toenail-trimming supplies**
  - Cauterizer or styptic powder
  - Cotton balls
  - Toenail clippers or nail grinder
- **Show supplies** (Chapter 18 provides a list.)

Chapter 4

Training Your Dog for Grooming

In This Chapter

▶ Drilling your dog on essential grooming manners

▶ Helping your dog accept being touched in sensitive areas such as paws and face

▶ Establishing a grooming routine

▶ Handling troublesome dogs

So you dread the idea of grooming your dog. All dog owners, at one time or another, have had a dog they just couldn't groom. Perhaps a dog's bad experience being brushed or combed was to blame, or maybe you cut a toenail too short (Ouch!) and your dog bled and now won't let you near him, or maybe your dog just doesn't like the bath. Whatever the reason, you're facing a dog who doesn't like to be groomed.

The truth is you still can have a dog who at least tolerates grooming. The trick is to train your dog to get him used to what you normally do when grooming him, such as putting him on the table or gently handling his mouth or feet. In this chapter, I give you great pointers on how to show your dog that the basics of grooming are not such a bad experience after all.

Refining Your Dog's Grooming Manners

Good grooming manners don't happen overnight. Familiarizing your dog with procedures is essential in anything you're trying to get your dog to do. Dogs need to be trained in good grooming manners so they get used to the idea of being cleaned and preened — they may even come to enjoy it! After all, grooming is attention and time spent with you.

Unfortunately, most dogs are introduced to grooming at the worst possible time, when they're either dirty, have mats in their hair, they need their toenails clipped, or all of the above. They struggle (Who wouldn't?) because they don't like being held or having their feet touched or their fur pulled. Remember when you were a kid and had a mat (or bubblegum) in your hair?

You know how unpleasant that is. I used to hate to have my mom comb my hair, because I always had so many tangles. Your dog feels the same way.

The best way to instill good grooming manners in your dog is to make the experience a pleasant one. Otherwise, your dog simply won't participate or will do so only grudgingly.

The best time to train a dog to accept any kind of grooming procedure is when he's a puppy. Puppies are more open to new things, and you have time to build up good experiences from this openness. When your dog hasn't had any bad experiences with grooming, he's more likely to be accepting of the procedures.

But even if you have a dog who has endured bad experiences with grooming, you still can retrain him to accept it. Your dog just needs more time and more training.

 Try spending about five to ten minutes a day training your dog to deal with grooming issues. Keep your sessions short and fun and always end them with a quick game of fetch or another activity that your dog enjoys.

Using positive reinforcement to train your dog

A great training method known as *positive reinforcement* works well with dogs in most situations. When using this method, you reward the dog's behavior that you want to see and ignore — don't acknowledge — what you don't want to see. For example, every time your dog hops onto the grooming table, give her a treat or high praise — "Good dog!" When your dog doesn't get on the table, don't give her any rewards or attention — but don't punish her, either. The trick is providing a good enough reward that your dog actually wants to get on the table each time.

Most dogs are food driven, so food is used in most positive reinforcement training, because it's easy to hand out and most dogs do what you want to do for the right kinds of treats. You may have to experiment a bit with your dog, especially if one treat isn't going to do it for her. You may have to think out-side the box and go with human food. I haven't yet found a dog who would pass up cooked steak, liver, or chicken. I'm sure they're out there, though. On the other hand, keeping a handful of your dog's regular kibble close at hand can be just what the vet ordered.

When handing out treats, make sure they're small enough so you can reward your dog with a bunch of them. Unless your dog is ultrathin, doling out medium to large treats is likely to make for a very fat dog in no time. Try splitting treats into thirds or buying treats made in tiny-sized portions.

Some dogs simply are not food driven. If yours truly isn't, try finding a toy that she's ecstatic about or a brief activity she really enjoys, and use that as your treat.

Showing your dog how to enjoy grooming procedures

If humans have one fault when it comes to their canine friends, it's that they can be a little impatient. Yes, dog owners have it all figured out, and somehow (perhaps by osmosis or by rote) they think their dogs have figured it out, too. What dog owners forget is that dogs sometimes find humans just as perplexing as humans sometimes find dogs. The problem: What translates well to humans doesn't translate at all to dogs, and that applies to grooming.

When you begin a grooming session, your dog probably won't understand that it's ultimately for his benefit — even if you try to explain it to him. He is, after all, a dog, and dogs don't come with the knowledge of combs, brushes, shampoo, and nail clippers.

Because you can't simply sit your dog on the couch and rationally explain grooming to him, you pretty much have to leave him in the dark about why it has to be done. You can, however, make your dog comfortable with tools and procedures simply by minimizing the scary and painful sides of grooming as much as possible and giving rewards and praise for behaving in the right way.

You go about this task by desensitizing your dog to smaller grooming issues that won't bother him as much by doing the following:

- **Choosing a time when your dog is a little tired and maybe a little hungry.** You want your dog to be willing to stand still for a while and to accept food from you when you want to initiate a grooming procedure, such as brushing or toenail trimming. However, you don't want your dog so tired that he's falling asleep.

- **Finding a quiet place around your house where you can spend some time alone with your dog.** The room in which you plan to groom your dog needs to be in an out-of-the-way area where neither you nor your dog is distracted.

- **Petting your dog gently all over his body.** Observe his reactions as you touch his legs, the sides of his body, his face, his tail, and his rear end.

✔ **Giving your dog small treats as you're petting him.** These morsels provide a distraction for your dog when you're touching him in areas he otherwise may find worrisome or uncomfortable.

If your dog shows signs of sensitivity or nervousness when you touch a particular area, don't push it. You may be tempted to insist on touching the spot your dog's reacting to harder, but don't. Lighten up on the pressure to find out whether the nervousness continues or abates. If it continues, move to another section of the body that he's more comfortable with you touching. As your dog relaxes, you can try to go back to the sensitive area with a gentler approach.

✔ **Keeping the petting sessions short — maybe one to two minutes, tops.** The length of these initial sessions isn't as important as the frequency. Intersperse them frequently throughout the day.

Gradually increase the length of the petting sessions as your dog relaxes and begins to enjoy them. You can also move the petting sessions into your grooming area, if you haven't done so already.

✔ **Getting your dog used to grooming objects, such as by running a brush or comb through his fur and against his skin.** Start with a soft slicker brush (see Chapter 3), substituting it for your hand and repeating the petting routines described earlier in this list.

If your dog is fearful of grooming procedures, you need to make the petting and brushing sessions extremely short at first. Use treats to coax your dog's attention away from the slicker brush so that he focuses instead on the food you're giving him and the pleasant sensation.

Whatever you do, don't push the sessions any longer than your dog can stand. If your dog reacts adversely to them, start out by holding a treat and letting him nibble at it. While he's distracted (tricky, eh?), slowly and gently use the slicker brush, praise him when he's reacts positively, and then stop. Work up to longer brushing sessions slowly.

Handling sensitive puppy feet

Dogs hate having their feet handled — possibly because they're ticklish but more likely because it just doesn't feel right to them. The fact is if you're going to groom your dog, at some point your dog must get used to having you hold her feet.

Being able to hold your dog's feet when grooming is essential. You need to hold them when you're:

🖝 Clipping your dog's toenails or trimming the fur between her paw pads

🖝 Checking your dog's feet for foreign bodies such as burrs, foxtails, thorns, and other stickers that can cause her to limp

🖝 Examining your dog for other injuries

You can help your dog acclimate to having her legs and feet touched in much the same way you work with her to accept grooming procedures (see previous section). After choosing a time when your dog's a little tired and maybe a little hungry and finding a quiet place where you can spend a little time together (your grooming place is a great spot), try the following:

1. **Pick up and then set down your dog's paws one at a time.**

   Observe her reactions as you pick up her feet. Don't hold them for any length of time — just a quick pickup, look-see, and then put them down.

   If she reacts negatively, try distracting her with a bit of food as you pick up the paws.

2. **Repeat the paw pick-up and put-down process several times a day.**

   Don't lengthen the sessions until your dog becomes comfortable with the procedure.

3. **Gradually lengthen the amount of time you're holding the paw when you pick it up.**

   Increase your holding time by a second or two until your dog is comfortable with you separately picking up all four feet. Distract her with food whenever necessary.

   If your dog shows any sensitivity or nervousness, don't push the process. Although you may be tempted, don't hang onto your dog's foot any longer, or hold it tighter, than your dog will allow. Reduce or increase the amount of time spent on this step according to whether your dog's nervousness continues or abates. If it continues, go back to Step 1 and work from there.

4. **Try a light one- or two-second massage as your dog becomes more comfortable with having her feet held.**

   Rub each toe individually rather than just holding the foot. The sensation may be new to your dog and a little scary, so be brief.

5. **Gradually increase the amount of time you spend massaging your dog's paws.**

   Your dog soon finds out that it's easy to relax and enjoy the massages. Be sure to move these sessions into your grooming area, if you haven't already done so.

Eventually your dog grows accustomed to having her feet handled. When you start clipping her toenails, try clipping the nails on only one paw at a time so you don't have to hold her in one place for so long. Just trim the tips; don't try to cut a lot off at this time. See Chapter 6 for more information about trimming toenails.

Manipulating your dog's mouth

Most dog owners never really have to handle a dog's mouth unless they need to give their dogs a pill — and then, watch out! As a dog owner, you soon learn that handling your pup's mouth can be a real struggle, and those pointy teeth can hurt like heck when you're on the receiving end.

The truth is that dog owners need to handle their dogs' mouths all along for good grooming reasons, such as:

- Brushing your dog's teeth
- Looking for foreign objects in your dog's mouth
- Giving your dog pills and liquid medication
- Checking your dog for health problems such as shock (gray gums) and dehydration (sticky gums)

The problem with your dog objecting to having his mouth handled is that he may consider letting you know his position in no uncertain terms — yes, ouch, big time — especially when his teeth are so close to you. You must be extremely careful when working around your dog's head, because snapping when frightened or in pain is an instinctive reaction for your dog. Go slowly and deliberately, and watch for signs of possible fear or even aggression when working with your dog's mouth.

Again, you can show your dog how to accept being touched on the mouth using a method similar to the way you persuade him to accept grooming procedures (see the previous section). Remember, slow and easy does the trick. After choosing a time when your dog's a little tired and maybe a little hungry and finding a quiet place where you can spend a little time together (your grooming place is a great spot), try the following:

1. **Touch the sides of your dog's mouth.**

   Observe his reactions as you're touching his mouth. Use light pressure — nothing major — and then give him a treat and as you touch his mouth, letting him work on the treat in your hand so that your fingers are touching his gums.

   Repeat this procedure a few times a session, several sessions a day, to get your dog used to it. If your dog reacts negatively, try distracting him with a bit of food as you touch his mouth.

2. **When your dog is comfortable with you touching his mouth, try pushing or flipping up his *flews* (upper gums) and letting them drop along each side of his mouth.**

   Don't lengthen the sessions until he becomes more comfortable with this procedure.

   Lengthen the flew-flip time by a second or two after your dog grows comfortable with that form of touching. Distract him with food if necessary.

3. **When your dog is accustomed to having his flews flipped up, you can lightly rub his gums with your fingers and a soft treat.**

   In place of the soft treat, you can try using a bit of doggie toothpaste that's flavored with chicken or malt.

   Don't force the issue if your dog shows any sensitivity or nervousness. Although you may be tempted to push on, don't. Instead, reduce the time spent rubbing his gums to find out whether the nervousness continues or abates. If it continues, go back to Step 1 and work from there.

4. **When your dog is more comfortable having his teeth and gums touched, try a light one- or two-second gum massage.**

   Rub the gum lightly rather than just touching it. This sensation may be a new one for your dog, and it may be a little scary, so be brief.

5. **Gradually increase the length of the massage sessions as your dog relaxes and starts to enjoy them.**

   Move them into your grooming area, if you haven't already done so.

As your dog relaxes and enjoys the attention, be sure to get him used to opening his mouth and having all his teeth and gums touched. Go slowly and gently — don't force.

Convincing your dog to accept eye contact

One mistake that dog owners sometimes make is not making proper eye contact with their dogs and then all of a sudden expecting the dog to accept eye contact. If your dog is uncomfortable with making eye contact, it may be because dogs sometimes consider eye contact as an aggressive, challenging, or domineering behavior.

However, when you're grooming your dog, you can't always avoid your dog's gaze, so you need to train your dog to accept eye contact as something pleasing and not challenging. You may see your dog avert her eyes when you look into them, but don't fret — she's only saying, "I know you're boss."

Training your dog to respond to the Watch-me cue can help you make better eye contact with your dog. Starting with a handful of treats and working with your dog when she's just a little tired and a little hungry, follow these steps:

1. **Get your dog's full attention by showing her one of the treats.**

   Hold a treat up to the bridge of your nose. Your dog should follow the treat with her eyes.

2. **When your dog makes eye contact, offer her praise and drop the treat so she can catch it.**

   Repeat this step several times to reinforce the pleasurable aspect of making eye contact.

   Practice Steps 1 and 2 several times a day.

3. **Pair the action in Steps 1 and 2 with a cue, such as "Watch me!"**

   Say, "Watch me!" show your dog the treat, and then give it to her when she makes eye contact.

The Watch-me cue is useful whenever you want to get your dog's attention.

Getting Your Dog to Help You Reach the Right Places

Grooming goes much more easily when your dog is willing to help you. Your dog doesn't necessarily have to compete in dog shows or attend obedience-training classes to know a few key cues that can make your job of grooming him that much easier.

Your dog needs to know how to

- Get onto and off of the grooming table
- Sit on command
- Lie down on one side or the other

Showing your dog how to do these things takes a certain amount of patience on your part and his. After he catches on, grooming will go much more quickly.

Helping your dog onto the grooming table

Getting your dog up on the grooming table is an important part of grooming. After all, you can't use the grooming table to groom your dog if you can't get your dog on it.

If you have a small- to medium-sized dog, picking her up and putting her on the grooming table isn't such a big chore. But if you have a large- or super-sized pooch, you're likely to schedule visits to your chiropractor after grooming sessions if you use that approach.

The two ways to coax your dog onto the table without hurting your back require training and may depend on whether your dog is capable. You can show your dog how to jump up on the table or provide accommodations that enable your dog to climb up on the table. Either way, after you show your dog how to get up on the table, you still need to make her stay there.

If your dog is arthritic, young, or just not athletic, a ramp or steps can be a handy solution. Several different kinds of steps and ramps are available.

Although most dogs love to hop onto the grooming table because they think they're getting away with climbing on the furniture, a few may be apprehensive. If you're trying to convince your dog to hop up onto the table and she just won't do it — even for the yummiest of treats — try using:

- ✔ **A lower table.** A shorter table, such as an old coffee table or other sturdy piece of furniture, can make hopping up easier for your dog. You then try working up to higher surfaces. Four cinder blocks and a heavy board or piece of plywood or adjustable agility equipment also work. After a little practice at lower heights, you can try the grooming table again.

- ✔ **A different surface.** Look at the surface of your grooming table. If it's slick, try putting a piece of rubber-backed carpet on it. The carpet won't slide, and neither will your dog when she jumps on it.

- ✔ **A sturdier grooming table.** Dogs hate wobbly things, and if your grooming table wobbles in any way, fix it or get a sturdier one. You don't want the table to wobble or (worse yet!) collapse while you're working on your dog.

Never force a puppy or an injured, old, arthritic, or small dog to jump onto the table. Doing so can cause the dog serious injury.

Regardless of whether your dog is capable of jumping onto the table or whether stature, age, or infirmity prohibit her from doing so, you can find a way to train your dog to get up on the table and stay there. All you need to do is choose a time when your dog is more attentive and maybe a little hungry, have plenty of treats on hand, and follow these steps:

1. **Bring your dog to the table.**

   Let her sniff it and become comfortable with it.

2. **Show your dog a treat and say "Table."**

   Use the treat to lure her up onto the table or the ramp or steps, depending on which method you're using.

   You may not get her full compliance, but that's okay. Reward your dog for any positive behavior toward getting onto the table, such as putting her front feet on the table or moving to the next step or farther up the ramp.

3. **When your dog hops up or climbs onto the table, give her a treat and plenty of praise.**

4. **Lengthen the time your dog is on the table by telling her to "Stay" and holding her there with a treat.**

   Start with only a few seconds and then gradually increase the time.

5. **Release your dog with the word "Okay," which means she can jump off (or walk back down the ramp or steps).**

Some dogs can injure themselves jumping off a table, even one as low as a grooming table. If you can, support the dog or carry her off so she doesn't get hurt.

Teaching Sit

The Sit cue should be one of the first cues your dog learns. If she hasn't learned it yet, teach it to her now. Sit is important because it gives you basic control over your dog. When your dog's moving around and not staying in one place, the Sit cue helps you regain that kind of control. What could be easier than showing your dog how to sit in one place?

When you start showing your dog the Sit cue, choose a quiet place with few distractions and show her while she's on the floor or the ground. Be sure to have some treats ready, and place your dog on a leash so you can keep her with you. To show your dog the Sit command, follow these steps:

1. **Hold a treat above your dog's nose and slowly move it toward your dog so that she follows it (see Figure 4-1).**

2. **As your dog follows the treat, put your opposite hand on your dog's rear end and gently apply downward pressure on the hindquarters.**

3. **As your dog starts to sit, give her the command to "Sit."**

4. **When your dog sits, give her the treat.**

   If your dog resists this method, try having her stand with a wall behind her. That way, as you move the treat back towards her, she has no place to go and will sit.

Figure 4-1:
Move the treat back toward your dog as you give the Sit cue.

Practice the Sit cue frequently to reinforce it. Get your dog completely comfortable with sitting before trying Sit in other areas such as on top of the grooming table.

Teaching your dog to lie on his side

One of the most useful cues for grooming your dog is a variant of the Down cue. At some point, you have to show your dog how to lie on his side so you can brush his sides and belly and work on his legs and paws. Show your dog the Down cue first, and then introduce the Side cue. Again, you need treats, a quiet place, and your dog on leash. Work at ground level before moving your training session up onto the grooming table. Your dog also needs to know the Sit cue before you start this exercise. Here's how you show your dog the Down cue:

1. **Put your dog in the Sit position (see the preceding section).**

2. **Show your dog a treat, and move it from in front of his nose downward to his chest while having him stay in the Sit position.**

   Your dog should follow the movement downward.

3. **Give your dog the cue "Down" as he moves into the down position (see Figure 4-2).**

4. **When your dog's elbows touch the floor, give him the treat.**

   Practice Steps 1 through 4 several times so your dog becomes comfortable with it.

Figure 4-2:
Teach your
dog the
Down cue
so it's easier
for him to lie
on his side.

Next, you need to get your dog to lie down on his side, so follow these steps:

1. **Put your dog in the Down position.**

2. **Show your dog a treat and move it sideways in an arc so that as your dog follows it, he puts the side of his head on the ground.**

   If your dog is stubborn and won't put his head down, try putting your hand along the opposite side of his head as you focus his attention on the treat (see Figure 4-3). Then, as you move the treat, move your hand, palm downward, so that your dog assumes there's no place to go on the other side.

3. **Issue your dog the "Side" cue as he starts rolling over onto his side.**

4. **Practice the Down and Side cues together and often.**

   Show your dog how to follow the Side cue on both sides so that he understands it can mean either one.

Figure 4-3:
Place your hand on the side of your dog's head as you gently help him lie on his side.

Teaching her Stay

One cue that's useful for grooming your dog is the Stay. When your dog is on the table, you probably want her to stay there for at least a few seconds. To get her to stay, try the following steps:

1. **With your dog on the table, preferably in a sitting or down position (see the preceding sections), tell her to "Stay."**

2. **As you vocalize the Stay command, hold your hand out in a stop or halt position, with palm flat and fingers extended upward.**

   Make a pushing motion toward your dog's nose for emphasis.

3. **Wait for a few seconds, and if your dog stays, reward her.**

   If she breaks her Stay, put her back in position without a treat and repeat Steps 1 through 3.

4. **Release your dog from the Stay command by saying "Okay" and giving her a treat.**

   "Okay" means she doesn't have to hold the Stay any longer. If she doesn't figure that out, make a happy fuss over her — she'll get it.

5. After your dog is successful at holding a Stay for a few seconds, gradually lengthen the amount of time.

If at any time she doesn't stay, go back to the previous shorter amount of time and try again.

Establishing a Grooming Routine

Do you feel like you're in a rut? Many people talk about being in a routine as a bad thing. Well, unlike humans, dogs don't see the situation that way. Routines make your dog feel comfortable and secure. An established routine gives your dog comfort in knowing that things are reliable at home.

You can make your dog happy by establishing a solid routine in his life that includes everything from feeding, training, and grooming to playing with and walking him. Sound boring? It isn't, really. When dogs have a routine, they know what to expect and often get ready for it before you do. For example, when you walk your dog first thing in the morning, I guarantee that by the third day, he's waking you up to go for that walk.

Plan your grooming sessions to become part of your dog's daily, twice-weekly, or even weekly routines. When you can make grooming sessions pleasant and routine, your dog will help you by anticipating the brushing or clipping session — just like the morning walk.

The ideal grooming calendar depends on how much work your dog routinely needs. You need to set it up and stick with it to find out whether it works for you and your dog. As a general rule, your grooming schedule may devote:

- ✔ Two days a week to brushing your dog's coat
- ✔ One day a week to brushing your dog's teeth
- ✔ One day a week to trimming toenails and inspecting teeth

Dealing with Difficult Dogs

If you're lucky and you've worked with your dog for some time, you don't have to worry about working with an uncooperative dog. Nevertheless, at some point, you may find yourself trying to groom a difficult dog. Maybe your best friend has a dog who's never been properly groomed before and needs help. Maybe you found a mutt on the street who has matted and dirty fur. Maybe a rescue group is having a dog-wash day and you're there to help. Or maybe she's your own dog, and you're just having problems with her. Whatever the reason, you're dealing with a difficult dog.

Handling an uncooperative dog

Before I explain how to handle a difficult dog, you first need to know how to handle *any* dog, because dogs don't react to things the way you and I do, and sometimes they do things that humans don't always expect.

When faced with a difficult dog, whether it's yours or someone else's, having this dog checked out by a veterinarian for possible underlying causes is always a good idea. Dogs who suffer from arthritis or hip dysplasia may snap when their pain threshold is pushed. Other behavior problems may have underlying medical conditions. When in doubt, get it checked out!

Exploring the wolf inside the poodle

Dogs inherit most of their behavior from a common ancestor, the wolf. Yes, even a dog such as a Poodle, who looks nothing like a wolf, has inherited the basic instincts from that ancestor. Looking at your dog's behavior from that perspective, you quickly understand why grooming with brushes, combs, and clippy things can be so distressing. In even the most docile Cocker Spaniel beats the heart of the wolf.

Because the dog has wolf-like preprogramming at the heart of her behavior, she automatically reverts to it whenever the civilized trappings fall by the wayside. Instinctive reactions to fear, hunger, anger, and pain all come not from the civilized dog but from the wolf inside; it's a survival mechanism. The wolf has been around a long time and knows how to deal with those feelings. The dog, on the other hand, has become civilized during only the last 20,000 years or so (125,000 years, if you believe the genetic mathematics). Regardless, wolves have been around much longer, and the domesticated dog is simply a descendant of the wolf.

Why is this history lesson so important? Because you need to understand that when you're faced with a frightened or angry dog, you're faced with an instinct as old as the wolf — not some sweet little puppy dog.

Reading dog behaviors

Be aware that any dog has the potential to bite — from the seemingly harmless Yorkshire Terrier to the so-called dangerous dogs like Pit Bulls. (I say so-called because plenty of nice Pit Bulls are out there — it's the training, not the breed.)

The truth is that getting bitten is unpleasant even when you're bitten by a small dog. (I've been bitten by a Schnauzer and a Keeshond, and it was very painful both times.) So you need to be aware of the signs of a frightened or angry dog before the dog gets an opportunity to bite. A dog may bite at various times, even while being groomed. In the sections that follow, I give you enough foresight to see a potential bite in the making, because most of the time, bites are reactions to fear, pain, or anger.

Handling fearful dogs (submissive behavior)

Fearful dogs usually become submissive first. They're tentative, shy, and usually don't want anything to do with you. A submissive dog — one who's crouching down with tail tucked between his legs, ears laid back flat, and eyes averting your gaze — may bite to try to get away from you in a real response to fear. Eyes of fearful dogs open wide to the point where you can actually see the whites of their eyes quite well. Pursuing such a dog is the worst thing you can do — whether you intend to grab him by the collar (a threatening gesture in the dog's mind) or corner him (providing no way out, which heightens the panic) or force him into submission (again, you've just pushed the wrong buttons).

Dogs who are fearful usually bite once or in a flurry, either way intent on telling the attacker (you, in their mind) to leave them alone. The dog just wants to get away and calm down.

When dealing with this type of dog, remove the threat — talk in an upbeat and happy tone, and offer treats and snacks. Or you can let him have his space for a while to calm down, and then try again to offer something positive.

Some dogs are natural fear biters, meaning they react by biting whenever anything unusual happens, because they're automatically left alone after they bite, thus reinforcing a very bad behavior. When dealing with that kind of dog, you need to use a muzzle to avoid becoming another victim.

You can greatly reduce a dog's anxiety by moving slowly and deliberately and not pushing. Keeping the atmosphere as upbeat and positive as possible goes a long way toward reducing a fearful dog's stress.

Dealing with dogs in pain

Dogs who are in pain are usually pretty obvious. They cry or whine from the pain and seek whatever way possible to relieve the pain. Dogs in pain don't know or care that you're there — they're just reacting out of instinct.

Never attempt to handle a dog who's in pain unless you're taking the dog to the veterinarian. In that case, you need to muzzle the dog and take her in for treatment immediately.

In some cases, something you do accidentally can cause a dog pain. When the pain is beyond the dog's threshold, she's going to snap, and that may injure you. For that reason, exercising care and using a muzzle are the best courses of action whenever you're doing any grooming procedure that may hurt your dog.

You will never be able to rationally confront a dog who's in pain. No matter how gentle the dog is (or you are), when she's in pain, she's going to snap just like the fearful dog. She doesn't have a clue what she's doing — she's just trying to protect herself. If you must handle a dog who's in pain, always use a muzzle. If you have no muzzle available, follow the directions for how to make one in Chapter 17.

Getting help for your aggressive dog

Dogs who are truly aggressive are angry at you for daring to do what you're doing. An aggressive dog may be:

- A dominant dog who looks on you as challenging his authority.
- A suspicious dog who's guarding a treat, bone, or other dog possession.
- A frustrated dog redirecting that frustration as aggression toward you.
- A prey-driven dog who views you as his next quarry.

A dog's aggressiveness is pretty obvious. Aggressive dogs bark and snarl at you in a challenging manner. Their hackles rise as they lift their lips in a snarl and gaze at you with hardened eyes, without any reservations about staring at you right in the eyes with their own challenge.

Needless to say, aggressive dogs are downright scary, and you should never handle them — at all. If you own one of these dogs, I suggest that you seek help from a dog behaviorist, a veterinarian, or other dog professional when it comes to working with an aggressive dog.

Considering muzzling versus medication

Deciding whether to muzzle or medicate a dog depends on you and the dog. Say, for example, that you have a difficult dog and perhaps he's fearful of the entire grooming process (bad experiences) or just struggles a lot. You've tried training the dog, but your valiant efforts have failed, or at least it's going to take a long time before you can coax your dog to cooperate.

You basically have two options; however, you may not consider either of them particularly satisfactory. One option is muzzling the dog, and the other is medicating the dog. I tell you about each method in the next two sections.

Muzzling

When muzzling your dog, you slip on a *muzzle,* a device that slips over your dog's nose and mouth to prevent him from biting you when you do a particular grooming procedure, such as brushing him out, clipping his coat, or trimming toenails. The positive sides of using a muzzle are that your dog isn't groggy or doped-up with potentially dangerous chemicals, and you're not bitten.

The downside is that muzzling can be dangerous during hot weather, when the dog can overheat. Muzzles also can force a dog to start behaving more aggressively, because you've restrained him. It also looks bad. People who may be watching you handle your dog can get the wrong impression about your dog, and your dog can develop a bad reputation when someone sees him restrained with a muzzle.

Muzzling should be done only as a last resort — for example, when you know that your dog is going to snap whenever you trim his toenails and that the only way to stop the snapping is to muzzle him. You slip the muzzle on, trim his toenails, and slip the muzzle off. The toenails are done, and neither of you are worse for wear.

But muzzling won't help you retrain your dog to accept the procedure. In fact, you may find him even more difficult, because now he knows he has no choice and you're going to restrain him. So unless there's really no way around it, leave the muzzle off.

If you have to muzzle your dog, choose a good groomer's/veterinarian's muzzle that fits your dog's head and the shape of his muzzle (foreface). They're usually made of nylon and are intended to prevent a dog from biting. They are not, however, supposed to be used for any length of time. Most muzzles aren't made to wear for any longer than a few minutes.

If you decide to muzzle your dog, put the muzzle on right before the procedure and take it right off afterwards. Never leave a dog with a muzzle unattended, and never leave him alone with a muzzle for any length of time. A dog can overheat while wearing a muzzle, because it restricts breathing and prevents panting. Furthermore, your dog can hurt himself trying to take the muzzle off, or he can catch it on something and it can choke him.

Medicating

With the exception of some homeopathic and herbal combinations (such as Bach Flower Rescue Remedy), you must obtain all medications from your veterinarian. The common medications used by veterinarians to calm dogs are acepromazine, diazepam (Valium), or other drugs such as cloricalm.

The problem with medications is that they can have adverse side effects. For example, acepromazine can cause seizures in seizure-prone dogs. In many cases, these medications can affect your dog's metabolism, making her more susceptible to chilling or overheating.

If you decide you must medicate your dog, talk it over with your veterinarian. Ask about possible side effects and problems associated with medicating your dog while grooming. Ask for possible alternatives — some newer medications may be available. The main thing is to understand how to use the medication and in what circumstances you can use it and to understand what alternatives may be available.

Holistic types of medications that you can try with your dog include Bach Flower remedies or homeopathic and herbal supplements that have little or no side effects. However, whether they actually work is debatable. I've had good luck with Bach Flower Rescue Remedy and Dr. Goodpet's calming medications, but that's just my own experience, which doesn't have any documented scientific basis behind it. Check with your vet before giving any holistic medicines to your dog.

Restraining a difficult dog

Restraining a dog is something you may have to do occasionally. No dog loves staying in the tub or on the grooming table for very long, so you have to restrain your dog once in a while to get the job done.

Crates

If you need to keep your dog in one place while you get your things together, use a travel carrier or crate. These are useful devices for keeping your dog in one place without forcing him to be tied up or restrained in any fashion.

The downside to crates is airflow. Don't leave your dog in a crate in the hot sun or in a place where he can't get good airflow and can accidentally overheat. You can't wash or brush a dog in a crate or do any other procedures on him.

Tub tie-outs and bathing nooses

Plenty of tie-outs and nooses are available for washing a dog. These devices generally work by hooking to your dog or your dog's collar to hold him in place. The idea is to keep a medium or big dog in the place where you need him to stay while you bathe him.

Never use training collars, choke chains, or other similar devices with tie-outs or nooses. Your dog can choke himself. Likewise, never leave your dog unattended in one for even a moment for the exact same reason.

Grooming table nooses and body restraints

Various gadgets are available for keeping your dog restrained while he's on the grooming table. Most involve grooming nooses that hook to the grooming arm of the table. These devices, which slip around your dog's neck, are cable nooses that hold the dog's head up while you work on him. Other body restraints hook off these nooses to keep a dog standing in place. A variety of slings are also fashioned for these purposes.

Grooming table nooses and body restraints are extremely dangerous when-ever a dog is left unattended while attached to one of them. Dogs can choke to death by hanging or even get terribly tangled. If you use one, be sure your dog doesn't struggle constantly while attached to it, and never leave him unattended in one of these devices for any reason. If you use a noose, get a nylon one with a quick snap release so you can quickly free your pooch in case of an emergency.

Body sacks and other devices

Body sacks and other restraining devices are usually used by groomers to handle small breeds and cats. They look like a mesh sack that you put your pet's head through. The idea is to restrain the dog or cat so you can bathe him. A few are equipped with holes so you can clip nails. Again, a body sack isn't an ideal tool for restraining the dog, and no dog (or any animal) should ever be left alone in one, because he can get tangled up, panic, or become overheated in one.

Part II
Making Your Dog Look Good: The Basics

The 5th Wave   By Rich Tennant

"I've got the salad spinner down here! I'm drying the dog."

In this part . . .

Part I tells you why grooming is so important, but in Part II it's time to find out how to actually groom your dog. In this part, you discover the basics of grooming virtually any dog, regardless of breed, whether pedigreed or a mutt. I show you the basics from brushing to bathing and from clipping hairs to clipping nails. All-in-all, the chapters in Part II give you the most useful everyday information about grooming your pooch.

Chapter 5

Mastering Brushing and Bathing Basics

In This Chapter

▶ Tackling brushing and combing basics for any breed

▶ Bathing and drying your dog without bother

G ood grooming is a part of caring for your dog, but most of what you do is just maintenance work — that is, just keeping your dog clean and healthy. If you start with a clean dog and maintain a clean and healthy coat, you prevent headaches and disasters later on.

In this chapter, I cover the proper techniques for brushing, combing, bathing, and drying your dog. You can find out about other grooming basics like clipping your dog's toenails and cleaning his ears and teeth in Chapter 6.

The key to a successful grooming session is making it a fun and enjoyable time for you and your dog. Read on for advice on how to do just that!

Brushing and Combing Basics

Brushing and combing form the foundation of good grooming. Most dogs don't actually need baths all that frequently. They usually need them only when they get noticeably dirty or have to go to a show. However, they must be brushed and combed often — usually twice weekly or more often, depending on the breed and coat (check out Part III of this book for specifics). Brushing and combing are great for your dog's skin and coat, because they distribute oils from the skin throughout the coat and get rid of bits of dirt, tangles, and loose hair. This aspect of grooming is the one thing you really need to do, even if you don't do anything else and decide to hire a groomer.

Always brush and comb a dog before you bathe her, because doing so helps prevent tangles and keeps your dog cleaner. See the section called "Rub-A-Dub-Dub: Washing Your Dog" later in this chapter.

Beyond pulling hairs: Making the experience pleasant

Brushing and combing can be an enjoyable experience or one that ends up as a total nightmare. Usually, dogs who hate to be brushed and combed are the ones with long hair or thick coats that tend to mat easily. Owners often don't tackle the thick coat early or often enough, and these sessions wind up being much more painful than they have to be. Brushing and combing don't have to become a hair-pulling event.

Here are a few tricks to brushing and combing your dog:

✔ **Start young.** When your dog is a puppy, get her used to the procedure. In many cases, dogs love the attention, and you'll enjoy working on her. However, even if you do start early, some dogs never quite take to grooming entirely. In many instances, you may have to work through some bad behaviors, and in other rare cases, you may need to muzzle or sedate the dog. (See Chapter 4 for more information about handling a difficult dog.)

✔ **Stick to a routine.** Where on your dog you first start brushing, combing, and grooming doesn't matter, but being consistent when you work *does*. By following the same routine every time you groom your dog, you won't forget to do anything, and your dog will be happy there aren't any surprises.

✔ **Relax with your dog.** Taking time to relax — both dog and owner — goes a long way toward calming your dog's fears. Your dog may get nervous when she senses it's grooming time, regardless of whether you're breaking out a grooming table (which I highly recommend using) or simply reaching for a brush and comb. Giving her treats, a good massage (see the "Massaging your dog" sidebar for advice), or just talking to her in a soothing tone helps relieve your dog's tension before and during a brushing session.

If you use a grooming table to groom your dog, never leave her unattended. She can hurt herself jumping off or even strangle herself if she's hooked into a noose.

✔ **Brush your dog after she's exercised — when she's a little bit tired.** She'll be calmer.

✔ **Never hurry, and always be gentle whenever possible.** One bad experience can be traumatic and turn your dog off grooming entirely.

✔ **Use the right tools.** The right tools make the job not only easier but also less stressful and less painful. Use the wrong tools and you're likely to pull on your dog's hairs — ouch! Chapter 3 introduces you to common grooming tools, and the section that follows suggests specific brushes and combs to use when grooming each type of dog.

Massaging your dog

Massaging your dog may sound a little odd, but it's a great way to bond with him and get him to relax. If your dog has never been massaged, he may find it a little strange at first. The first goal when massaging your dog is to get him to relax. Start with gentle stroking movements in areas where he's normally accustomed to being petted. Don't touch areas that your dog isn't quite comfortable with you touching, and don't use a lot of pressure until your dog gets used to it. Pick up a copy of *How to Massage Your Dog* by Jane Buckle (Wiley, 1995) or *Dog Massage* by Maryjean Ballner (St. Martin's Press, 2001) for the basics of massaging your dog.

Gathering the tools you need

Before you get started with brushing or combing your dog, gather all the tools you need for the session. Having everything you need in one place and within reach makes the brushing and combing session go much more smoothly; it can make all the difference between a pleasant experience and one that's not so pleasant.

If you live in a flea-prone area, make sure that you have a flea comb handy, especially during flea season. (Flea season often begins in spring. If you live in the U.S., www.nofleas.com/Flea-Index.asp can give you a general idea of when to be especially on guard.)

If your dog has a long coat, you need the following tools (Chapter 3 includes some illustrations and descriptions):

- **An undercoat rake or long comb:** To remove the loose undercoat hairs.

  Some groomers prefer using wide-toothed combs first and then changing to progressively narrower or finer-toothed ones. This strategy is good whenever your dog has really snarly hair. However, if you're simply maintaining your dog's coat, you can choose to go over her with a fine- or medium-toothed comb and then a slicker brush.

- **Detangler solution and a mat splitter or mat rake:** For tangles and mats (electric clippers can be used in extreme cases).

- **A shedding tool:** For removing the soft undercoat when the dog is blowing coat (shedding profusely).

- **A slicker brush:** For removing dead hair and stimulating the skin and coat.

If your dog has a shorter coat, you need these grooming tools:

- ✔ **A Zoom Groom or short curry brush:** For removing dead hair and polishing the coat.
- ✔ **A short-toothed comb:** For removing dead hair and getting through any tangles.
- ✔ **A slicker brush:** For removing dead hair and stimulating the skin and coat.

Brushing up on basic techniques

Some groomers like to work from tail to head, but others prefer to work from head to tail. No sensible reason exists for doing it one way over the other, except to say that you need to work whichever way is more comfortable for you and your dog. Nevertheless, you do need to start at one end and work your way to the other so you can be sure that you don't miss anything in between.

Various methods of brushing include *line brushing and combing* — that is, parting the fur and combing and brushing out each section (which works well on long coats addressed in Chapter 13) — and *spiral brushing,* in which the dog's hair is brushed and combed in a circular pattern. Spiral brushing works well on any coat.

Regardless of the method of brushing and combing you use, you need to brush all the hair and not just the top coat. That means getting down to the skin and brushing upward.

You can brush out your dog's coat in a variety of ways. One common way is to brush backward against the lay of the fur and then brush it back into place (see Figure 5-1). Brushing that way usually loosens and removes dead hair and stimulates your dog's skin. Some breeds have hair types that won't allow the use of this method. Breeds with corded hair, in particular, just can't be brushed backward, so make sure you remove all the tangles as you go. For more about specific breed coats, check out the chapters in Part III of this book.

Dealing with the dreaded mat

Because brushing or combing out mats and tangles can cause any dog a great deal of discomfort, don't keep pulling on them after you find them. Instead, follow these instructions to gently remove tangles and mats:

Figure 5-1:
Brushing against the grain to remove dead hair and stimulate the dog's skin.

1. **Spray the mat with detangler solution and use an appropriate comb to slowly work the hairs in the mat free.**

   Work from the outside of the mat (where the hair isn't tangled) and slowly untangle the hair. Hold the base of the mat (closest to your dog's skin) as you work to avoid pulling your dog's skin.

2. **If the mat doesn't come out with the comb, try using a mat rake next.**

   Mat rakes are equipped with sharp teeth that work at cutting through the mat. You use the mat rake the same way you would a comb but simply rake along the lay of the hair. The teeth will cut through the mat.

3. **If the mat rake doesn't cut it (so to speak), try using a mat splitter — but don't put away the rake just yet.**

   Start by splitting the mat of hair in horizontal or vertical strips and then using either a mat rake or a comb to tackle those smaller pieces individually. Watch to make sure no skin is pulled up into the mat as you work.

   Be careful when using mat rakes or mat splitters. They're quite sharp and can cause cuts if used improperly.

4. **In the worst conditions (that means the rake and the splitter have failed), use electric clippers (any blade should work) to slowly shave away the mat.**

   Be aware that this step should be considered as a last resort and that it can leave a bare patch that will ruin a show coat until it can grow out again.

   Short of that, you can also ask a professional groomer or veterinarian to help you get rid of the mat.

Whatever you do, don't use scissors to cut out a mat! No matter how careful you think you are, accidentally cutting your dog's skin is all too easy, and that means a trip to the emergency vet for a suture.

Heading down the right grooming path

If your dog's coat or the hair on her face is short, use a soft slicker that's made specifically for the face, and even then, brush gently. The skin and hair around a dog's face are particularly sensitive.

Be especially careful when working around a dog's eyes. It's easy to scratch a dog's eyes with a sharp implement like a dog comb or brush.

On the other hand, if your dog has long hair on the face, such as the fall (hair over the eyes) or beard found in breeds such as Old English Sheepdogs or Soft-Coated Wheaten Terriers, put your fingers behind the long hair and gently comb it out. You need to place your fingers behind these long facial hairs to protect your dog's sensitive skin and face from the sharp, pointed teeth of the comb.

If you find mats or tangles around your dog's face, don't spray them with detangler solution, because you risk getting some in your dog's eyes. Instead, dip a washcloth into the detangler solution, gently rub it into the hair, and then gently comb out the tangle, starting from the bottom of the hair. If the mat is really serious — yes, they sometimes have minds of their own — use an electric clipper with a guarded blade to clip out the mat while also guarding your dog's face and skin (and keeping her reassured and still) with your other hand.

When your dog has long hair on her ears, you can use a comb to hold the hair so that your hand is between the comb and your dog's tender skin. If the ear fur is matted or in knots, use the washcloth dipped in detangler solution to slowly try to comb out the tangles. If the knots of ear fur are too big, (many dogs get them behind the ears), use electric clippers (sliding your hand between the skin and the clipper) to remove them or just ask a professional to do it for you to avoid cutting the skin.

Never use scissors to cut out a mat or a knot, because you can seriously injure your dog, even if you *are* careful about it. If you don't have grooming clippers, ask a vet or a professional groomer to remove the mat for you. Most are happy to remove the mat or knot at little or no charge.

Smoothing the ruff-les on the nape of your dog's neck

The neck and ruff areas of your dog's coat (see Chapter 2 for more about your dog's anatomy and appearance) may also be sensitive, so start brushing them with a soft slicker. Brush backward against the lay of the hair (if appropriate — otherwise, brush with the grain). If your dog is shedding, the slicker may fill up quickly. You can use the comb to dislodge the hair from the slicker and deposit the hair in the trash. If your dog has a *ruff* (the longer, thicker fur around the neck, shoulders, and chest), pay particular attention to it; you need to use a comb or undercoat rake whenever your dog has a long or thick double coat in those areas. Comb through the hair you just brushed before brushing it back the way it should lay.

Brushing and trimming feathered forelegs

Short hair on a dog's forelegs usually doesn't need to be brushed, but if your dog has *feathering* — that is, long hair on the backs of the legs that runs from armpit to paw — you have to comb it out. Feathering, like the hair behind the ears, has a tendency to tangle more so than the rest of your dog's coat, so use a detangler solution whenever the feathering on your dog's legs is tangled and comb it out carefully, or use a mat splitter or mat comb.

If your dog isn't a show dog but nevertheless has feathering that's either too matted or too much of a pain to brush out all the time, consider using a guarded clipper to remove the feathering on each side for a cleaner look. Be sure to keep your fingers between the clippers and your dog to protect his skin, trimming the hair so that it looks neat.

Belly-rubbin' for laughs

The next step is to brush out your dog's chest and belly. Use a slicker to brush against the lay of the hair (if appropriate — otherwise, brush with the grain), remaining keenly aware that your dog's underside is sensitive, especially around the belly and private parts. If you can get your dog to lie down on one side — as explained in Chapter 4 — do so. Be gentle while brushing around your dog's privates — she will appreciate the care taken.

Don't pull on any mats on your dog's sensitive underbelly, and don't use a mat rake, because one slip can cause problems in these sensitive regions. If you find any mats, take your dog to your vet or a professional groomer who can use electric clippers to carefully remove them.

Sidewinding and backing up

Your dog's sides and top are probably the easiest areas to brush and comb. Take the slicker and brush backwards against the lay of the fur (if appropriate — otherwise, brush with the grain) and follow up with a comb. Use detangler and mat splitters as required for removing any mats.

No butts about it

Like the belly and underside, your dog's rear end can be particularly sensitive, but it's also often the first area from which a dog may shed. Use a slicker brush first to find out how tolerant of being touched your dog is, especially along the back legs, where the fur may be feathered or in *pantaloons*, tufts of hair that make your dog look like she's wearing bloomers. Anyway, brush the fur against the lay (if appropriate — otherwise, brush with the grain) and then follow up with a comb. Use detangler solution and a mat rake if you run into any mats, but be extremely careful around the base of the tail near the anus and around the dog's, um, equipment.

Handling those hind legs

Like the forelegs, your dog's hind legs shouldn't require much brushing, but if your dog has feathering, you have to comb it out. Feathering, like the hair behind the ears, tends to tangle a lot, so use a detangler solution if needed and comb the feathering out carefully or use a mat splitter or mat comb.

If your dog isn't a show dog and has feathering down her back legs, you can trim it just like you trim the front legs in the earlier section "Brushing and trimming feathered forelegs." Removing the feathering makes your job easier when it comes to grooming. Don't forget to use an electric clipper with a guarded blade, and carefully trim the feathering back so that it's nice and neat.

Tweaking that dratted tail

Depending on what your dog's tail is like — smooth and sleek or furry or like a plume — you may need to carefully comb it out. If it's short, fuggetaboutit! Otherwise, if it's long and furry, you need to use a comb. If you find mats in your dog's tail, use detangler solution and a mat splitter or mat rake.

Shedding time

Some double-coated breeds shed profusely once or twice a year. Others shed year-round. If your dog has little tufts of hair that look like pieces of cotton candy scattered throughout his coat, he's *blowing coat,* or shedding. You can pluck these tufts of hair out, but most dogs find that annoying. A better solution is to use a shedding blade or an undercoat rake.

The shedding blade looks like something you'd use on a horse. It's a flexible piece of steel with little saw-like teeth that catch the hairs. You can operate the blade in a one-handed U-shaped configuration, or you can keep the blade straight and use two hands. The undercoat rake is a rake with either long sets of teeth to pull the dead hair out or a dual set of teeth that work both the undercoat and top coat.

Be forewarned that shedding blades need to be used carefully on thin-coated dogs because the blades can scratch the skin. However, if you own a thick-coated dog, you're not likely to have this problem.

Getting pesky fleas to flee!

During flea season, which varies from one region to the next, you'll be using a flea comb in addition to the other grooming implements. After you brush out your dog's coat, you want to go over her again with a flea comb.

At one time, I would have recommended that you use old-fashioned flea control substances such as flea dips and powders while grooming, but no longer! Unless you have an extremely bad flea problem (and even then, the following recommendations hold true), you need to talk with your veterinarian about putting your dog on a systemic flea-control product, which is what the name implies — a flea-control product that's distributed throughout your dog's system either in topical (spot-on) form or pill form. The topical products are usually applied between your dog's shoulder blades and at the base of her tail; you feed products in pill form to your dog. These systemics have rendered other flea-control substances virtually obsolete, except when a dog exhibits undesirable side effects from using systemics. Ask your veterinarian what's right for your dog.

When using any systemic, read the directions thoroughly and follow them carefully. Otherwise, the product may be ineffective. For example, some topical systemics can be ineffective if you wet your dog shortly after you apply them. Use common sense, and if you're not sure, ask your vet. Also, dosages and the amount of time the systemic is effective vary, so always have a clear understanding of the product you're using.

These flea products likewise often control ticks. Talk to your vet for other possible tick-control solutions as needed. See Chapter 16 for more information concerning ticks.

Rub-A-Dub-Dub: Washing Your Dog

One of the old wives' tales about grooming dogs is that you shouldn't bathe your dog unless he's really dirty or stinky. The story goes that if you do, you'll remove essential oils and dry out his coat.

This story is so prevalent among dog people that it's repeated as a mantra by folks who should know better, namely breeders and dog experts. Even I used to prattle on about this nonsense.

At one time, dog shampoo really was pretty harsh stuff that could strip a dog's coat, leaving it feeling pretty icky. However, show people (and groomers) needed to be able to bathe dogs frequently to get them ready for dog shows without ruining their coats.

Today, dogs enjoy some pretty decent shampoos, conditioners, cream rinses, mousses, gels, detanglers, and just about any other hair-care products that humans enjoy, only formulated for dogs. Although I think bathing your dog every day probably is a bad idea (plenty of work, to say the least), don't think that you're hurting your dog's coat just because you're bathing him.

Bathing, like brushing, doesn't have to be a pain, but it tends to be a pretty traumatic experience for many dogs. Most dogs try to avoid a bath when they've had bad experiences with it. Again, patience is the key.

Just (rubber) ducky: Making bath time a pleasant experience

Because most dogs hate baths, getting your dog to a point where he actually likes them can be rough.

Here are a few tricks that can help you smooth over those rough spots when bathing your dog:

- **Start young.** Get your dog used to bathing at an early age, when he's just a pup. Like with brushing and combing, experience is key to preventing bad bath-time behavior. In many instances, you may have to work through the bad behavior. In fact, in some rare cases, you may have to muzzle or sedate the dog. Sound familiar? It is; I say the same thing about brushing and combing.

- **Use the right tub, and give your dog easy access.** If you're using your bathtub, putting your dog in it may be as easy as walking him in. With a groomer's tub, you may have to use a ramp or stairs to walk a big dog into it, especially if you have a bad back (or if you have a good back and don't want to have a bad back). Use the sink only for small or toy-sized dogs. Don't use the shower for any dog.

  Although you may be tempted to use an outdoor hose for bathing, resist the temptation. It isn't ideal because the water is usually too cold, and the dog will get dirty all over again from being outside.

- **Keep your dog in one place in the tub.** Most dogs don't like to stay still in the tub, so you may want to use a special tub or bathing noose that attaches to the tub to keep him in place (see Chapter 3).

  As is true of the nooses used on grooming tables, you should never leave a dog restrained by a tub noose alone.

- **Don't hurry, and be gentle whenever possible.** One bad experience can be traumatic.

- **Make bathing as comfortable as possible.** To prevent a painful experience, gently put some cotton balls in your dog's ears — don't shove them into the aural canal at the base of the ear, mind you. The cotton balls merely help keep water out of your dog's inner ears. You can also protect your dog's eyes by applying an optic ointment before bathing him.

Gathering the tools you need

Before you start to bathe your dog, make sure that you gather all the tools you need. (Chapter 3 describes the necessary tools in more detail.) Having everything in one place makes the bathing process much smoother and makes all the difference between a pleasant experience and one that's not so pleasant.

When bathing your dog, you need the following supplies:

- A pH-balanced shampoo for dogs (and possibly a pH-balanced conditioner for dogs)
- Cotton balls for ears
- Bathing noose (if required)
- Washcloth
- Blow-dryer
- Towels for drying

You may want to look into the tearless variety of shampoo if you're not used to bathing dogs.

Scrubbing bubbles

No, I'm not recommending that you use a toilet bowl cleaner to wash your dog, but before you think about wetting down and lathering up your pooch, remember that you need to thoroughly brush and comb your dog's coat. If you don't brush dogs out before you bathe them, most dogs end up with nasty tangles and mats from those scrubbing bubbles. The same is true for a dog who's shedding heavily. Although warm water loosens the hair, clumps of shedded hair tend to mat and make for a grooming nightmare.

Some dogs' coats require a prebath clipping. After thoroughly brushing out your dog and getting rid of all the tangles, you may need to use the clippers to lop off frizzy or flyaway split ends so they don't become a tangled nuisance during the wash. You can find out more about taking just a little off the top with the clippers in Chapter 7.

The following steps explain the basics of bathing. Before you begin, you may want to place sterile cotton balls inside your dog's ears to keep water out while bathing. Just don't forget to take them out when you're done!

1. **To start, place your dog in a tub that's an appropriate size for your breed of dog.**

2. **Wet down your dog's hair thoroughly with tepid water (that's a fancy way of saying lukewarm water); use a washcloth to gently wet your dog's face.**

   You may like a hot shower, but that temperature is too high for your pooch!

   Some bathtubs nowadays come equipped with sprayer attachments that enable you to focus the flow of the water. They're great for soaking your dog's coat and for being gentle around the face.

   While your dog's wet but before you apply shampoo is as great a time as any to express your dog's anal sacs, if you were planning to do it as part of your grooming routine (see Chapter 6). Who said dog grooming wasn't fun . . . ? Yuck!

3. **Apply enough pH-balanced dog shampoo to lather up your dog's coat thoroughly except around the face and sensitive eyes — which you must do separately with a wet cloth (see Chapter 6).**

4. **Rinse thoroughly sliding your fingers along your dog's skin so that you get out all that soap.**

   Soap attracts dirt, and a dog with dried soap in his hair is prone to those dreaded mats.

5. **Apply a good pH-balanced conditioner or cream rinse for dogs.**

   Using a conditioner that prevents tangles and also keeps the coat from drying out is a good idea for most coat types (see Part III).

6. **Thoroughly rinse away the conditioner.**

   With regard to attracting dirt and causing mats, conditioner residues are equally as bad for your dog's hair as soap residues, so rinse even better than you did in Step 4.

7. **Get out those towels and start drying.**

   As you squeeze the towels into the coat, look for soapy water. If you find any, go back to rinsing. The next section provides addition advice about drying your dog.

Drying

After you've thoroughly rinsed your dog, dry his coat off as thoroughly as possible first using towels. Blot the coat. If you've managed not to get wet thus far while bathing your dog, you will get wet at this point, because he will shake off all that excess water and shake some more. After toweling off and allowing for a few shakes, you can move your dog onto the grooming table for a blow-dry and style.

Some professional groomers like to use cage dryers. They're devices that attach to the outside of a cage or crate and force warm air inside to dry off your dog. Cage dryers can be efficient, but watch your dog carefully when using them. A dog can quickly overheat in a warm area he can't escape.

Whenever you use a cage dryer, never leave a dog unattended in it. Dogs have overheated and died because the groomers forgot to watch them. Unless you're planning to open a grooming shop (or you care for several dogs), I suggest you skip the cage dryer and work with the hand-held blow-dryers only.

When using a blow-dryer, make sure you use one that's made specifically for dogs (see Figure 5-2) or one that doesn't use any heat. Hot air from human blow-dryers is much too hot and can hurt your dog's skin and frazzle the fur. You can use a human hair dryer on the no-heat setting to dry small dogs, but blow-dryers intended for humans don't have enough power to handle drying a larger, long-haired dog.

Always thoroughly dry your dog before you let him outside.

After your dog is dry, you need to brush him again. At this time, you can use mousse or other leave-in coat conditioners if you're getting him ready for a show.

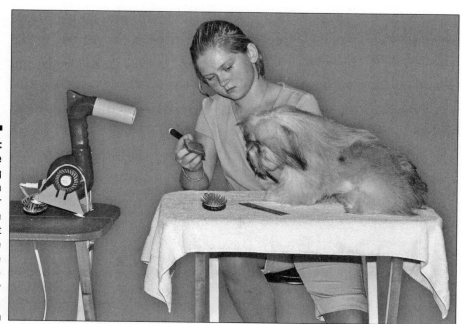

Figure 5-2:
The epitome of a drying dog. Use a blow-dryer that has a no-heat setting, like this one made specifically for dogs.

Chapter 6

Caring for Your Canine's Teeth, Toes, Ears, Face, and Ahem, Other Areas

After you discover the basics of dog grooming — brushing, combing, and bathing — you have to tackle some tougher jobs, like brushing your dog's teeth, cleaning his ears and face, trimming his toenails, and yes, some less glamorous and even gross tasks. Don't panic! All dogs need these essential grooming tasks done regularly. In this chapter, I show you how you can do them without a struggle.

Toe (Nail) Tapping

Many dogs' toenails have a habit of rapidly growing long. Unless your dog runs around on hard surfaces that help keep toenails short, you have to clip them. But clipping a canine's claws can be an agonizing chore, especially if your dog has had a bad experience with the nail clippers.

Making toenail trimming a pleasant experience

Despite your best intentions and skill level, your dog may never be comfortable having her nails trimmed. Even now, I have dogs who fuss as though I'm pulling their toenails out with a pair of pliers, even though I've never caused them any pain when I've trimmed their nails. Knowing that you have a few options helps. If you can't do all your dog's nails at once, never fear — you can clip them one paw at a time, with other activities or a resting period in between. The trick is to be diligent so that you're trimming your dog's nails before they're overgrown. And if all else fails, there's no shame in having a professional groomer or veterinarian trim them.

Some tricks you can try when trimming your dog's toenails include

- ✔ **Getting your dog used to your handling her feet:** Getting your dog used to having her paws handled is of utmost importance (see Chapter 4). Most dogs simply detest having their feet handled, so the sooner you get your dog used to enduring it, the better (and easier) giving your dog a weekly manicure can be.

- ✔ **Asking for help getting started:** If your dog's nails are too long the first time you think about trimming them yourself, ask your veterinarian or a groomer to show you how to trim them to the right length. After that, you can trim them every week or so.

- ✔ **Trimming one paw at a time:** This technique is a good one for fussy dogs. You can trim one paw at a time, giving your dog a rest before moving on to another paw.

- ✔ **Providing a treat:** Giving your dog a yummy treat after trimming her toenails also helps, and so do big hugs, a boisterous "Good dog!" and a healthy scratch behind the ears.

- ✔ **Trying a nail grinder instead of clippers:** Some dogs who can't tolerate nail trimmers sometimes can deal with a nail grinder. If you're experiencing major problems clipping toenails, a nail grinder (which looks like a rotary tool) may work.

- ✔ **Trimming your dog's nails once a week:** Ideally, you need to trim your dog's nails once a week. Weekly nail trimming not only helps keep them in good shape and prevents problems like broken nails but also gets your dog used to having a routine manicure.

If you hear your dog's nails clicking as they touch a hard surface (floor or sidewalk), it's time for a nail trim.

Gathering the tools you need

Before wielding any sharp instruments like nail clippers, make sure that you gather all the tools you need for the toenail-trimming session (see Chapter 3). Having everything you need within reach can make the nail-trimming session go more smoothly, may ease much of the tension associated with it, and can make all the difference between a pleasant experience and one that isn't so pleasant.

Here's what you need to trim your dog's toenails:

- ✔ **Nail cutters for dogs:** You can use either the guillotine or scissors styles.

- ✔ **Styptic powder or a nail cauterizing tool:** You need one or the other of these products in case you cut the quick (blood supply in the nail) and your dog's toenail begins to bleed. Find out more about this problem in the following section.

- ✔ **A slightly damp washcloth:** Use a washcloth to clean up any styptic powder or other messes you may make.

- ✔ **A nail file or nail grinder:** The file or grinder is used to smooth off rough edges of the nail.

- ✔ **Cotton swabs:** If you need to apply styptic powder, you also need a cotton swab to apply it.

- ✔ **A batch of those yummy treats:** Rewarding your best bud for a toenail-trimming job well done helps ease your dog through this procedure.

Just a little off the tip: Trimming basics

A dog's toenail is made up of the nail and the quick. The *quick* is the pink (when it's visible) part of your dog's toenails; it's similar to the pink part of your own fingernails and toenails. It provides the blood supply to the nail. When trimming your dog's nails, you must avoid cutting into the quick, because it bleeds quite a bit and it's quite sensitive (see Figure 6-1).

If your dog has white nails, you'll be able to see the quick. However, many dogs have black or dark-colored nails, and no matter what tricks you've heard about, seeing the quick in them is impossible. You have to snip carefully and look at the nail. If the nail feels spongy while you're trying to cut it, stop immediately!

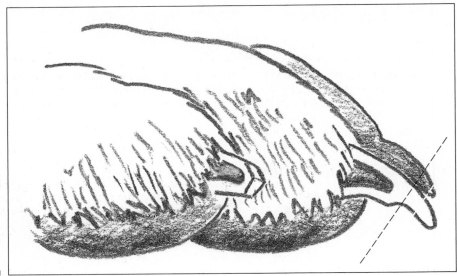

Figure 6-1:
Be sure
to trim the
nail below
the quick.

If you cut the quick (often called *quicking*), you'll have an unhappy dog and a bloody mess. The quick bleeds a great deal, so if you cut it, you need either a nail cauterizer or styptic powder (see Chapter 3) to stop the bleeding. Pack the nail with the styptic powder or use the cauterizer on the nail. Quicking hurts a lot, and most dogs remember the experience long afterward.

To trim your dog's nails, you must

1. **Hold the foot steady.**

   However, be sure and hold your dog's foot gently.

2. **Snip off a small bit of the end of each toenail.**

   Place a tiny bit of the nail in the nail clipper and snip.

   Most people prefer to have their dog lying down or sitting when they cut the toenails. Use whatever method's most comfortable for you and your dog.

If you use a nail grinder rather than clippers, the same method more or less applies. Hold your dog's foot, turn on the grinder, and grind a little off each nail.

The best time to trim nails is, of course, when they need to be trimmed; however, some people like to do the trimming before a bath so that if they do happen to quick the dog, they can wash off the blood. I simply do nail trimming as a weekly routine.

Doing the dew

Some canine breed standards require dew-claws for animals that are intended for the show ring. Rear double dewclaws are the standard for Great Pyrenees, for example. Other standards say that rear dewclaws need to be removed. Check the breed standard on the AKC Web site at www.akc.org.

Before removing dewclaws on a puppy, you need to check with the breed standard to find out whether removal is allowable, if you plan to enter your puppy in the show ring.

In working dogs, dewclaws need to be removed by the breeder or vet when the puppy is 3 to 5 days old to prevent injuries that can occur when dewclaws are torn. Removal of dewclaws any time after that requires surgery and anesthesia at the vet's office.

If you plan to remove the dewclaws from a litter, have your vet show you how. If dewclaw removal isn't done right, you can end up with malformed dewclaws or worse — an injured or crippled puppy!

Don't forget the dewclaws. Some dogs have dewclaws; others don't. If your dog has dewclaws, pay special attention when trimming them. They tend to grow long because they don't normally touch the ground. If you fail to cut them, they will eventually grow back into your dog's foot, which is quite painful.

The dewclaws are a dog's thumbs. But unlike your opposable thumbs, they're not really useful. They're located a little bit higher on the inside of the leg above the foot. Most dogs have dewclaws in the front; some also have them in the rear.

Do You Hear What 1 Hear?

All dogs have sensitive ears, and some of them can develop ear problems frequently. Others never seem to have any problems whatsoever. Breeds that have a predilection for ear infections and injuries tend to be sporting dogs and hounds because of their dropped (hanging or drooping) ears. Dropped ears make an ideal place for bacteria to grow and mites to hide.

Regardless of whether your dog has pricked up or dropped ears (see Chapter 2 for more about ear types), you have to keep them clean and sweet smelling. If an odor is present around your dog's ears, they may be infected.

Dog owners (usually Poodle owners) often pluck the hair inside their dog's ears. They use ear powder to dry the ear and yank the hair out. Ouch! I don't like this procedure, and I'm sure dogs don't either. But if your dog has hair growing in his ears and has a lot of infections, plucking may be something you have to do. Ask your vet.

Making ear cleaning a pleasurable experience

Dogs hate to have things stuck in their ears, so you're not likely to win the battle of making this an enjoyable experience. Nevertheless, you can try to make it as comfortable as possible by:

- ✔ **Getting your dog used to your gently handling his ears:** Get him used to your touching his ears (a gentle ear scratch), holding his ears, flipping up the ear flaps (if he has hanging or dropped ears), and looking into his ears.

- ✔ **Cleaning your dog's ears when he's a bit tired:** The less your dog fights with you, the less he's going to have his ears pulled.

- ✔ **Cleaning your dog's ears once a week:** The longer you wait to perform a grooming task like this one, the longer it takes and the worse the experience is likely to be for the dog and for you.

- ✔ **Giving your dog treats for behaving while you clean his ears:** Give him a goody even if he's good only long enough for you to touch his ears.

- ✔ **Never pulling on your dog's ears or jabbing anything deep into them:** It's painful, and if you do it, your dog will never let you near his ears again. Ears aren't doggie handles, no matter what a former president may have done with his dog's ears.

Gathering the tools you need

Before you get started, gather all the tools you need for the ear-cleaning session. (For more about grooming tools, see Chapter 3.) Doing so makes the ear-cleaning session go more smoothly. Having all your implements in one place makes all the difference between a pleasant experience and one that isn't so pleasant.

Here's what you need to clean your dog's ears:

- ✔ **Mild otic (ear-cleaning) solution for dogs:** Don't use anything with insecticides. Otic solution is available at groomer's supply houses.

✔ **Sterile gauze or sponges:** Use the gauze or sponges for removing the otic solution or cleaner.

✔ **Surgical forceps or clamps:** No, you're not doing surgery. You wrap the clamp or forceps with the gauze and then wipe the gauze inside the ears to clean out any dirt and otic solution.

Cleaning your dog's ears

Cleaning your dog's ears is a fairly uncomplicated job. The main ideas you need to keep in mind are proceeding slowly and exercising care not to enter the ear canal (which would be hard to do anyway because of the way the ear canal is situated in a dog's head).

Follow these steps when cleaning your pup's ears:

1. **Gently hold your dog's head so that the open ear is exposed.**

   Sitting down beside your dog usually works.

2. **Squeeze some otic solution into your dog's ear (follow the label directions).**

   Gently massage the outside of the ear canal to enable the solution to do its work

3. **Using a sterile gauze pad or sponge, gently wipe out the excess solution.**

   You can wrap the gauze or sponge completely around the forceps or the clamp (mentioned in the preceding section) to wipe around the ear.

   Don't leave any excess solution behind; it can lead to an ear infection. And don't use insecticides or mite treatments, because they can cause irritation. If you notice any red dirt, anything that looks like coffee grounds, or a waxy buildup and you suspect ear mites (see Chapter 16), see your vet for the appropriate treatment.

4. **While your dog's ears are exposed, gently trim any excess hair from around the openings.**

Recognizing an ear problem

Ear infections sometimes may be difficult to clear up. Doing so takes commitment and determination. Watch your dog for the following signs of potential ear problems that may need to be addressed by a veterinarian:

✔ Blisters or abrasions on the ears

✔ Crusty or red ears

- ✔ Excessive waxy buildup
- ✔ Foul-smelling odor coming from the ears
- ✔ Red or black waxy buildup
- ✔ Scratching at or pawing his ears or shaking his head
- ✔ Yelping when you touch his ears

Unclogging Anal Sacs

Has your dog suddenly taken to using your nice, new Berber carpet as a roll of toilet paper? If so, you may be in for a real treat. You may have the distinct pleasure of helping your dog remove the fluid from his anal sacs (and you thought dog grooming wouldn't be any fun!).

Anal sacs, or a dog's anal glands, are located around or on either side of the dog's anus. These sacs carry some smelly fluid and occasionally need to be *expressed,* or emptied. Many dogs express them by themselves every time they poop, but occasionally these sacs fill with fluid, and your dog may need some help from you to release the fluid. Some dogs need their anal sacs expressed a lot; others don't. Expressing the anal sacs too often can lead to impacted anal glands, and failing to care for them may lead to infection. Whether you need to express the anal sacs is really a matter of what your dog is feeling.

You can tell when your dog needs to have his anal sacs expressed. When you see him sliding his backside across the cut pile, or when he chews or licks at his rear end or tail, you know it's time.

Ask your vet before attempting to express your dog's anal sacs for the first time, because although the procedure is harmless in most cases, in some dogs you can cause impacted anal glands and in really bizarre instances can rupture the sacs.

Making anal sac expression a pleasurable experience (Yeah, sure)

I'm skipping the "Making it pleasurable" section for this particular task (for obvious reasons) other than to say that it won't be pleasant for either you or your dog until it's done. It's just something you have to do. I recommend expressing your dog's anal sacs when you're bathing him. That way, you can wash away the smelly liquid and you don't really care whether it misses the paper towel you're using.

Gathering the tools you need

For those of you with, say, *Fear Factor* constitutions, if you have a thumb and forefinger, you have all the tools you need. For normal folks and those with really weak constitutions, in addition to your two phalanges (smart word for finger bones), I recommend using

- **Paper towels:** Having plenty of paper towels for any type of cleanup always helps. Heck, you may even want to try a diaper wipe or other moistened cleansing wipe.

- **A clothespin, heavy-duty rubber gloves, welder's apron, rubber boots, and tongs:** With these tools you can glove up, cover up, and thus avoid the gag reflex the way Michael Keaton does while changing diapers in *Mr. Mom.*

Expressing yourself

Expressing anal sacs is relatively simple work. You simply

1. **Fold several paper towels together (about like the huge wad you normally need to take care of a spider or bug).**

   Doing so provides an absorbent pad to catch the liquid.

2. **Lift your dog's tail and place the paper towels over his back side (and wonder when commercial television will pick up on this type of ad).**

   Note the position of his anus in relation to the paper towels.

3. **Press gently on the 4 o'clock and 8 o'clock positions in relation to his anus (see Figure 6-2).**

   Keep your face out of the way! (You're welcome!)

   Throw away the paper towels.

4. **Wash and rinse your dog's rear end really well.**

   A clean doggie rump is a healthy doggie rump.

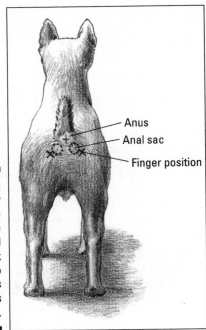

Figure 6-2:
Apply
pressure
at the
4 o'clock and
8 o'clock
positions to
express
your dog's
anal sacs.

Anus
Anal sac
Finger position

If your dog shows discomfort back by his butt and his anal sacs aren't producing any fluid, he may have an impacted anal sac, which requires veterinary intervention.

Pearly Whites — Tooth Brushing

Dogs don't get cavities the way humans do, but they do get plaque, tartar, and gingivitis — all of which can cause foul breath and tooth problems. Trips to the doggie dentist can end up being costly, and your dog will have to be put under anesthesia, because no dog ever "opens wide" for any dentist or vet.

Brushing your dog's teeth obviously is important, but how often you do it depends on your dog and your motivation factor. Poor doggie dental care, however, can lead to dental infections that can travel to your pooch's heart, causing major problems and even death. How's that for motivation to brush your dog's teeth?

Making brushing dog teeth a pleasurable experience

Now that you're working with the end of your dog that has the teeth, your concerns lie not only with your dog's dental health in mind but also with the safety of your fingers and hands. Working anywhere near your dog's mouth puts you at risk of an occasional frustrated nip or two. Here are some hints and steps you can take to make brushing your dog's teeth a little less tedious:

- **Brush frequently.** Ultimately, you need to brush your dog's teeth every day, but realistically, you're better than most pet owners if you can brush them once or twice a week. Frequent brushing gets your dog used to the brushing routine and to the idea of having her mouth handled by you.

- **Choose the best time.** A great time for brushing is right after your dog has exercised and is a little tired. At least, that time's preferable to when she's willing to fight with you over handling her mouth.

- **Train your dog to allow you to touch her mouth.** You can get her to tolerate having her mouth handled by following the instructions in Chapter 4.

- **Get her ready to have her teeth brushed by**

    1. Flipping up her lips (see how to do so in Chapter 4 and Figure 6-3).

    2. Wetting the edge of a clean washcloth so you can rub your dog's gums and teeth; hold a corner of the wet portion of the washcloth with your index finger and use a gentle, circular motion.

    3. Talking to your dog in calm, soothing tones.

    4. If your dog grows impatient, do Steps 1 through 3 for only a few seconds, and then stop and give her a treat.

    5. Repeat Steps 1 through 4 again tomorrow, gradually lengthening the amount of time you spend doing them.

Eventually, you'll be able to build up the amount of time your dog allows you to touch her mouth to where you're giving your dog a nice tooth and gum massage without any fuss.

Gathering the tools you need

Before you get started, gather all the tools you need for the tooth-brushing session (check out Chapter 3 for more about these tools). Doing so makes the tooth-brushing session go more smoothly. Having all your implements in one place also makes all the difference between a pleasant experience and one that isn't so pleasant. Here's what you need:

- ✔ **Toothpaste for dogs:** Don't ever use human toothpaste! Doggie toothpaste is flavored with malt, chicken, or some other yummy flavor that dogs can't resist. It makes the experience a little more enjoyable. (Imagine your dentist offering to clean your teeth with chocolate? Mmm. I'd wait in line for that dentist, wouldn't you?)

- ✔ **Toothbrush for dogs:** A finger toothbrush that's made for pets is best (see Chapter 3). You can use a human toothbrush, but it isn't as good as a finger brush.

Both of these items are available at the pet supply store or through mail-order catalogs.

Twice a day and between meals: The lowdown on brushing a dog's teeth

After your dog's used to getting a gum massage with a wet washcloth, the next step is getting her used to the finger brush and pet toothpaste. You can start brushing your dog's teeth by using a technique similar to the way you use the washcloth in the section "Making brushing dog teeth a pleasurable experience."

At the risk of repeating this information, never use human toothpaste on a dog. Human toothpaste contains fluoride, which in large quantities is poisonous to dogs. Dogs can't rinse and spit, so they pretty much swallow everything you put on their teeth. Follow these steps to properly brush your dog's teeth:

1. **Squeeze some doggie toothpaste onto the brush and allow your dog to lick it off.**

   Most dogs like the flavor, but some don't. Don't worry about it one way or the other.

2. **Flip up your dog's lips and gently rub the toothbrush and toothpaste against your dog's teeth and gums for a few seconds (see Figure 6-3).**

3. **Give your dog a treat, even if she allows you to work on her teeth for only a few seconds.**

4. **Repeat Steps 1 through 3 again tomorrow, gradually lengthening the amount of time spent brushing.**

If you gradually increase the amount of time you spend working on this four-step process, you'll eventually build up enough time to give your dog's teeth a thorough brushing.

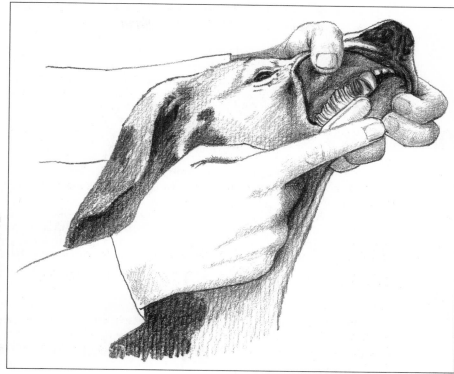

Figure 6-3:
Flip up your dog's lips as you gently brush her teeth, an important grooming task.

Some people like to purchase a *dental scalar,* a device they use to scrape away plaque from their dogs' teeth. Unfortunately, if you're not careful, you can injure your dog's gums, not to mention make one unhappy pooch. That form of teeth-cleaning is better left to your vet, especially when your dog has a lot of tartar and buildup and big teeth!

If your dog has loads of tartar buildup, get your dog to a vet first to have her teeth cleaned.

Spotting a dental problem

Watch your dog for these signs of potential tooth or gum problems that need to be addressed by a veterinarian:

- A lump above or below a particular tooth
- Bad breath
- Loss of appetite
- Nasal discharge

- Red, swollen gums
- Sudden, unexpected chewing on inappropriate items
- A grayish or darkened tooth

The Eyes Have It: Keeping Your Dog's Eyes Shiny and Bright

Dogs' eyes, for the most part, are pretty much self-maintaining, but occasionally you do run into problems with their eyes and the areas surrounding them.

As dogs have various head types (see Chapter 2), dogs likewise have various eye shapes and sizes. Some dogs, especially those with brachycephalic (short, pushed-in) heads — Pugs and Pekinese — tend to have large, protruding eyes that are more susceptible to accidental injury. Other dogs have almond-shaped eyes — Alaskan Malamutes, Siberian Huskies, and still others have rounded eyes.

Exploring ways to keep your dog's teeth white

If your dog doesn't handle brushing well, you can use one of several methods for keeping your dog's teeth clean. Most of these methods have something to do with feeding him the right kind of food and giving him appropriate kinds of chews. Here are some of the items you can use to clean those pearly whites:

- **Dental toys intended to reduce plaque and tartar:** Some of these toys actually are made so that doggie toothpaste can be squeezed into them, so they sometimes take the place of brushing. Busy Buddy, Kong toys, and Nylabone all have products intended to clean teeth.

- **Certain premium dog foods:** Some premium dog foods have additives that make their products more dental friendly by making them more abrasive. Hill's and Iams each market a dental dog food, and so do many other brands.

- **Tartar-control biscuits:** Many pet food manufacturers have come up with tartar-control biscuits and snacks.

- **Appropriate kinds of dog chews:** Some chews, such as Greenies and Pedigree's Dentabone, are made to help reduce plaque and tartar.

- **Large bones:** Giving your dog a big marrow bone or knucklebone from a cow often helps clean canine teeth. Some veterinarians recommend boiling them for safety or freezing them raw to make them harder. Bones are controversial, because they harbor bacteria and can cause blockages when chewed or swallowed. Never give a dog small sharp bones that can splinter.

Regardless of type, red eyes, lacerated eyes, and eyes that tear excessively are *not* normal, and dogs with these conditions need to visit the veterinarian as soon as possible. Excessive tearing, for example, may be caused by ear infection, tonsillitis, or infected teeth.

Making cleansing your dog's eyes a pleasurable experience

A dog's eyes are particularly sensitive, so you want to avoid bringing them into contact with soaps, chemicals, or anything that may cause irritation or abrasions. Unless directed by a veterinarian, avoid using eyedrops altogether. When you do use eyedrops, make sure they're made specifically for a dog's eyes.

When you clean around your dog's eyes, you need to do so in the gentlest way possible. Because you have to be able to touch your dog around and close to his eyes, here are some ways to help your dog get used to it:

✔ **Try cleaning the accumulated gunk from your dog's eyes.** Use a soft cloth or cotton ball moistened only with water. You'll be cleaning off gunk deposits that my mom called "sleep" (as in *"rub the sleep from your eyes . . . "*) and other deposits that accumulate.

✔ **Avoid directly touching your dog's eyes.** Do you like having your eyeballs touched? I think not.

✔ **Gently rub your pooch's jowls and forehead, and give him a scratch or two behind the ears as you talk to him in a calm, gentle, and reassuring voice.** Setting your dog at ease like this gives you better access for cleaning the areas around those sensitive orbs.

If you encounter excessive deposits (and I mean lots) of gunk, it's time for a trip to the vet to have it checked out and to make sure nothing's wrong. Dogs don't cry, so if your dog's eyes are watering all the time, that's also another reason to visit the vet.

Don't cry for me Argentina: Tear stains

Tear stains show up as brown gunky stuff that runs from the tear duct on the inside corner of the dog's eye and go down the muzzle. Although they're unsightly, not very pretty at all, with some dogs they're natural, and there's plenty you can do to get rid of them.

If your dog has tear stains, take him to a vet first to make sure there isn't some other problem. Tear stains are natural for certain breeds but not for most.

Dogs who are prone to tear stains usually are white or have light-colored coats and usually are single-coated with long hair (see Figure 6-4a). Many dogs with brachycephalic heads (where their eyes protrude) are going to pick up more gunk (see Figure 6-4b). In fact, the problem has a name. *Poodle eye,* as the name suggests, is common among Poodles, but that doesn't mean other dogs don't have tear stains. You probably don't notice it as much in other dogs because their fur is darker or seems to get rid of the gunk better.

In some breeds with serious congenital eye problems, the tear ducts can get clogged and require surgery. (See your vet if your dog shows any problems with his eyes or his tear ducts.)

Figure 6-4: Get rid of icky tear stains. Some dogs develop tear stains more than others.

Gathering the tools you need to clear up minor tear stains

A vet can help you get rid of Poodle eye (tear stains) — if that's indeed what the problem is — with a course of tetracycline, which usually helps get rid of the staining but not the tears.

Grooming products you need to help you get rid of tear stains include

- ✔ **A soft cloth, makeup pad, or cotton ball:** These materials, or others like them that don't contain any soaps or chemicals, can be used to apply grooming products to rid your dog of tear stains.

- ✔ **A 10-percent solution of hydrogen peroxide with water, or other grooming products for getting rid of stains:** These stain removers may or may not get the total stain out, depending how bad it is.

  Always be extremely careful not to get any of these products in your dog's eyes.

- ✔ **Face cream, powder, cornstarch, or other cover-up products:** Yes, you have a choice of either getting rid of the tear-stained hair or covering it up.

- ✔ **Electric clipper with an appropriate clipper guard or guarded blade:** Use this tool with extreme care if you choose to get rid of stained fur altogether.

Getting rid of your dog's tear stains

As you may have already guessed, you can get rid of tear stains by either wiping them clean, covering them up, or clipping or plucking them off. You've probably also surmised that tear stains are the nemesis of show dogs and their owners. Here's how to get rid of tear stains:

- ✔ **Wiping them off:** If you choose to wipe off the tear stains, use the 10-percent solution of hydrogen peroxide or another stain-removal product for dogs. Gently swab the solution over the tear stain, but don't get any of these products in your dog's eyes. Make sure that you rinse the residues from your dog's fur.

- ✔ **Clipping them off:** If you decide to clip out the stain, do so very carefully with guarded clippers, or try plucking the stained fur. *Note:* Your dog must be extremely tolerant of clippers to remove tear-stained fur; otherwise, using the clippers can spell disaster.

  Never use scissors around your dog's eyes or face for any reason.

- ✔ **Covering them up:** If you choose the face cream, powder, or cornstarch coverup route, you've chosen the safer but less permanent way. Here's how those products work:

  - • **Cornstarch:** Use it in a pinch, because it can whiten or lighten the stained area.

  - • **Face cream/powder:** Dampen the area and then use a small bit of cream or mousse to apply the powder. (Make sure none gets in the eyes!) Then you can gently brush out the area. Some of the powder will stick, thus making your dog's face more appealing.

Technically, a show dog is never supposed to have chalk or powder left over. The truth is that some stays in, but the handler must get most of it out so that it doesn't *appear* that the chalk is still there.

Eyeing other eye issues

Some breeds are prone to eyelid conditions, such as *entropion* (eyelids that roll in) and *ectropion* (eyelids that roll out), in which the eyelids are malformed. These conditions aren't just cosmetic, and they can be quite painful. In most cases, surgery is needed to correct them. Other types of eye and eyelid problems include cherry eye, distichiasis, and conjunctivitis (pinkeye). Again, these are not conditions that you can correct by yourself, so be sure to seek out the advice of your vet.

As your dog grows older, he may develop eyelid tumors (such as papillomas) or clouding of the eye (or crystal eye) caused by cataracts. If your dog has any of these conditions, a trip to the vet is in order.

Knowing when your dog has an eye problem

Eyes are one area of your dog's grooming that you don't want to ignore, especially if your dog has an eye problem. It's time to take your dog to the vet if your dog is squinting or pawing an eye or if your dog's eye

✔ Bulges or is out of its socket (that one is a no-brainer!)

✔ Is red or tearing profusely

✔ Is lacerated or exhibits another apparent abnormality

✔ Appears opaque or cloudy

✔ Bleeds or shows other signs of injury

✔ Has foreign matter in it

Face Time

Your dog's face is the first thing you and other people see, so keeping her face clean and looking great makes sense, right? Some of the problems many dogs have in maintaining that glow usually have to do with wrinkles (if they have them) and beards (if they have them).

Making cleaning your dog's face a pleasurable experience

Get your dog used to your touching her face. Unless your dog is really comfortable with looking you right in the eyes, avoid making direct eye contact, because doing so exhibits a challenging behavior. Move slowly and carefully around her face, which is extremely sensitive.

Gathering the tools you need

Before you get started, gather all the tools you need for the face-washing session. Doing so makes washing your dog's face go much more smoothly. Having all your implements in one place also makes the difference between a pleasant face-washing experience and one that isn't so pleasant.

Here's what you need to wash your dog's face:

- A damp washcloth

- A mild soap, dog shampoo (the tearless variety works well), or groomer's *blue shampoo* (a great cleansing product that you don't have to rinse out)

- Cotton swab

Facing off

When cleaning your dog's face, use a damp washcloth (wet but not dripping) and some mild soap. I like to use dog groomer's blue soap (waterless shampoo) because you don't have to rinse it off. When using any kind of soap, your main objective is keeping it away from your dog's eyes, because it can sting. Gently go over your dog's face with the washcloth until it's clean. Be sure to wash the *flews,* or the hanging skin around the mouth.

If your dog has wrinkles, the crevices can harbor bacteria and can become infected. Clean wrinkles carefully. If your dog is small, like a Pug, you can use a cotton swab dipped in blue soap to go over the wrinkles.

Long hair and beards need to be brushed out first. If your dog naturally has long hair over her eyes (a fall), brush out the hair first and then use a ponytail-type band to bunch it and get it out of your dog's face. Any stained hair that isn't going to fall back in the eyes can be washed with soap and water. Trim any discolored hair unless it's absolutely necessary for the show ring. If you can't trim the hair, then try the hydrogen peroxide solution mentioned in the "Getting rid of your dog's tear stains" section earlier in this chapter, or try to cover it with chalk.

Chapter 7

Giving Your Dog a Great 'Do: Clipping Basics

In This Chapter

▶ Knowing which dogs need to be clipped

▶ Choosing the right tools: Clippers, blades, and scissors

▶ Clipping your pooch

*C*lipping a dog is one of the more daunting tasks for pet owners. If you have a dog who needs to be clipped or one who needs a touch-up here or there, this chapter's for you.

Several breeds need to be clipped. Most of these dogs have single coats, the kind without an undercoat. The hair of these dogs grows like yours and mine, and because these pooches don't shed, they're bound to look like a terrible mess of hair if you don't clip their coats. Other breeds are clipped for show or style reasons, or maybe just because the pet owner doesn't want to deal with all that hair.

Don't fear the electric clippers. You can discover the basics of using them and what you can do with all those strange blades and plastic snap-on thingies in this chapter. You can also discover how to safely handle scissors (also called shears in the grooming world), and I even explain how to give your dog a basic clip.

After you gain a good grasp of the basics in this chapter, you can check out Part III, where I tell you about the specifics of grooming the different types of dog coats.

Deciding Whether to Clip Your Dog

Before I tell you about clipping your dog, you need to determine whether your dog actually needs to be clipped. Although many breeds need only a cursory neatening up, the following breeds generally need more serious clipping:

- American Cocker Spaniel
- American Water Spaniel
- Bedlington Terrier
- Bichon Frise
- Black Russian Terrier
- Bouvier de Flandres
- Brittany
- Cesky Terrier
- Cocker Spaniel (American and English)
- Curly-coated Retriever
- English Setter
- English Springer Spaniel
- Field Spaniel
- Gordon Setter
- Irish Setter
- Irish Water Spaniel
- Kerry Blue Terrier
- Löwchen
- Poodle (all sizes)
- Portuguese Water Dog
- Soft Coated Wheaten Terrier
- Springer Spaniel

At first, you may be surprised that more breeds aren't on this list, but that's because some breeds aren't exactly clipped breeds — they're *stripped breeds,* or dogs from whose coats you need to strip excess hair to attain the proper look. Most dog owners, however, aren't into time-consuming stripping procedures (see Chapter 12), so they opt to use the clippers on their dogs instead. Nothing is wrong with using the clippers in that manner, but you won't get the right look for your breed if you intend to show your dog (see Chapter 18).

Getting Acquainted with Your Tools

A dizzying array of electric clippers and blades are sold in the grooming-tool market these days. Open up a grooming catalog and you'll see a bunch of different clippers ranging from the basic home-use, pet-grooming clippers to the fancy-schmancy ones the pros use. I'm sure that broad range has you asking, "What do I really need to clip my dog?"

Clip, clip! Deciding which clippers to buy

The kind of clippers you need depends on how much clipping needs to be done with your particular dog. Here are three hints that can help you choose wisely:

- ✔ If you're using clippers just to neaten up Fido's feet or clean up a stray hair here or there, you're likely to need only a set of inexpensive home clippers that won't see a lot of use.

- ✔ If you want to maintain a nice show coat (or even a good pet coat) between trips to the groomer, you're probably looking at medium-priced clippers with which you can use a variety of blades, depending on your dog's needs.

- ✔ If you want to trim and style your own dog and perhaps other dogs, you're looking at getting professional-style clippers, maybe with more than one speed and certainly with more than a few blades. Some of these clippers also are cordless, so you don't always have to have an outlet handy.

Depending on how much work you have on hand, the type of clippers, and the speed at which you do your clipping, you may run out of battery power partway through your clipping job when using cordless clippers. Keep that in mind when you consider cordless clippers.

Several different manufacturers make clippers, including Oster, Wahl, Andis, and Conair, among others. Oster is pretty much the leader when it comes to clippers, and its blades are universal enough that other manufacturers make their clippers so that Oster-style blades fit them. In fact, almost all clipper blades are made to fit Oster or similar products.

If you decide to purchase a clipper other than an Oster, make sure that it's equipped to use Oster-style blades. Most clippers are, but you need to be sure; otherwise, you're stuck buying proprietary blades that may cost more. Besides, if your clipper breaks, you're forced to choose between buying new clippers of a brand that matches the blades you already have or tossing everything and starting from scratch.

Becoming a blade-runner

Most clippers come with blades, but some don't. These blades are typically marked either by the closeness of the cut or by their Oster number (size 10, for example).

You can tell how close an Oster blade cuts by the size of the number. The higher the number, the closer or finer the cut. The lower the number, the more hair you'll have on your dog after each clipping. So a size 40 blade (surgical cut) produces a much finer cut than a size 5 blade (¼-inch cut).

Choosing your blades is a bit of an art form and depends on your dog's breed and coat type. Look at your breed standard, talk to other owners of your breed, and check out Part III of this book to determine what kind of blades are best for your dog's coat. Table 7-1 describes what blades are out there and what they're used for.

Most blades are full-toothed, but you can also find some skip-tooth blades. *Skip tooth blades* are for stand up coats (Poodle type coats). *Full-tooth blades* are for smooth or drop-coated dogs (Spaniel type coats).

Table 7-1	Clipper Blade Types, Cuts, and Uses	
Blade Size	**Cut Length/Type**	**Uses**
40	¹⁄₁₀₀-inch/surgical	Trimming hair from around wounds; can be used for ears and face as well
30	¹⁄₅₀-inch/very close	Show clips
15	³⁄₆₄-inch/medium	General use; this blade is also referred to as a Poodle blade
10	¹⁄₁₆-inch/medium	General use, including trimming hair from around and between your dog's paw pads
9	⁵⁄₆₄-inch/medium	Smooth finish, general use
8½	⁷⁄₆₄-inch/medium	General use; this blade is also referred to as a Terrier blade
7F	⅛-inch	Full tooth, body clipping
7	⅛-inch	Skip tooth, body clipping
5F	¼-inch	Full tooth, body clipping
5	¼-inch	Skip tooth, body clipping
4F	⅜-inch	Full tooth, body clipping
4	⅜-inch	Skip tooth, body clipping

Blade Size	Cut Length/Type	Uses
3F	½-inch	Full tooth, body clipping
3	½-inch	Skip tooth, body clipping
⅝	$\frac{1}{32}$–⅝-inch/wide	For trimming and finishing
⅞	$\frac{1}{32}$–⅞-inch/wide	For trimming and finishing

Snapping on guide combs

Snap-on guide combs (shown in Figure 7-1 along with electric clippers, blade lubricating oil, and a cleaning brush) are plastic combs that you attach to your electric clippers to provide an even cut. So if you get a half-inch guide comb, you'll get a half-inch cut. Pretty simple, isn't it?

Some guide combs come with the clippers. Others you'll have to buy separately.

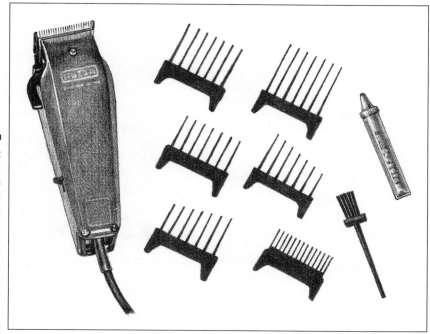

Figure 7-1:
Electric clippers (with oil and a cleaning brush) and guide combs help maintain your pooch's coat.

Using scissors

When you just can't get your dog's coat to even out with clippers, no matter how hard you try, use scissors or shears (a fancy name for scissors), but do so only with extreme caution. Scissors can injure you and your dog if you're not careful.

You can find plenty of reasons for using scissors on your dog's coat. One is that you just don't have the same control with clippers that you do using scissors. If you need to trim whiskers or stray hairs from your dog, for example, scissors probably are better than clippers. Scissors are best used on dogs who are already groomed properly and just need touch-ups. Here are some tips about using scissors:

- Choose scissors that are sharp and made for dogs.

- Never use dull scissors on a dog's coat.

- Go slowly when using the scissors.

- Always keep your fingers between the scissors and your dog's skin. Otherwise, mishaps that require you to take your dog to the emergency vet can happen easily.

- Train your dog to stay still when you're using scissors (see Chapter 4). Otherwise, you can accidentally hurt him.

- Avoid distractions when using scissors. That means no TV, no chatty friends, and no talk radio. Remember, you're working closely with your dog's coat using sharp instruments.

Thinning scissors (also called thinning shears) are used to thin the coat or blend in one layer of hair with another. The scissors have rows of skipped teeth that cut only every other hair. Like all scissors, thinning scissors can be dangerous if used incorrectly or without care, so use caution when handling and using them.

Getting Down to Clipping Business

Before you cut your first dog hair, make sure you treat your dog safely and plan how you're going to clip her. Your dog needs to be clean and have all mats and tangles brushed out of her coat before you start clipping. Doing so makes clipping the coat evenly easier for you.

Preparing for success

You have your clippers and your dog. Now, what do you do to keep from running afoul while using the clippers? Here are some handy tips for getting your dog used to the clippers and keeping your dog looking good:

- ✔ **Start clipping your dog as early as possible, even as a puppy.** Getting an older dog used to the clippers is much harder than training a puppy to accept them.

    Using quieter clippers can be helpful. Loud buzzing would scare me, too!

- ✔ **Read your dog's breed standard.** Often, you can get clues about how your dog's coat should look and how to make it look that way.

- ✔ **Check out the breed club's Web site for tips on how club members clip their dogs.** Some breed clubs provide free guidelines on how their dogs should look.

- ✔ **Have a professional groomer or a breeder show you how your dog's coat needs to be clipped.** Most groomers and breeders are happy to spend a little time helping you get it right.

If you make a mistake, don't fret. Your dog may have a bad hair day, but it'll eventually grow out. The main thing to be concerned with is using your clippers safely.

Using clippers safely

Here are some handy guidelines for safely using clippers on your dog's coat:

- ✔ Be sure your clipper blades are sharp. Dull clippers pull hair more.

- ✔ Choose the clipper blade that works best with the specific type of coat your dog has so you achieve the result you want.

    If you're not sure about the cut of the blade you're using, you can try using one of the many snap-on guide combs that are available. These combs help you make a uniform cut.

- ✔ Always use clipper coolant or lubricant on your blades to keep them from getting too warm and burning your dog. Coolant or lubricant is available separately through pet supply catalogs and on the Internet. Clipper blades can become extremely hot, especially when you use them for a long time. If you burn your dog, she won't soon forget, and I guarantee she'll decide that clippers are no fun. Make sure that you wipe off any excess lubricant, or you'll end up getting oil all over that nice clean coat.

Frequently turn your clippers off and touch them to make sure they're not too hot. If they become too warm, simply spray on the coolant. It's made especially for cooling down hot clippers. (Follow the directions on the canister.) When the clippers become too warm, you can also

- Switch blades and let the hot ones cool down.

- Switch to another clipper (if you have one).

- Place the blade on a metal surface, which quickly cools it off (a cookie or baking sheet works).

Making your first clip

The best way to find out how to use your clippers is to start by neatening up areas where your dog already has been trimmed but where the fur has grown a little untidy.

Before jumping into the deep fur, however, make sure that you've chosen the clipper size that works best for your dog's coat and the right blade, and make sure that your dog is clean and free of tangles and mats.

Hold the clippers in a way that feels comfortable in your hand and gives you the most control over the clippers. Check out Figure 7-2 to get a better idea.

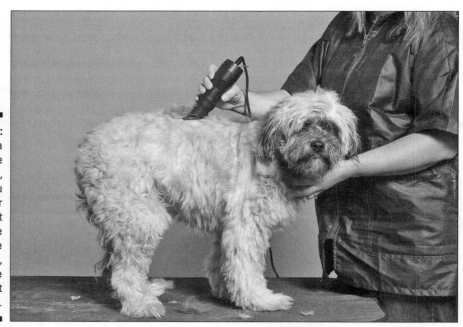

Figure 7-2: Clipping a dog can be daunting, but after you and your dog get comfortable with the clippers, it can be downright fun.

By starting with an inconspicuous area that needs some neatening up, you can easily find out how much hair your clipper and blade take off. If the amount of hair you removed is too much or too little, you can adjust by switching to a more appropriate blade. **Remember:** The higher the number of the blade, the shorter and finer the cut.

Always appraise your work as your clipping progresses — after you've trimmed a bit. That way, you know whether you're taking off too much or too little. Don't forget, however, that taking off too little is better than taking off too much. After all, you can always trim more off, but you can't glue it back on.

And don't forget to trim the hair that sticks out around and between your dog's paw pads if you like a neater look. Simply use an electric clipper with a size 10 blade and hold the foot in its normal shape (not splayed). Trim the hair that sticks out beyond the pads (don't clip the hair down between the pads), and then use the clippers to trim any other hair around the foot that ruins a neat presentation.

Attempting a Pet cut

Unless you're set on your dog's having a show cut (usually because you're showing your dog), sometimes the best thing to do is to clip your dog in an easy-to-maintain cut. Often called a *Puppy cut,* a *Teddy Bear cut,* or *Pet cut,* this cut doesn't require much work (see Figure 7-3). Follow these steps for giving your pooch a Pet cut:

1. **Equip your clippers with a size 30 or 40 blade and an appropriate snap-on guide comb to set the length at which you want to clip your dog's coat.**

2. **Go over your dog's body with the clippers, trimming her coat to an even length.**

3. **Remove the snap-on guide comb, and gently trim the ears with either a size 10 blade or size 15 blade (if you want a closer shave).**

   Trim to the ear flaps, thus following the line of the ear.

4. **Using the size 10 or size 15 blade without the snap-on guide comb, gently trim your dog's underside — especially around the genitals and anus, to keep them clean.**

Figure 7-3:
Most owners like the simplicity of a Pet cut, because keeping it looking good doesn't take too much effort.

Oops! Righting a wrong

Everyone makes mistakes. It's a normal part of being human. Occasionally, you're going to make goof-ups that aren't going to hurt your dog but will make her look pretty silly. No matter how hard you try, you make a mess, and now your dog looks like she's having a bad hair day. What do you do?

Take a deep breath before you panic, and try to relax. If your dog is injured, with cuts to the skin, see Chapter 17 on how to handle them. If your dog has suffered clipper burn, you can use a little aloe vera on the burn, and remember to keep your clippers cool next time.

If, on the other hand, your dog has not been injured, remember that the mess you've made is only hair, and hair *does* grow back. You just need to figure out how to fix the problem so your dog won't be the laughingstock at the dog park.

Assess the problem first. What did you do that looks so awful? In most cases, you're probably looking at an uneven spot or two, so check to see whether there's any way to blend the two layers of hair together. Thinning scissors (or shears — see the "Using scissors" section earlier in this chapter and Chapter 3) can sometimes fix a problem; sometimes they can't. Sometimes you can trim the area around the uneven spot to match, or vice versa. Your dog's coat may be a little short for a while, and she may have to wear a sweater, but what the heck?

If you're afraid you're going to end up with a bald dog, put away all your grooming tools, take your dog off the table, and have a cup of coffee (or tea). After you've relaxed, evaluate your dog. Is this something you can realistically fix? Or do you need to call in the pros? Try not to clip your dog's coat to the point where the only thing a pro *can* do is shave her.

Part III
Grooming by Coat Type: Beyond the Basics

The 5th Wave   By Rich Tennant

©RICHTENNANT

"Okay, okay— maybe it's not a good idea. I just thought since Huskies were bred for winter weather, part of the grooming process might include having them flocked."

In this part . . .

*I*n the first two parts of *Dog Grooming For Dummies* you discovered the basics, but now you need to tackle some particulars that apply to the many different breeds of dogs. You must consider your dog's particular coat. Is your dog bald and beautiful or does she have flowing long hair that's the envy of runway models? Is he short coated and bristly or curly coated? Or maybe your dog has cords? No matter what breed your dog is, I have you covered in this part.

Chapter 8

Spiffing Up Short- and Medium-Coated Breeds

ogs with short or medium coats are the wash-and-wear dogs of the canine world. They're the least grooming intensive, needing almost no clipping and minimal brushing when compared to long-coated breeds (see Chapter 13).

Now, I said these dogs have shorter coats, but I never said they were low shedding or low maintenance. When pondering a short coat, you may think your troubles are over when it comes to shedding. After all, less fur on the dog means less hair on your pants and couch, right? Wrong. If you've ever owned a short-coated dog for any length of time, you know that hair is simply another condiment and that these dogs can shed profusely. Only hairless dogs won't shed; nevertheless, they do lose hair in some ways. If you're looking for a low-shedding dog, try a Poodle, Kerry Blue Terrier, Soft Coated Wheaten Terrier, or any one of the single-coated breeds. Be forewarned, however, that low-shedding dogs still need a considerable amount of grooming to keep their coats looking good.

In this chapter, you find out everything you need for grooming your dog's short or medium coat so that it looks its very best.

Introducing the Wash-and-Wear Breeds

When I talk about the wash-and-wear dog, I'm often referring to short-coated breeds. These dogs typically have hair that doesn't require much brushing and almost never mats. In this section, I actually cover these breeds in three categories — dogs with no hair, dogs with short hair, and dogs with medium-length hair.

Arguably these dogs can appear in other groupings by coat types. For example, a good number of medium-coated dogs actually have double coats and fall into the double-coat breeds; however, their coats require less maintenance than their longer-haired double-coated counterparts who cannot be lumped together with short-coated breeds.

The bald breeds

Make no mistake, hairless breeds have their own set of grooming requirements. These dogs are characterized by having little or no hair at all (see Figure 8-1), but an occasional powder puff coat shows up in their litters. *Powder puffs* are bald-breed dogs that actually have hair. The bald breeds include the:

- American Hairless Terrier
- Chinese Crested
- Hairless Khala
- Peruvian Inca Orchid
- Xoloitzcuintli

But I thought they were hairless

When you look at so-called hairless breeds, you may be surprised to see dogs with tufts of hair. In the case of the Powder Puff Chinese Crested, you may even see a dog completely covered with hair.

Hairless dogs are the result of a genetic variation, so hairy dogs naturally show up from time to time in these breeds. Indeed, many of the hairless breeds have peach fuzz, if you will, on their bodies, making them a little less hairless than you may have imagined. When compared to other dogs, however, these dogs are certainly bald and beautiful, but because of that, they require special care, which I discuss throughout this chapter.

Figure 8-1:
The Chinese
Crested is a
popular
hairless
breed.

The short coats

Dogs with short coats have the typical wash-and-wear fur that you imagine
when you think of short-haired breeds (see Figure 8-2). But make no mistake
about it, short-coated dogs still require maintenance. The short coats include:

- American Foxhound
- American Pit Bull Terrier
- American Staffordshire Terrier
- Australian Kelpie
- Basenji
- Basset Hound
- Beagle
- Beauceron
- Belgian Malinois
- Black and Tan Coonhound
- Bloodhound
- Bluetick Coonhound
- Boston Terrier
- Boxer
- Bracco Italiano
- Bulldog
- Bullmastiff
- Bull Terrier
- Chihuahua (smooth coat)

- Chinese Shar-Pei
- Dachshund (smooth coat)
- Dalmatian
- Doberman Pinscher
- English Foxhound
- French Bulldog
- German Shorthaired Pointer
- Great Dane
- Greater Swiss Mountain Dog
- Greyhound
- Harrier
- Ibizan Hound
- Italian Greyhound
- Labrador Retriever
- Manchester Terrier
- Mastiff
- Miniature Pincher
- Neapolitan Mastiff
- Pharaoh Hound
- Pointer
- Pug
- Redboned Treehound (a type of Coonhound)
- Rhodesian Ridgeback
- Rottweiler
- Saluki
- Staffordshire Bull Terrier
- Vizsla
- Weimaraner
- Whippet

Figure 8-2:
The Beagle has a short coat that makes grooming a snap.

The medium coats

Dogs with medium coats don't quite have short coats, but they aren't long-haired dogs either (see Figure 8-3). For lack of a better term, they have medium coats that make them easier to groom than the double-coated and long-haired breeds, yet they still need some attention. The medium-coated dogs include:

- Australian Cattle Dog
- Australian Shepherd
- Border Collie
- Brittany
- Canaan Dog
- Cardigan Welsh Corgi
- Collie (Smooth)
- Flat-Coated Retriever
- German Shepherd Dog

- Glen of Imaal Terrier
- Golden Retriever
- Irish Wolfhound
- New Guinea Singing Dog
- Nova Scotia Duck Tolling Retriever
- Pembroke Welsh Corgi
- Petit Basset Griffon Vendeen
- Scottish Deerhound

Figure 8-3: The Golden Retriever has a medium coat that requires more grooming attention than short-coated breeds to avoid mats.

Brushing

Just because your dog has short- or medium-length hair doesn't mean you can avoid using a brush altogether. Many short- and medium-coated dogs have undercoats, and that means they'll shed them out once a year or in some cases year-round.

You may look at your short-coated dog and wonder how in the heck did a dog with such a short coat produce so much hair? But then you'll realize that it takes less time for you to brush your dog, because short coats (for the most part) aren't as susceptible to mats and tangles except in the worst conditions.

With medium-coated dogs, you can expect a bit more brushing and combing than you do with short coats. And you'll need to watch more closely for mats and tangles with a medium coat.

The sections that follow look at some of the details about brushing bald to medium-length coats.

Hairless breeds

You're probably wondering how on earth you brush a hairless-breed dog — let alone why. The truth is the hairless dog isn't going to have much hair beyond a *crest* (along the top of the head) or perhaps some peach fuzz. But *powder puffs* — no not what you find in your compact, but rather hairier versions of hairless dogs — are out there, so I address them here, too.

Crested dogs

Owners of hairless dogs don't do a lot of brushing, but they often shave their dogs with human razors; however, this practice is dangerous and can cut your dog's skin. You can get a smooth cut by using clippers with a No. 40 (surgical cut) blade (see Chapter 7).

For bald dogs with crests, use a very soft (fine) slicker or pin brush on the hair patches to keep them free from tangling. You can get by with brushing them only once or twice a week. If you encounter a tangle, gently untangle it following the instructions in Chapter 5.

Be very gentle because the pins on those pin brushes can hurt!

Powder puffs

Powder puffs are hairless breed dogs that are born with hair all over their bodies. Unlike their hairless counterparts, you'll have a bunch of brushing ahead of you with a powder puff. (Think long-haired dogs.) You can probably get by brushing your powder puff three times a week when he's mature, but you may have to brush every day when he's young, when the fur tends to tangle more.

The hair of the powder puff usually is long, so it should be treated the way you'd treat a long-haired, single-coat dog (see Chapter 13).

To brush out a powder puff:

1. **Look for and gently remove mats and tangles on your powder puff by combing and brushing him and by using a detangler solution first with a medium-toothed comb and then eventually with a fine-toothed comb.**

   If this method doesn't work, try using a mat splitter or mat rake (see Chapter 5).

2. **Working from one end of the dog to the other, separate the hair in layers and brush out with either a soft (fine) slicker brush or a pin brush.**

   Brush out the coat by backbrushing and then brushing along the lay (Chapter 5 explains how).

   When using a pin brush, be careful not to scrape our dog's skin with the pins.

3. **These coats are prone to matting, so you may need to take a second pass through the coat using a medium-toothed comb to find any other tangles.**

   Use detangler solution and the comb to remove the tangles.

4. **Go over the dog's coat with a flea comb to be sure no fleas are evident.**

5. **Feel your dog's paw pads for tangles in the hair between the pads.**

   If you find any tangles or hair that grows beyond the paw pad, trim it with electric clippers and a No. 10 blade (see Chapter 7).

Short coats

Short-coated dogs are relatively easy to care for. In most circumstances, these dogs can get away with a quick brushing once a week. The only time you really need to brush them more often is when they're shedding. If your

Avoiding the tough-to-groom big, hairy coats

If you enjoy the easy-grooming lifestyle, you may want to avoid owning breeds that are tough to groom in the future, because they can require clipping, stripping, or the necessity of (almost) daily brushing. Some tough-to-groom breeds to avoid include

- Afghan Hound
- Bichon Frise
- Briard
- Cocker Spaniel
- Keeshond
- Newfoundland
- Old English Sheepdog
- Poodle
- Schnauzer
- Soft Coated Wheaten Terrier

dog sheds year-round, well I'm sorry, you're probably going to have to brush him more frequently, unless you really don't mind dog hair everywhere.

Here's how to brush your short-haired dog:

1. **Give your dog a good rubdown using a hound glove.**

2. **Using either a curry brush or Zoom Groom, brush your dog's coat with the grain of the hair (the way it grows).**

   You generally don't backbrush short-haired breeds because there isn't enough hair.

3. **Go over your dog's coat with a flea comb to look for fleas.**

4. **Use a hound glove to finish the brushing.**

Medium-length coats

Dogs with medium-length hair are a bit harder to care for than dogs with short coats; however, they aren't as much work as the longer-haired and double-coated breeds. Medium-coated dogs usually need a brushing twice a week and more when shedding or when they're adolescents — changing from their puppy to adult coats.

Here's how to brush your medium-haired dog (single or double coated):

1. **Look for any tangles or mats and first try removing them using detangler solution and a medium-toothed comb.**

   You may find more mats on a medium coat than a short coat. If this method doesn't work, try using a mat splitter or mat rake (see Chapter 5 for specific mat removing instructions).

2. **Backbrush (or brush against the lay of the hair) first using a slicker brush and then again using a fine- or medium-toothed comb.**

   Using a slicker brush removes the loose hairs, and using a comb helps you make sure no tangles are present and removes more hair.

3. **Brush your dog's coat with the lay of the hair using a slicker brush.**

4. **Go over your dog's coat with a flea comb to look for fleas and to make sure there are no tangles forming — unusual in a short coat but a necessity with a medium coat.**

5. **Assuming you don't plan to show your dog (or your dog is shown in an untrimmed coat), use electric clippers with a No. 10 blade to trim hair that grows between paw pads and any other excessive hair for a finished look.**

Bathing

Bathing your dog regularly with a pH-balanced dog shampoo is one of the necessities of life. A number of the short- and medium-coated dogs tend to have oilier skin and hair and can become dirty quickly. Short- and medium-coated sporting breeds are examples. For that reason, regular bathing is essential.

How often and when, really?

How often do you really have to bathe your hairless, short-coated, or medium-coated dog? Well, like most other things, it depends. But keep these points in mind:

- Hairless dogs require weekly bathing followed by moisturizers and sunscreen. Remember, they're as unprotected from the elements as you are, so put them in T-shirts or sweaters to keep them warm after a bath and at night.

- Short-coated dogs usually need more baths than medium-coated dogs. Bathe your short-haired dog when his coat gets dirty or feels oily.

- Medium-coated dogs need to be bathed when dirty, but they also need to be brushed more, depending on the dog's skin type and how often the coat gets oily.

If you use pH-balanced shampoo and conditioner made for dogs, you can bathe your dog as much as you want. And you can make bath time less stressful by protecting your dog's ear canals. Simply place a cotton ball in each ear prior to bathing him to keep water out of his sensitive inner ear. Also, if you have a short-coated dog and you think his coat is getting dry, you can finish up with an oil-based coat conditioner. Be aware that this attracts serious amounts of dirt, and you'll need to bathe your dog again much sooner.

The basics

After performing the pre-bath brush (see the "Brushing" section earlier in this chapter), follow these step-by-step instructions for bathing your short- or medium-coated pooch:

1. **Wet down your dog thoroughly with tepid water in a tub that's an appropriate size for your breed of dog.**

   Although you wouldn't think it, one of the toughest parts of bathing a short- or medium-coated dog is getting the dog completely wet. I know that sounds really odd, but if you want a dog with a natural weather-resistant coat, soaking him down to the skin can be harder than you think. Medium coats can be especially dense.

   Buy a hand-held shower head or tub faucet attachment for bathing your dog; it's made to soak a dog to the skin, *provided* you have enough water pressure.

2. **Soap up your dog with a good pH-balanced dog shampoo except around the face and eyes — which you must do separately with a wet cloth.**

3. **Rinse your dog's coat thoroughly.**

   Leaving soap in a medium coat will cause it to collect dirt, so be sure to rinse carefully.

4. **Apply a good conditioner for dogs.**

5. **Rinse really well.**

   Feel for any soapy, slimy spots next to the skin, and continue rinsing until they are gone. Rub your hands through your dog's coat to help rinse the soap away. A thorough rinse is important for all dogs, but it's especially important for dogs with wrinkles such as Shar-Pei and Pugs (see the nearby "Dealing with those wrinkles" sidebar). You need to be extra careful to ensure dirt and soap residue aren't trapped in their wrinkles.

6. **Dry your dog thoroughly. (See the "Drying" section later in this chapter.)**

7. **Brush out your dog's coat thoroughly to prevent tangles.**

Of course, washing a bald dog isn't as hard because there isn't much of a coat to worry about. But you do have to apply moisturizers to prevent the skin from drying out.

Dealing with those wrinkles

If you own a dog that has wrinkles on the face and forehead (Pugs, Boxers) or maybe all over the body (Shar-Pei), you've probably heard (or experienced) that those wrinkles can be a nightmare. Well that's true only if you allow sore-causing bacteria to form within them. When bathing your dog, you need to make sure that you clean inside the wrinkles and then dry them thoroughly so moisture doesn't have a chance to foster the bacteria.

With small wrinkles, you can use a cotton swab to make sure they're completely cleaned and then wiped dry with a clean, dry swab. Larger wrinkles require sterile cotton balls for cleaning and drying.

If you find sores on your dog, be sure to have your veterinarian treat them. Your vet can also provide you with an ointment or topical steroids to prevent sores from flaring up.

Drying

When you dry your short- to medium-coated dog, always start by pulling as much water off him as possible with thick cotton terry cloth towels. After you towel-dry your dog, it's a good idea to blow-dry him, too. (If your dog is hairless, you won't need a blow-dryer, unless you want to fluff his crests.) Just make sure that you use either a blow-dryer specifically intended for use with dogs or a human-style dryer equipped with a "no-heat" setting. Even though he looks only a little damp, that dampness can attract dirt and can cause your dog to become chilled quickly. Short- to medium-coated dogs normally don't take long to dry, but you need to check the ones with dense short hair to make sure that their hair is dry to the skin.

A chilled dog can become hypothermic in cool or cold weather. Always dry your dog thoroughly.

Preparing for Show

Earlier sections of this chapter explain the basics of getting your short- and medium-coated dog cleaned up and groomed. But what if you're planning to show your dog? Well, here are some tricks of the trade for getting your dog ready for the show.

When showing your dog, understanding the breed standard and the correct coat type your dog should be wearing, if you will, are essential. A good place to look for breed standards is on the Internet at www.akc.org.

Getting short- and medium-coated dogs ready for a show is pretty easy. The basic things you have to do are:

- Trimming toenails

- Brushing out your dog's coat

- Bathing and drying your dog

- Brushing out your clean, dry dog

- Clipping stray hairs and keeping a clean line as allowed by the breed standard

- Dressing the coat with coat conditioners that are available from pet-supply catalogs and stores. These conditioners help give your dog's coat the right feel and can help the coat puff out, if the breed standard so requires. For example, some show folks use mink oil, lanolin, mineral oil, and other oil-based coat conditioners for their short-coated dogs.

Is that all? Well, yes, in a nutshell it is. The best thing to do is to ask people who show your breed what they recommend and then experiment.

Chapter 9

Warming Up to Double-Coated Breeds

*I*t's time to talk big hair. If the short-coated breeds are the wash-and-wear dogs of the canine world (see Chapter 8), the double-coated breeds probably are the biggest headaches as far as the grooming world is concerned. It isn't so much that double-coated dogs are extremely grooming intensive, except (of course) when they blow their coats, or shed, but rather it's what happens to their coats when you don't care for them — mats!

When I talk about double-coated dogs, I'm referring to dogs that are specifically bred to deal with colder climates. These dogs have what I call natural to woolly coats. I say *natural* because they are coats like you might see on a wolf, minus the coloring — thick, with an undercoat and a top coat equipped with guard hairs that can be fairly coarse. The woolly coat is an extension of the natural coat — sort of a natural coat on steroids. These thick, heavy coats can be real nightmares when you're trying to remove mats from them.

If you own a double-coated breed, you're probably wondering what you're in for, and that's what I tell you about in this chapter. You'll find out everything you need to do to groom your double coat and make him the best looking pooch on the block.

Introducing the Big Hairy Deal: Double-Coated Breeds

Technically many dog breeds that aren't discussed at length here in this chapter actually have double coats. Among them are breeds like Labrador Retrievers, Golden Retrievers, and even Pugs. But unlike the hairy dudes I'm going to tell you about, those breeds are not as difficult to groom (see Chapter 8). Big hairy double coats are dogs that are typically characterized as having dense double coats that shed once or twice a year (see Figure 9-1). Some breeds in this category actually can shed year-round, especially in warmer climates.

Here's the list of the double-coated dogs that I'm talking about:

- Akita
- Alaskan Husky
- Alaskan Malamute
- Belgian Sheepdog
- Belgian Tervuren
- Bernese Mountain Dog
- Canadian Inuit Dog
- Chinook
- Collie (Rough)
- Finnish Lapphund
- Finnish Spitz
- German Spitz
- Great Pyrenees
- Jindo
- Keeshond
- Leonberger
- Lundehund
- Newfoundland
- Norwegian Buhund
- Norwegian Elkhound
- Pomeranian
- Saint Bernard
- Samoyed
- Shiba Inu
- Siberian Husky

As I talk about these double-coated breeds, you may notice a huge variation in length of their coats. Some breeds, like the Norwegian Buhund and the Siberian Husky, can have relatively short, dense coats, but others, like the Keeshond and the Samoyed can be downright woolly. So the coat length usually is somewhere between one and four inches.

Woolly coats probably are the most difficult to groom, because there's just so much fur to deal with. Not only are wooly coats long, but they also usually have a dense, thick undercoat. If you're talking wicked mats, you're probably talking about a woolly dog — and dozens of breeds qualify. Woolly fur is so long and thick, you may feel like grabbing the sheep shears instead of a brush.

Figure 9-1:
An Akita (a) and a Bernese Mountain Dog (b) don the bulky characteristics that come with wearing a double fur coat.

You have to brush and comb a wooly double-coated dog every day to keep his coat from looking ratty. During shedding season, you're in for a royal headache. The undercoat becomes matted with guard hairs, making it nearly impossible to comb through.

If you're wondering why you can't just shave your double-coated pooch, well, doing so essentially defeats the purpose of having a double-coated breed. After all, if you didn't like the look of the breed, why own a double-coated dog in the first place? Other more important reasons for not shaving your double-coated breed include:

- **Skin protection:** Double-coated dogs aren't made to walk around without their coats (truly naked) and can be more susceptible to sunburn, hypothermia, and heat stroke without them. When a double-coated dog's fur is brushed and free of blown or shedded hairs and mats, the guard hairs (or top coat) provide shade to the body and enable air to circulate closer to the dog's skin. With a well-maintained coat, your dog can actually remain cooler than she can with a shaved coat.

- **Skin health:** Don't forget that your dog needs time to regrow his coat. After you shave him to the skin, he's starting at square one. Health conditions can impede your dog's ability to regrow his coat, and that can spell trouble, especially with fall and winter approaching.

Caring for your dog's coat is better for him than shaving it. The following sections explain how.

Brushing

As you may have guessed, brushing is a big hairy deal with these dogs. They won't look their best unless you brush and comb them at least twice a week. In some cases, you'll be brushing them almost every day to remove loose fur from that undercoat, especially when they're shedding.

The basics

Here are the basics of how to brush your double-coated dog:

1. **Look for tangles or mats and remove them using detangler solution and a medium-toothed comb (see Chapter 5 for specific instructions).**

   The best way to deal with mats — especially with a double-coated dog — is to not let them form in the first place. You can do that by brushing and combing your dog regularly. If you take care of your double-coated dog's hair, it's probably going to look good and be free from tangles and mats.

2. **Backbrush, or brush against the lay of your dog's hair, first using a slicker brush and then again with a medium- or coarse-toothed comb — depending on the thickness and length of your dog's coat.**

   Using a slicker brush removes the loose hairs, and using a comb helps you make sure no tangles are present and removes more hair.

3. **Brush your dog's coat with the lay of the hair using a slicker brush.**

   Be sure to get all the way to the skin as you brush your dog this way.

4. **Go over your dog's coat with a flea comb both to look for fleas and remove tangles.**

   You can best use a flea comb by parting the coat, starting at the root, and combing through.

5. **Depending on how hairy your dog's pads are, you can either leave them natural or clip them by running electric clippers with a No. 10 blade over the paw pads to remove any excess hair.**

   Don't clip the hair between the pads — just any excess that otherwise may get in the way or inhibit a neater appearance.

Grooming easy-going wash-and-wear dogs

As you're brushing your huge and hairy dog, you may be wishing for (or dreaming of) a wash-and-wear type pooch. Well, being the sadistic author I am, I've decided to list those just plain easier-to-groom breeds right here in this sidebar amid your long-coated agony:

✔ Basenji

✔ Chinese Crested (for those who think bald is beautiful)

✔ Dalmation

✔ Doberman Pinscher

✔ Great Dane

✔ Mastiff

✔ Pharaoh Hound

✔ Pointer

✔ Rhodesian Ridgeback

Nonetheless, you love the look of your long-haired, double-coated breed, don't you? I do, too. I have Alaskan Malamutes. Still, we're allowed to look longingly at the easier-to-groom breeds — don't you agree?

These steps are merely the basics of brushing out a double-coated dog. If your dog is shedding, you're faced with much more to do — keep reading!

Surviving shedding season

Double-coated dogs usually shed out their undercoats once or twice a year. Occasionally, depending on the breed and the geographic climate, you may see double coats shedding year-round. (Lovely, isn't it?) Dogs that shed year-round usually are found in temperate climates (think south).

When the shedding season starts, you know it . . . oh boy, do you know it! Shedding starts innocently enough. Cotton tufts of hair poke through the top coat here and there. Usually you first find it around your dog's flank. When you see that, you need to watch out! You're going to have to start brushing and combing every day to get rid of all that excessive fur; otherwise, you're going to be hip deep in it.

If you own an intact female dog, she usually *blows coat,* or sheds, right before or during her heat or season. In fact, that usually was the sign I looked for so I knew when one of my intact females was ready to come into season. (I've since spayed them all.) But some females don't follow this menstrual schedule, or they blow their coats only after their season, so you can't rely on this hint as a solid tip.

There isn't a comb, slicker brush, or other grooming device made that can hold as much hair as a big dog releases when blowing coat. I swear when they're in full blow, they cast off enough fur to knit three more dogs. A good tool to invest in (if you haven't already) is a shedding blade (see Chapter 3). These blades pull hair from the dog with a single stroke, depositing the hair on the ground. Then, you can bag up the hair and throw it out or hand it to someone who spins dog hair — I'm serious; see the nearby "Puttin' on the dog: Spinning dog hair" sidebar. Just never use a shedding blade on your dog in the living room, or you'll be wishing you hadn't. You'll end up going through many vacuum cleaners.

Some people recommend bathing a dog in warm water to loosen the hair and facilitate shedding. Although this works to a certain degree, you're more likely to have clogged sewer pipes and a tangled mess for a dog if you do it. Better to bite the bullet and brush and comb out your dog before and after bathing. Having a hair strainer in your drain helps, though.

Start where the problem is worst, and use the shedding blade to pull the hair out in a downward motion. Most double-coated dogs are pretty tolerant of having their coats pulled in this manner, but they may not be as tolerant when you pluck the tufts from their coat. I've also noticed that Zoom-Groom combs also pull loose hair out with minimal problems.

After you get a fair amount of fur pulled off the dog, bag it up as soon as possible. I use grocery store bags that I can tie off and throw away. They help keep the hair problem under control. Or you can use a shop vac to tidy up.

Puttin' on the dog: Spinning dog hair

You may be amazed (and amused) to discover that like wool, dog hair can be spun into yarn. The fur is called *chiengora*, (*SHEE-en-gora*) which is just a fancy term for dog hair. (That way your mom won't balk when you hand her a *chiengora* hat for Christmas.

Here are some Web sites that cover knitting with dog hair. These Web sites are for information only; I don't specifically endorse any of them:

✔ Handspinning Dog Hair Homepage — www.mdnpd.com/pd/default.htm

✔ VIP Fibers — www.vipfibers.com/index.php

✔ Betty Burian Kirk Dog Hair Yarn Custom Spun — www.bbkirk.com/Dog%20 Hair%20Yarn.htm

✔ Wolf Tales/Wolf Yarn — www.inet design.com/wolfdunn/wolfyarn/

✔ Woofspuns — www.dettasspindle. com/WoofspunDogYarn/Woofspun DogYarn.html

One book a knitter friend of mine recommends is *Knitting With Dog Hair: Better A Sweater From A Dog You Know and Love Than From A Sheep You'll Never Meet* by Kendal Crolius (St. Martin's Griffin, 1997). My friend considers it the bible of dog-hair knitting.

Bathing

Bathing can be easy or a big hairy deal when it comes to double-coated dogs. The double-coated dogs that I deal with consider bathwater akin to a near-death experience, so they can be really difficult in the tub. The good news is that with proper brushing and coat care, you don't really have to bathe a double coat as much as you do a single coat or a short-haired dog. All that brushing and blowing out their coat gives long-haired, double-coated dogs a better chance of keeping clean (or at least cleaner).

Some people swear that many of the dogs with natural coats don't have a doggie smell. I can't swear that's true, because my first dogs as an adult were northern breed dogs (Samoyed crosses, Keeshonden, and Alaskan Malamutes), but I do notice that some shorter-coated breeds have a houndy type smell. So, maybe there's something to that natural-coat characteristic.

How often and when, really?

How often you bathe your double coat depends a great deal on how dirty he gets and how often you brush and comb him. Most people get by with a bath once a month, but your mileage may vary. Here are some factors to keep in mind when deciding when to bathe a double-coated dog:

- You can bathe your dog as much as you want provided you use a pH-balanced shampoo for dogs. You won't ruin his coat by bathing him too often. Forget that old wives' tale.
- If your dog gets dirty digging a hole or getting into other filthy things, it's time for a bath; otherwise, the dirt will just cause mats.
- Bathing your dog will take a fair amount of time, because he needs to be brushed, bathed, dried, and then brushed again, and you may even want to add a clipping session or two. That mean's you need to plan ahead for your pup's baths.

The basics

After performing the pre-bath brush (see the "Brushing" section earlier in this chapter), follow these step-by-step bathing instructions:

1. **Wet down your dog thoroughly with tepid water in a tub that's an appropriate size for your breed of dog.**

   When bathing your double-coated dog, be sure to wet your dog all the way to the skin. Some coats are so dense they keep water away from the skin, so be sure to feel all the way down to the skin to make sure your dog's all wet.

A handheld shower head or tub faucet attachment is ideal for wetting down dogs if you have good water pressure.

2. **Using a pH-balanced dog shampoo, thoroughly lather up your dog's entire coat except around the face and eyes — which you must do separately with a wet cloth.**

3. **Rinse your dog's coat thoroughly.**

   Be sure to rinse the residue from the skin and undercoat.

4. **Apply a good conditioner for dogs.**

   One made to keep the hair from tangling is good. No-residue conditioners are good, too.

5. **Rinse really well.**

   Feel for any soapy, slimy spots next to the skin, and continue rinsing until they are gone. Although billed as no-residue conditioners, these products will leave a residue, if you don't rinse them out.

6. **Dry your dog thoroughly. (See the section on "Drying" your long coat later in this chapter.)**

7. **Brush out your dog's coat thoroughly.**

Preventing tangles and mats

A double-coated dog's fur may easily tangle, or it may not, depending on how fine or coarse his hair is. The tricks to preventing tangles and mats from forming include keeping the following points in mind when grooming your double-coated dog:

✔ Brushing out your dog's coat before bathing is imperative. Yes, I know, she may be filthy or stink beyond belief, or she may be shedding worse than anything you've ever seen. Brush and comb her; otherwise, after you get that double coat wet, it will mat and tangle worse than a preschooler's hair. Do you and your dog a favor and brush and comb her out before her bath.

✔ Detangler solution is your next best friend. Removing all mats, foreign objects (twigs, burrs), and blown coat before you bathe your dog prevents tangles from forming after the bath.

✔ Use a mat rake and mat cutter to eliminate tangles that can become serious mats.

✔ Use a coat conditioner that prevents tangles and matting.

✔ Rinse your dog thoroughly when bathing. Any leftover residues will attract dirt and cause mats.

✔ After bathing, always blow-dry your double coat in a clean area where he's unlikely to pick up more dirt that can cause tangles.

✔ Dry your dog thoroughly. Wet hair picks up dirt and thus causes tangles.

Drying

If you have a sopping wet dog in your tub, grab the towels and start drying, blotting and squeezing as much water from the thick coat as you can. *Hint:* You'll need plenty (a lot) of towels.

Preventing collar marks

One big problem with double-coated breeds is the marks that collars can leave on their necks. If you're a conscientious owner, you know that you must have a collar and tags on your dog at all times so you can identify him if he accidentally slips away from you and so he can then be returned to you. The problem is that most collars rub the fur in such a way that a mark is left where the collar was worn — even after you clean up and brush out his coat.

Many show dog owners don't make their dogs wear collars, preferring instead to rely on microchip or tattoo identification of their dogs. However, this form of identification can be risky, because many people don't know to look for tattoos and microchips. Someone may find a dog and not bother to take him to a vet or humane shelter, because no tags were present and the person who found him may not be aware of microchip IDs. Another issue with microchips is that the devices that read the information on the chips haven't been standardized; not all readers read all microchips. So if you decide on microchipping your dog, be sure that it is a common microchip. Check with your vet.

You *can* keep a collar on your dog without ruining his fur. Rolled leather collars do a minimal amount of damage to the neck fur. They come in buckle and slip styles (ones that tighten when the collar is pulled on), and you can use either type. Be aware, however, that when these collars get wet, some of them can stain your dog's fur.

As a note or warning: You should never leave a slip-style collar on an unattended dog.

After your dog is no longer dripping, move him to your grooming table and doggie blow-dryer and start drying. At first the coat will be too moisture-laden and heavy to comb or brush as you're drying it, but as it begins to dry, you can begin combing it with a medium-toothed comb and then eventually move to a slicker brush. Lift the outer hair with the comb so that you can dry your dog's top coat and undercoat.

As you dry your dog, be mindful of how you're using the brush and comb. Like blow-drying your own hair, a dog's hair follows the style you set as you dry. So, for example, if you want a stand-up coat, you have to backbrush with a comb to get it to stand up away from the lay of the hair. If the coat is to lay flat, you brush with the grain, not against it.

After your dog is dry, backbrush his coat with a comb and a slicker brush, and then brush the hair forward.

Preparing for Show

Getting a double-coated dog ready for a confirmation show isn't necessarily a big deal if you maintain his coat, but the process is time-consuming.

When showing your dog, understanding the breed standard and the correct coat type your dog should be wearing, if you will, are essential. A good place to look for breed standards is on the Internet at www.akc.org.

The list that follows contains the basics of what you have to do to get your dog ready for the show:

- ✔ Trim your dog's toenails.
- ✔ Brush out your dog.
- ✔ Remove any mats.
- ✔ Bathe your dog.
- ✔ Dry your dog.
- ✔ Brush out your dog again.
- ✔ Clip stray hairs and trim your dog's coat to keep the clean line that is allowed by his breed standard.
- ✔ Use coat dressing to spruce up you dog's coat, whenever appropriate.

If you want to show your dog, you'll need to know some of the finer points of getting your dog's double coat ready. I tell you about them in the sections that follow.

Mousse and a spritz — Conditioning the coat

Plenty of good coat conditioners are available to get dogs ready for show. Most, like coat dressings and bodifiers, are used to add volume to your dog's hair. Texturizers also are available to give your dog's coat the proper feel.

You need all this stuff, because using it has to do with giving your dog the proper coat type. For example, certain breeds are supposed to have what's called a harsh coat. That means the dog's coat feels a little stiff to the touch and is weatherproof. When you bathe and condition your dog frequently, that feel can be lost because of coat maintenance, or the dog's coat simply may not have the right feel. Whatever the reason, you need to adjust the coat so that it feels as close to the way the breed standard dictates as possible, and that requires some coat dressing.

Coat conditioners won't make a bad coat perfect, but they will improve it tremendously, especially when you do all the other good-grooming tasks correctly. Coat conditioners won't necessarily make your dog into a show winner, but they will keep you from losing badly because your dog's coat looks awful.

Making the hair stand up

Now that you've conditioned your dog with enough mousse and coat texturizer to saturate her coat, you may be wondering just how to get her fur to puff out like the other show dogs you see. If you have a dog with a stand-up coat (meaning, she puffs out naturally), you're in luck! Your dog has a natural show coat. But if yours doesn't puff, here are some tricks you can try to make your dog look like she has a stand-up coat:

- ✔ While your dog's coat is drying, use your blow-dryer against the lay of the hair and backbrush your dog's coat (using a brush or comb) to puff it out.

- ✔ Spray bodifier over your dog's coat, backbrush again, and let the coat air dry.

- ✔ If the hair starts to lay back down, use a bodifier or water mister to spray on the coat and backbrush the hair as required.

All of these tips are legitimate tricks you can use to get your dog's hair to stand up and look pretty for the show.

Chapter 10

Clarifying the Corded Breed's Coif

In This Chapter

▶ Discovering the corded breeds

▶ Developing those doggie dreadlocks

▶ Bathing (and drying) the corded canine coiffure

▶ Preparing your corded dog for show

*I*f you've never seen a corded dog, the first time you run into one you're likely to think that you've met up with a mop with four feet, a wet nose, and a tail. But make no mistake about it, these dogs are cool to watch and look fabulous when their coats are in full cords.

Cords on these breeds form naturally. The undercoats naturally entwine with the top coat, creating a type of cording or felting (another fancy name for cording). The cords usually begin to form when the puppy is shedding out his puppy coat and growing in his adult coat at 9 months or thereabouts. Depending on the breed, cords can take from two to five years to mature. During this maturation process, owners of corded dogs need to make sure that their pups' coats don't form mats and instead separate into cords.

Most owners choose these dogs because of the distinctive look the cords have, plus they love the personalities of the corded dogs. If you have a corded dog, chances are you want to keep the cords in as good of shape as possible and keep them long. Ultimately that means you need to encourage a show-type coat, which requires a considerable amount (almost daily) of maintenance. Lucky for you, this chapter explains everything you need to know about grooming your dog's corded coat to keep it looking its very best.

Introducing the Corded Breeds

So you've never seen a four-legged, wet-nosed mop, eh? Well, take a look at the Komondor in Figure 10-1, who is joined by four other breeds on the corded list:

- Bergamasco
- Corded Poodle (Poodles can be shown with corded coats)
- Komondor
- Puli
- Spanish Water Dog

Corded dogs are water dogs or herding dogs, primarily because their corded coats provide good protection against the elements.

Figure 10-1:
Yah mahn! The Komondor, he's got the best of canine dreads.

Brushing

Until your puppy starts developing cords, brushing and combing are imperative for keeping your uncorded puppy looking good.

Caring for the coat before cords form

You need to brush and comb your puppy every day before the cords form. That's the reality of the breed.

Without cords, corded puppies need to be brushed and combed the same way you would any other dog with curly hair. Here's how:

1. **Look for tangles or mats and remove them using detangler solution and a medium-toothed comb (see Chapter 5 for specific instructions).**

   The tricky part is telling a mat from a forming cord. If the hair is trying to form longwise, it's a cord; otherwise it's a mat and needs to be detangled.

2. **Backbrush, or brush against the lay of your dog's hair, first using a slicker brush and then again with a medium- or coarse-toothed comb — depending on the thickness and length of your dog's coat.**

   Using a slicker brush removes the loose hairs, and using a comb helps you make sure no tangles are present and removes more hair.

3. **Brush your dog's coat with the lay of the hair using a slicker brush.**

   Be sure to get all the way to the skin as you brush your dog this way.

4. **Go over your dog's coat with a flea comb to detangle any mats and to look for fleas.**

   You can best use a flea comb by parting the coat, starting at the root, and combing through.

5. **Depending on how hairy your dog's pads are, you can either leave them natural or clip them by running electric clippers with a No. 10 blade over the paw pads to remove any excess hair.**

   Don't clip the hair between the pads — just any excess that otherwise may get in the way or inhibit a neater appearance.

6. **If you wish, use a No. 10 blade to trim around the anal area and belly to avoid a mess.**

As the cords form

At some point, your puppy's coat is going to start forming cords (see Figure 10-2). They usually begin to form at the skin first as the puppy starts shedding his puppy fluff, and the coat begins to mature.

After the cords start forming, you need to separate them from the other hair with your fingers to make sure that they don't form mats. Separating the cords is a daily task together with brushing out any other hair that hasn't yet become part of a cord with a slicker brush and a comb. Cords form pretty much on their own – it just happens; you can't do much to stop the process or encourage it.

Figure 10-2:
Here's what
you may
start with —
a Puli pup
before
cords have
fully formed.

As you might expect, mats and tangles are common with corded dogs until the cords form. After all, that's how the cords are formed — sort of. If you think about it, cords are just elongated pieces of twisted hair that clump together, almost exactly as a mat would, except that they form a cord instead. If you find a smaller mat that isn't cording, you can try to remove it by using detangler solution and a comb to gently tease it out, but you may have to use your fingers to get between the hairs and untangle them. After you do, you can try to separate the cords again and encourage them to stay corded. If the mat is seriously large, the best thing to do is consult a professional groomer to help you remove it.

Be patient with the cording process. It usually takes several years and daily grooming to coax the cords to mature properly. The coats of most corded breeds will cord naturally, but the fur still needs your help to prevent it from forming mats and terrible tangles rather than cords.

Maintaining healthy cords

If you've been a conscientious corded-breed owner, you've been separating cords so that they don't become entangled. At some point, nothing is left but cords (see Figure 10-3). Now that your corded dog has a mature coat, I'm sure you're wondering: "What do I do with the cords now?"

Figure 10-3:
Body (a)
and paw
(b) cords
close up.

After the cords form, your main responsibility becomes keeping the cords separated and free from dirt and debris. That's no minor task for any kind of mop-like object or being. (If you don't keep the cords clean, you end up with the kind of horrible mess that only clippers can solve.)

Put away the brush and comb and break out your clippers, pH-balanced shampoo, and conditioner — the basic tools you need to keep a corded dog clean and looking good.

You can use the clippers or scissors (remember to be careful) to trim away fuzzies that form on the ends of the cords and keep them neat and tidy. Trimming the cords also makes sure that the dirt these dogs naturally pick up off the floor doesn't cause mats. Many pet owners prefer to have their dog's underside and the area around the genitals and anus clipped to avoid obvious problems.

If you decide that cords are too much of a hassle (as many pet owners have), you can keep the cords trimmed back to about four inches, thus keeping them off the ground. In extreme cases, you can clip your dog's cords back to whatever length you feel comfortable maintaining.

Keeping Cords Clean

The best way to keep your corded dog clean is to keep him away from the stuff that gets him dirty to begin with. But that means keeping him from being what he really is — a dog. You can expect a corded coat to pick up an extraordinary amount of dirt and debris that definitely requires thorough cleaning. Yes, corded breeds do need to be bathed, so in the sections that follow, I tell you how.

How often and when, really?

Corded dogs need to be bathed frequently to keep the cords clean and to maintain a healthy skin and coat. You may have to bathe your corded dog as often as once a week. If your dog can stay clean, you maybe can get by with bathing only once every other week. It just depends.

Bath time for corded dogs can be a lengthy ordeal — not because of washing, per se, but rather because of drying. Think in terms of hours when it comes to washing and drying a corded dog. Your arms will hurt, your dog will get bored, and you'll start dreaming of dogs with no coats. An entire afternoon or morning may work — figure an hour to wash and two to three hours to dry.

Bathing basics

No one part of bathing a corded breed is tougher than the other. They all present unique problems that the corded breed owner must overcome. Getting the dog completely wet, completely washed and conditioned, completely rinsed, and then completely dried are what make bathing a corded dog really tough.

Never wash a corded dog outside or in a dirty room. You end up undoing all that you've done to wash your dog.

Here are the steps to follow when washing your dog's corded coat:

1. **Wet down your dog thoroughly in a tub that's an appropriate size for your breed of dog.**

   Accomplishing this task can be rough. Those cords can sop up a lot of water, and soaking your dog down to the skin may prove to be harder and more time consuming than you think.

Use a shower spray attachment or even fill a container and pour water from it into the cords then feel the skin and the cords to make sure they're soaking wet.

2. **Using a pH-balanced shampoo, thoroughly lather up your dog's entire coat.**

   You need to make sure that the shampoo penetrates the cords by squeezing the suds into each one.

3. **Starting from the skin and working outward to ensure that you leave no residue, thoroughly rinse the shampoo from the corded dog's coat.**

   Always rub your hands through your dog's cords down to the skin and through the cords again to rinse shampoo residue away. You must run clean water through each of the cords to make sure they're totally rinsed.

   Rinsing your corded dog's coat is extremely important, because leaving any residues in it is likely to result in a very dirty dog in a very short time. Dirt in the cords likewise can trap water and other nasty stuff, making them perfect breeding grounds for bacteria and mildew.

4. **Repeat Steps 2 and 3, but this time in place of shampoo, apply a good conditioner to keep the cords feeling their best.**

5. **Rinse the conditioner from the corded coat really well (in the same way described in Step 3).**

6. **Dry your dog's corded coat (check out the next section).**

Drying the cords

Now that you've washed your corded dog, you must take these steps in the daunting process of drying your dog's dreads:

1. **Gently twist handfuls of cords in a wringing motion to remove the excess water while the dog is still in the tub.**

   Repeat this step on all of the cords, starting from the top of your dog and working your way down.

   If the excess water is too soapy, rinse the cords again.

   Wring the cords out several times until you can't get any more water out.

2. **Using towels, squeeze the water out of each cord down to the skin.**

   Take this step while your dog is still in the tub.

Pining over towel-dry-and-go dogs

Whenever you've had to spend hours drying your corded dog, you're probably thinking that a bald dog might be the way to go. All righty then: Although these dogs must be bathed weekly, drying them is a breeze:

✔ American Hairless Terrier

✔ Chinese Crested

✔ Hairless Khala

✔ Peruvian Inca Orchid

✔ Xoloitzcuintli

---

3. **Remove your dog from the tub and repeat Step 2 using dry towels.**

4. **Using a strong dog hair dryer without heat, blow-dry the corded coat from the skin outward.**

   Dry the cords in layers from the top to the bottom of the dog.

   Remain patient. Drying a corded dog's coat takes an extraordinary amount of time.

Remember to thoroughly dry your dog; otherwise, he will mildew — yuk! If your dog smells like rotting vegetation or his coat turns odd colors and smells of mold or mildew, it's time to clip the cords. Depending on how bad the mildew problem is, you may have to trim only a small section, or it may end up being the entire coat. If the entire coat is involved, I recommend seeking help from a professional groomer and a veterinarian. If the mildew isn't too bad, you can try a medicated antifungal shampoo on your dog — which may get rid of the problem, but you must make sure your dog is completely dry to avoid the possibility of the mildew coming back.

Now that you know what bathing a corded dog entails, if you're dead set on allowing your dog to play outside, either clip the cords back or provide your pooch with some kind of doggiewear that keeps most of the offending brush and dirt out of his coat.

Preparing for Show

If you're thinking about entering your corded breed in the big show, a thorough understanding of the breed standard helps immensely. A good place to look for breed standards is on the Internet at www.akc.org.

Here are some basic preparations that are essential:

- ✔ Trimming toenails
- ✔ Trimming frayed cords
- ✔ Bathing the dog
- ✔ Drying the dog
- ✔ Keeping the dog clean

The last two items are probably the most daunting of tasks where the corded dog is concerned. You might find it helpful to ask people who show corded breeds what grooming tips and tricks they recommend and then experiment to establish your own show routine.

Chapter 11

Shaping Up the Clipped Breeds

*I*n this chapter, I discuss the clipped breeds, with the exception of Poodles (I devote Chapter 14 to that special breed). Certain dogs need clipping because their coats require it (being single coat) or because the breed standard calls for it.

Clipping a dog is a bit of an art form that requires a considerable amount of trial and error — not so much, it is hoped, however, on the error side.

If you have a clipped breed, you already know you have plenty of work ahead of you. Clipping takes time to practice and get good at — no book can teach you what experience and practice will.

Many of the stripped-breed dogs that I discuss in Chapter 12 arguably can also be considered among the clipped breeds within this chapter. However, for convenience, I distribute them between truly traditional clipped versus stripped lines within the two chapters and leave the decision up to you about which method of grooming you want to use for your particular dog.

That means here in Chapter 11, you're going to find out everything you need to groom your traditionally clipped breed to look his very best.

Taking a Little off the Top: Introducing the Clipped Breeds

Somewhere along the evolutionary ladder between wolves and dogs, humans discovered that certain types of coats lurked in canine *(canis lupus familiaris)* genetics. Although I'm sure a bald wolf, one in need of a haircut, or one whose coat became naturally tangled didn't last long in the wild, after humans started tinkering with these unusual canine breed characteristics, those kinds of dogs became popular. People not only liked the look and feel of the various coats, but in some circumstances, they actually sought out the right coat for the job. Here, however, I address the ones that need haircuts.

Clipped-breed dogs (see Figure 11-1) typically and primarily are characterized as being single-coated (or without an undercoat), although some sport double coats. Their coats also may be curly or straight, and they traditionally are clipped according to their standards. Dogs who fit this category include

- American Cocker Spaniel
- American Water Spaniel
- Bedlington Terrier
- Bichon Frise
- Black Russian Terrier
- Bouvier de Flandres
- Brittany
- Cesky Terrier
- Cocker Spaniel (American and English)
- Curly-coated Retriever
- English Setter
- English Springer Spaniel
- Field Spaniel
- Gordon Setter
- Irish Setter
- Irish Water Spaniel
- Kerry Blue Terrier
- Löwchen
- Poodle (all sizes)
- Portuguese Water Dog
- Soft Coated Wheaten Terrier
- Springer Spaniel

As I indicated in the introduction to this chapter, you can include the stripped-breed dogs from Chapter 12 in this list — in a less traditional sense.

Figure 11-1: Clipped breed dogs include Field Spaniels (a) and Soft Coated Wheaten Terriers (b).

Brushing Basics

The way you brush a clipped-breed dog often depends on the specific coat of each individual dog. If your dog has a curlier coat, you may find yourself reaching more for a pin brush rather than a slicker. Even so, you can find different ways to brush these kinds of dogs, depending on the specific coats.

Terrier-type coats

Terrier-type coats usually are wire-haired, but oddly enough, the five Terriers that I mention in this chapter don't have the traditional Terrier coat. (Go figure!) However, some of the dogs listed in the chapter on stripped breeds (Chapter 12) have wire-haired coats that can be clipped, and that's why I talk about them here.

Nevertheless, a proper way to brush out a wire-haired (Terrier) coat does exist. Harsh, wire-haired coats tend to resist tangles a bit more than other breeds, and you can usually get by brushing these dogs only twice a week — except when the dog's coat is in need of clipping — when the dog starts looking ratty. Here's how to brush a Terrier-type coat:

1. **Brush the entire dog with a slicker brush.**

   You can skip a second pass with a comb because these dogs usually don't mat the way other breeds do because of the wire hair.

2. **Backbrush, or brush against the lay of your dog's fur, with a slicker brush if your dog's coat type permits, and then brush it back into place.**

   Short-coated terriers such as Parson Russell Terriers may be harder to backbrush.

3. **Remove any loose hairs your dog has using a shedding blade or undercoat rake.**

4. **Using a medium- or fine-toothed comb, finish brushing and combing out your dog's coat.**

5. **Check for fleas by running a flea comb through your entire dog's coat.**

   Be sure to comb from the roots of the hair to the tips.

Spaniel-type coats

When I refer to spaniel-type coats, I'm talking about the coats that you see on Cocker Spaniels, English Setters, Soft Coated Wheaten Terriers, and Field Spaniels. The spaniel-type coat is like the long-haired dogs (see Chapter 13) and needs to be treated as such. They need daily brushing to keep them clean and free of mats. Follow these instructions for brushing:

1. **Check for and remove any tangles or mats with detangler solution and a medium-toothed comb.**

   If this method doesn't work, try using a mat splitter or mat rake (see Chapter 5 for specific mat removing instructions).

2. **Backbrush, or brush against the lay of your dog's hair, first using a slicker brush and then again with a medium-toothed comb.**

3. **Then brush again with the lay of the hair using a slicker brush.**

4. **Check for fleas by going over your dog's entire coat with a flea comb.**

Poodle-type coats

What about the curly coats, that is, the Poodle-like coats? These dogs include the Portuguese Water Dog, the Kerry Blue Terrier, and the Bichon Frise, and they need special brushing. Poodle-type coats have a propensity for getting tangled and matted, so you must brush and comb them every day. Here's how:

1. **Check for tangles or mats and remove them using detangler solution and a medium-toothed comb.**

   If this method doesn't remove the mat, consider using a mat splitter or mat rake (see Chapter 5).

2. **Gently brush through the curly coat with a pin brush, and follow up with a slicker brush.**

   These two passes will help remove any loose hair and keep tangles from forming.

3. **Comb through the curls using a medium-tooth comb.**

4. **Check for fleas and make sure you get out any tangles by running a flea comb through your dog's entire coat.**

Bathing

Clipped-breed dogs need baths about once every two weeks — more often when they get dirty. Because their hair acts like a dirt magnet, these dogs can end up looking dingy within only a short amount of time. In most cases, these dogs have hair that is similar to and behaves much like human hair. So, you need to give your dog a bath at least once every two weeks to be sure that he's clean and sweet smelling.

The prebath clip

Many groomers like to do a prebath clip after the prebath brushing for clipped breeds. By doing so, you can get rid of the frizzy hair and split ends here, and you'll have less hair to wash when you're done.

Most of the prebath clip is just for neatening or tidying up the coat — not for a full clipping unless the hair is really frizzy and is going to tangle badly during subsequent grooming without it.

If you do a prebath clip, make sure your dog is thoroughly brushed out before-hand. Clip only what needs to be clipped until after the bath when your dog is clean. If your dog is really dirty, you need to skip the prebath clip entirely and take your lumps after the bath, doing a full clipping then.

Knowing when a dog needs to be clipped is mostly a judgment call on your part. If your dog starts looking like an amorphous, hairy blob, well, that's a pretty good indication it's time for some trimming. However, most people like to clip their dogs about once a month to keep them looking good and maybe even once a week, as needed.

When doing a prebath clip, use the type of clipper blade that matches the type of clip your dog previously was given. Remember, the prebath clipping is just a trim, and the real work occurs after the bath. A prebath clip concentrates on trimming out-of-place hairs and the frizzy stuff.

Bathing basics

Bathing a clipped dog is very similar to bathing other dogs (see Chapter 5). Just be sure to do the following:

1. **Wet down your dog thoroughly with tepid water in a tub that's an appropriate size for your breed of dog.**

   Make sure that your dog's coat gets wet all the way down to the skin. This requires you to totally soak down your dog either with a handheld shower head or tub faucet attachment or by pouring water over your dog. Feel the skin to find out whether your dog is completely wet.

2. **Using a pH-balanced dog shampoo, thoroughly lather up your dog's entire coat except around the face and eyes — which you must do separately with a wet cloth.**

   Keep the shampoo out of your dog's eyes — ouch. Many shampoos are tearless, but you shouldn't count on them not stinging your dog's eyes.

3. **Thoroughly rinse your dog's coat.**

4. **Apply an excellent dog coat conditioner that prevents tangles and keeps the coat from drying out.**

5. **Repeat Step 3, squeezing out the excess water and rinsing again.**

   When rinsing your dog's coat, be sure to remove all soap and conditioner residues. Even no-residue conditioners leave residues when not rinsed properly.

6. **Dry your dog's coat thoroughly before clipping.**

   You can use a doggie hair dryer or one intended for human use that has a "no-heat" setting if your dog is small enough. Otherwise use a no-heat force hair dryer for dogs.

Clipping

You can clip your clipped-breed dog in a variety of ways, depending, of course, on which kind of dog you have. You can check out other same-breed dogs and ask their owners how they groom them so you have a good idea of how you'd like your dog to look and how you can get the job done.

Even so, you can work with some basic, everyday cuts, including Terrier cuts (for Terrier-type coats), Spaniel cuts (for sporting dogs), and Poodle-type cuts (for those curly-coated dogs).

Please take note that the cuts described in the following sections aren't intended to be show quality. If you want to do show-quality cuts, your best bet is to study the breed standard and have a show person demonstrate the correct cut for your dog.

Some general guidelines apply pretty much across the board when clipping your dog's coat in virtually all of the cuts described in this section. Here are two important ones:

✔ A shorter coat is easier to maintain than a longer coat.

✔ Snapping a guide comb onto your clippers (see Chapter 7) can help you guide the clippers over your dog's coat so that you cut it at a uniform length.

Never dig your clippers into your dog's skin. Even though they are guarded, a serious dig can cut and will *hurt* your dog. Clipper blades should run flat on the dog to avoid digging into the skin. You also need to make sure that the length of the blade is set accurately.

Terrier-type coats

If you have a Terrier (or a Terrier-like dog — and many of them are), you're probably wondering what you can do to keep him looking good without stripping (see Chapter 12) his coat. The three types of clips you can try with a Terrier are a single-length clip, a large-Terrier clip, and a small Terrier clip.

Finding the no-clip zone

You may be wondering what kind of dogs you can own that don't have to be clipped. Well, guess what? Plenty of them are out there. Here are ten no-clip dogs:

✔ Golden Retriever

✔ Siberian Husky

✔ Pug

✔ Labrador Retriever

✔ Rottweiler

✔ German Shepherd Dog

✔ Bulldog

✔ Beagle

✔ Samoyed

✔ Greyhound

Single-length clip

The single-length clip (see Figure 11-2) is probably the easiest to do, and it's one you can use on just about any dog, because you clip most of your dog's coat at only one length. You may, however, need to trim the coat closer around specific areas — the abdomen, anus, ears, face, genitals, and so on. A single-length clip is just as the name sounds, you use a single blade or snap-on a guide comb and run it all over the dog's body so most of the hair is one length. Use these steps to give your dog a single-length clip:

1. **Select a clipper blade that works well with the type of coat your dog or breed of dog has.**

   A No. 10 usually is ideal for close trimming around the genitals and abdomen, and a No. 7 or wider (smaller number) is best for body cuts.

2. **Trim the face with a No. 10 blade, starting from behind the eyebrows to the occiput (or the highest point on the dog's skull; see Chapter 2).**

   You can trim along the cheek but leave the moustache and beard.

3. **Trim the hair around the ears closely with a No. 10 blade, so that the ears look like triangles.**

   Trim the fur with the lay of the hair. Working against the grain can be very dangerous because you can cut the skin.

4. **Switching to a body clipper blade (the one you chose earlier in Step 1 for your specific dog), trim the coat evenly down the legs and across the back, chest, and loin.**

   Even up any discrepancies in length by carefully using either the clippers or scissors.

Figure 11-2:
The single-
length cut.

5. **Switch back to the No. 10 blade and trim the abdomen, around the genitals and anus, and the feet for a neater look.**

   Be careful not to touch any sensitive areas with the clippers.

Large-Terrier clip

The large-Terrier clip (see Figure 11-3) is seen on many larger Terriers such as Airedale and Welsh Terriers, and it looks pretty impressive even if it isn't standard. The Terrier coats are stripped to meet the breed standard for showing.

1. **Select a clipper blade that will work well with your dog.**

   Use a No. 10, No. 8½, or No. 7 blade.

2. **Using a No. 10 blade, trim your dog's face from behind the eyebrows to the occiput (or the highest point on the dog's skull; see Chapter 2).**

   You can trim along the cheek but leave the moustache and beard.

3. **Trim the hair around the ears closely with a No. 10 blade, so that the ears look like triangles.**

4. **Trim the coat evenly down the neck, back, chest, and loin.**

   Most groomers recommend a ¼-inch cut.

5. **Trim the tail and leave the legs untrimmed at this time.**

   Blend in the transition from the body to the legs so that it doesn't look like you just stopped with the clippers. Even up any discrepancies in length either with the clippers or *carefully* with scissors.

6. **Trim the abdomen and around the genitals and anus.**

   Be careful not to touch any sensitive areas with the clippers.

7. **Trim the legs so that they look more or less like columns.**

   If the legs look unkempt as you're trimming them, switch to a larger body-type blade, such as a No. 3 or No. 4, and trim the legs evenly so they look like columns.

Small-Terrier clip

Here's a small Terrier clip you might enjoy seeing on your dog (see Figure 11-4):

1. **Select a clipper blade that works well with your dog.**

   Use a No. 5, No. 7, or No. 8½. You'll also need a No. 10 clipper blade, if your dog has a standard Terrier head.

Figure 11-4:
The small-
Terrier clip.

2. **If your breed has a standard Terrier look, meaning it has the look of a basic Terrier, start by trimming the face with a No. 10 blade starting from behind the eyebrows to the occiput (or the highest point on the dog's skull; see Chapter 2).**

   You can trim along the cheek but leave the moustache and beard.

   If your dog has a natural-looking face (one that is not usually trimmed up) skip the more intense trimming and only use a No. 3 or a No.4 blade to trim away unruly facial hair.

3. **Trim the hair around the ears closely with a No. 10 blade, so that the ears look like triangles.**

4. **Trim the coat evenly down the neck, back, chest, and loin.**

   Most groomers recommend using a ¼-inch cut.

5. **Trim the tail, and leave the legs untrimmed at this time.**

   Blend in the transition so it doesn't look like you just stopped with the clippers. Even up any discrepancies in length carefully with either the clippers or scissors.

Falling over yourself?

Some breeds don't have moustaches and eyebrows, but instead they have falls. A fall is simply long hair similar to bangs that covers the dog's eyes. Soft Coated Wheaten Terriers, Black Russian Terriers, Kerry Blue Terriers, Lakeland Terriers, and Sealyham Terriers all have falls that extend from the occiput, eyebrows, or somewhere in between down over the eyes.

To be technically correct, if you have one of these breeds, your dog needs to have a fall, but if your dog is a pet and isn't being prepped for the show ring, you can skip the fall so you can see your dog's gorgeously expressive eyes.

To keep a fall, trim the hair from the occiput (or the highest point on the dog's skull; see Chapter 2) to the eyebrows in the shape of a *V*, so it falls over the eyes. Keep the fall trimmed so it looks nice.

   6. Trim around the genitals and anus.

   Be careful not to touch any sensitive areas with the clippers.

   7. Trim the legs so that they look more or less like columns.

   If the legs look unkempt as you're trimming them, switch to a larger body-type blade, such as a No. 3 or No. 4, and trim the legs evenly to look like columns.

Spaniel-type coats

Spaniels are part of the Sporting Group and many dogs, such as Irish Setters and Gordon Setters, have Spaniel-type coats. Here's the general way for you to clip your Spaniel-type dog (see Figure 11-5):

   1. Select a clipper blade that will work well with your dog.

   Use a No. 5 or No. 7 blade.

   You'll also need a No. 10 clipper blade for a close-in trim to the head and ears.

   2. Trim the face with a No. 10 clipper blade.

   You'll trim the cheek, jaw, and up to the occiput (or the highest point on the dog's skull; see Chapter 2). Trim the top third of the ears.

   3. Trim the throat down to the breastbone.

   4. Trim the coat evenly down the neck, back, chest, and loin.

   Blend in the transition so it doesn't look like you just stopped with the clippers, but leave the legs untrimmed.

Even up any discrepancies in length either with the clippers or *carefully* with scissors.

5. **Trim around the genitals and anus.**

   Be careful not to touch any sensitive areas with the clippers.

6. **Although the legs need to look more or less natural, if they appear unkempt, switch to a larger body-type blade, such as a No. 3 or No. 4, and trim them evenly.**

   The Spaniel cut looks different than the Terrier cut because you keep the Spaniel leg hair long and straight.

Poodle-type coats

Dogs with Poodle-type coats include Bichon Frise, Kerry Blue Terriers, and Portuguese Water Dogs. Each has its own style and look.

Kerry Blue Terriers and Bedlington Terriers are trimmed similar to the standard Terrier cuts, but their heads and ears are trimmed differently. Check the breed standards for the correct show look.

Classic Retriever cut

The classic Retriever cut (see Figure 11-6) looks good on longer-bodied dogs like the Portuguese Water Dog and Poodles (see Chapter 14 for more about other popular Poodle cuts). Here's how you clip a dog in the classic Retriever cut:

1. **Select a clipper blade that will work well with your dog.**

   Use a No. 5 or No. 7 blade for the body and a No. 10 blade for close-in trimming around the genitals and anus.

2. **Trim the coat evenly all over your dog's body. You need to leave about an inch of hair.**

   You can either leave the tail natural or trim it if you like a clean look.

3. **Trim around the genitals and anus.**

   Use a No. 10 blade, but be careful not to touch any sensitive areas with the clippers.

4. **If you like a clean face, trim it with either a No. 10 or a No. 15 blade.**

Figure 11-6: The classic Retriever cut.

Bichon-type cut

The Bichon-type cut looks great on Bichon Frise, but it looks great on any toy breed dog with curly hair, such as a Toy Poodle or a mixed breed of toy size (see Figure 11-7). When trimming a dog in this cut, you need to do the following:

1. **Select a clipper blade that will work well with your dog.**

   Use a No. 3 or No. 4 blade for the body and a No. 10 blade for close-in trimming.

   You need scissors to trim the Bichon-like coat.

   Be exceedingly careful with scissors, because they can seriously hurt a dog.

2. **Trim the coat in a snowball configuration all over your dog's body. By snowball configuration, I mean rounding the poofy fur, you know, like a snowball.**

   Use scissors to shape the fur so it has a uniform rounded look, but leave the tail natural.

   If you're not comfortable using scissors, you can use the clippers for this step.

   You should leave as much hair as needed to obtain a rounded look.

Figure 11-7: The Bichon-type cut

3. **Trim around the genitals and anus.**

    Use a No. 10 blade, but be careful not to touch any sensitive areas with the clippers.

4. **If you like a clean face, trim the face with either a No. 10 or No. 15 blade.**

Preparing for Show

If you have a clipped breed that you plan to show in competition, you need to have your dog clipped in a cut that is appropriate for showing dogs of his particular breed. Remember the cuts I describe earlier in this chapter are pet cuts, not show cuts. Show cuts require much more attention to detail with regard to the breed standard and the appearance that standard dictates.

Always ask breeders and other people who show your breed what cuts are appropriate for your breed and be sure that you know your breed's standard. A good place to look for breed standards is on the Internet at www.akc.org.

If you're working with a clipped dog, you already know you have a lot of work ahead of you just maintaining the coat. Now, just imagine maintaining a *show* coat. For one thing, show cuts are usually specific. Each cut is more or less defined by the breed standard, which makes them precisely specific.

In most cases, you won't simply make a dog's pet cut into a show cut. A show cut usually takes anywhere from three to six months to start and maintain — until it is ready for show. Maintaining a show coat means clipping sometimes on a weekly basis to make sure that the coat is styled according to the breed standard.

Few professional groomers actually know how to groom a dog properly for shows, and the ones who do, charge a fair amount of money for this expertise. Still, it's worth the hassle to pay someone who can put your dog into a professional show cut that you can simply maintain.

To prepare for show, you must:

1. **Make sure your dog's clip is correct a week before the show.**

    Make any final corrections at that point.

2. **Bathe and dry your dog, clean his teeth, brush out his coat, perform a coat maintenance clip, and trim his toenails the night before the show.**

3. **Add leave-in coat conditioners (if applicable) to your dog's coat, and remove any tear stains right before the show.**

Chapter 12

Beautifying the Stripped Breeds

As it pertains to dogs, *stripping* in a nutshell involves removing the dead undercoat from the rest of a dog's coat. Most stripped breeds are terriers and almost all are wire-haired dogs, which makes stripping the old-growth hair a necessity. Otherwise your dog's coat will look dull and wooly.

You can strip a dog's coat by using either a stripping knife, shedding blade, or even your fingers. Stripping a canine coat is time consuming; it can take hours (if you strip your dog's entire coat all at once) or days (if you choose to *roll the coat,* or strip it in sections).

You're probably wondering why you should bother stripping a dog's coat when you can much more easily clip it in a few minutes. After all, you can use clippers on the dog and get pretty much the same results, can't you? Well, not exactly. Using clippers on a stripped-breed dog tends to make the hair softer and less consistent with the coat type recommended by the standards for stripped breeds. If adhering to the breed standard is a big deal for you either because you're showing your dog or because you want your dog to look right, then you must find out how to strip your dog properly. Lucky for you, this chapter explains how to strip dog breeds that traditionally are stripped. Arguably many of these dogs can fall into the clipped breeds (see Chapter 11), so after reading this chapter, you can decide whether you want to strip or clip your dog.

Introducing the Stripped Breeds

Most of the dog breeds that need to be stripped are terriers, although a few other breeds fall into the stripped-breed category. In fact, many dogs with two-ply or double coats can be stripped in much the same way when they're blowing coat, or shedding their undercoats. Dogs that traditionally are stripped include:

- Affenpinscher
- Airedale Terrier
- Australian Terrier
- Border Terrier
- Bouvier de Flandres
- Brussels Griffon
- Cairn Terrier
- Wirehaired Dachshund
- Dandie Dinmont Terrier
- Wirehaired Fox Terrier
- German Wirehaired Pointer
- Giant Schnauzer
- Irish Terrier
- Irish Wolfhound
- Jack Russell Terrier

- Lakeland Terrier
- Miniature Schnauzer
- Norfolk Terrier
- Norwich Terrier
- Otterhound
- Parson Russell Terrier
- Petit Basset Griffon Vendéen
- Scottish Deerhound
- Scottish Terrier
- Sealyham Terrier
- Smooth Fox Terrier
- Standard Schnauzer
- Welsh Terrier
- West Highland White Terrier
- Wirehaired Pointing Griffon

Can't I pay someone to do this for me?

Stripping a dog is a daunting task, which is why you may be thinking, "Hey, that's what professional groomers are for." Well, I have bad news for you. Many professional groomers simply don't do stripping. And if they do, you're bound to pay a hefty amount of money, because it's a really time-consuming task. Instead, many pro groomers are more likely to clip your stripped-breed dog. If clipping isn't something that you want, you must either ask around for a groomer who will strip your dog and pay the money or learn to do it yourself.

Figure 12-1: Brussels Griffons (a) and Miniature Schnauzers (b) are two of the breeds with coats that need to be stripped.

Brushing

Brushing a stripped-breed or wire-haired dog isn't necessarily a big deal. You need to brush him at least twice a week to be certain his coat is in top condition.

The basics

Brushing your wirehair in preparation to be stripped is different than the method used for clipped-breed dogs in Chapter 11, because the coats are maintained differently. Here's what you do:

1. **Check for tangles or mats and remove them using detangler solution and a medium-toothed comb.**

   If this method doesn't work, try using a mat splitter or mat rake (see Chapter 5 for specific mat removing instructions).

2. **Backbrush your dog's coat, or brush against the lay of the hair, first using a slicker brush and then again with a medium- or coarse-toothed comb.**

3. **Brush your dog's coat with the lay of the hair using a slicker brush.**

   Also use a slicker brush on any thick hairs, such as those along the legs (like Airedale Terriers and other similar breeds may have).

4. **Check for fleas by running a flea comb over your dog's entire coat.**

Knowing when it's time to strip

Maybe your dog is looking a little ratty, or maybe your dog's hair is looking a little long. Regardless, you can always tell that he needs his coat stripped when you see the hair forming in little cotton ball–like clumps. Try gently plucking the fur by hand, and if it comes out easily, you know it's time to strip your dog's coat. Here's another way to tell: The coat is supposed to lay tightly against the dog's body (like a jacket). When it doesn't, it's time to strip it.

Most breeders and show people fully strip their dogs twice a year, but if you decide to roll your dog's coat (see the "Rolling the coat" section later in this chapter), you then work on the stripping process every time you brush your dog.

Bathing

Bathing is important for stripped-breed (or wire-haired) dogs. Although they don't need quite as much bathing as clipped-breed dogs (see Chapter 11), a bath once or twice a month is a good idea to keep your dog looking and smelling great.

The prebath strip

Before you pour your dog's tepid bath water, you're going to have to strip your dog's coat, if it needs it. As you find out from the "Bathing basics" section, you first have to brush and comb out your dog's coat to remove any tangles and get your dog's hair ready for a bath. In addition to brushing and combing out your dog before his bath, stripped-breed dogs also need a prebath stripping to remove the loose hairs. Doing so actually makes bathing your dog much easier.

Start with either a stripping knife, a shedding blade, or even your hands to hand strip (or pluck) your dog's coat. Removing the loose hairs guarantees a cleaner dog and less hair going down the drain. You'll find out exactly how to strip a dog in the "Stripping Your Dog" section later in this chapter.

Bathing basics

Bathing a stripped breed isn't much different than bathing any other breed. Here's how:

1. **Wet down your dog thoroughly with tepid water in a tub that's an appropriate size for your breed of dog.**

   Make sure that your dog's coat gets wet all the way down to the skin, which should be fairly easy if you've maintained a good stripped coat.

2. **Using a pH-balanced dog shampoo, thoroughly lather up your dog's entire coat except around the face and eyes — which you must do separately with a wet cloth to help keep the shampoo out of his eyes.**

3. **Thoroughly rinse your dog's coat.**

   Soap is a dirt attractant even for a wire-haired breed, so be sure to rinse your dog's coat carefully and thoroughly down to the skin.

4. **Apply an excellent pH-balanced dog coat conditioner that prevents tangles and keeps the coat from drying out.**

   Make sure you use a conditioner that doesn't make the hair too soft. *Remember:* Wire-haired dogs are supposed to have harsh coats.

5. **Repeat Step 3, squeeze out excess water, and rinse again.**

   When rinsing your dog's coat, be sure to remove all soap and conditioner residues. If you don't rinse your dog's coat, it'll get dirty quicker and it may leave the wrong feel for a harsh (stripped) coat.

6. **Dry your dog's coat thoroughly before stripping.**

   You can use a doggie blow-dryer or one intended for human use that has a "no-heat" setting.

Stripping Your Dog

If you're wondering why you should bother stripping your dog's coat when he will lose his undercoat on his own, remember that he also will look ratty if you don't help remove it (see Figure 12-2). Besides, an unstripped coat can be uncomfortable, because that much loose hair can easily form tangles or mats if it isn't stripped.

Figure 12-2: Check out this pooch's coat before stripping (a) and after stripping (b) — big difference!

You can strip a dog's coat using either a stripping knife, a shedding blade, or just your fingers, and one of these two methods:

- ✔ **Taking the coat down:** This method removes all the loose hair on the dog's body at one time.

- ✔ **Rolling:** This method removes a little bit of the loose coat in sections and not all at once. Rolling the coat means stripping it in one section and then the next. Although easier and less time consuming (in one session, anyway), rolling stretches out the time required to work your stripped breed's entire coat into show condition (think a half year to a year).

Using a stripping knife

Probably the easiest way to strip a dog's coat — that yields pretty good results — is stripping it with a stripping knife. Stripping knives are not truly knives and should never be sharp enough to cut or otherwise injure the person using it. Instead a stripping knife looks something like a putty knife that a plumber might use, except it has short teeth on one side.

Using a stripping knife is pretty simple. Run the knife through a bit of your dog's hair by grasping some of the hair between your thumb (the one on the hand in which you're holding the knife) and the knife blade (see Figure 12-3) and then pulling the knife away from your dog's body and in the direction of the hair growth. Don't hold the hair too firmly, or you end up yanking out too much good hair. Just pull out the loose hairs. Repeat this step throughout your dog's coat.

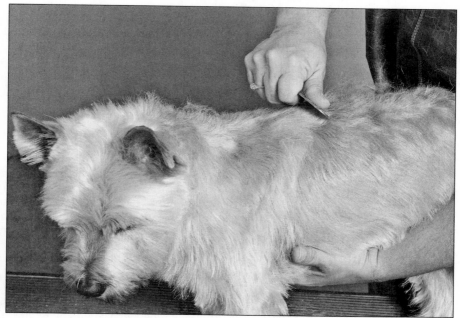

Figure 12-3:
Using a stripping knife.

The stripping knife doesn't work as well as hand stripping, but if you're short on time or have a big dog, it does a pretty good job. Remember, time is relative here. Stripping with a stripping knife still takes a lot of time, but because it takes more hair out than hand stripping, it's faster.

Using a shedding blade

Another tool in your coat-stripping arsenal is a shedding blade. Using one is not as precise as a stripping knife, but if you have a big job of getting rid of a lot of hair all at once, the shedding blade can help.

Shedding blades usually are large blades that can be held in a folded position or straight. You basically drag the small teeth of the blade over the dog, and they pull out the hair onto the floor. Be careful not to scrape your dog's skin with the blade!

When you have a big job (a big dog, a lot of hair, or both), use the shedding blade on the dog first, and then finish up with the stripping knife.

Hand stripping

Almost all groomers agree that the best stripping is done with your bare hands, because it's more precise. Known as *hand stripping,* or plucking, when using this method, you go over your dog's coat slowly and look for any loose hairs or undercoat that looks like little cotton tufts. With your thumb and forefinger, you grasp the tuft and gently but firmly pull out (the direction you pull or the amount of hair you pull at one time doesn't matter). Repeat as needed.

Rolling the coat

Rolling is a term used by groomers to describe a certain type of stripping. It's generally done by hand, but it can be done using a knife. You start on one section and strip or pluck that section on one day. Then the next day or in a few days, you strip another section. Because you usually move from one section to the next in a pattern that ultimately covers your dog's entire body, it's called *rolling*.

One positive side effect of rolling is that you strip only a little bit of your dog's coat at one time rather than taking hours to strip the entire dog. The negative side of rolling is that whenever you're planning to show your dog within a few months, you're out of luck, because rolling by itself can take six months or more to work a coat into show quality. However, after you get your dog's coat into show shape, rolling can keep it in show shape all the time.

Determining whether stripping is cruel

Some groomers are of the opinion that hand stripping or hand plucking a coat causes a lot of discomfort for the dog, and they simply prefer to clip rather than strip their dogs. To be honest with you, some dogs do have problems with the procedure, probably because the tufts of dead hair often catch and pull on live hairs.

I've noticed that this coat pulling occurs more often with hand-plucking than it does when a shedding blade or a stripping knife is used. If your dog tends to have sensitive skin, you need to use one or the other of these implements to facilitate the stripping process.

Dog owners who show stripped-breed dogs generally strip their dogs' entire coats and then use rolling to maintain them.

Preparing for Show

Preparing a stripped dog for show literally requires you to work months in advance of the show. If you own a dog who simply must be stripped, you can expect to strip him at least two months before the show or begin rolling (see previous section) the dog's coat at least six months ahead of the show.

When showing your dog, understanding the breed standard and the correct coat type your dog should be wearing, if you will, are essential. A good place to look for breed standards is on the Internet at www.akc.org.

The basic coat care that you have to perform to prepare a stripped breed for show includes

- Trimming your dog's toenails
- Brushing out your dog
- Removing any mats
- Stripping your dog's coat prior to bathing
- Bathing your dog
- Drying your dog
- Brushing out your dog
- Stripping your dog
- Clipping stray hairs and keeping a clean line if allowed by the breed standard
- Using coat dressing whenever appropriate

In between shows, you need to hand roll your dog's coat to keep it looking 100 percent. Every time you groom your dog, do the following:

1. **Starting at your dog's head and working down the head and neck, gently pluck out (with your hand) any hairs that ruin the clean line.**

2. **Moving on to the back and sides, pluck out any stray hair you find there.**

3. **Look and feel down your dog's front legs and chest, plucking any stray hairs.**

4. **Search for and pluck stray hairs that dogs usually lose along their rear ends and the backs of their legs.**

5. **Check along the belly and abdomen for stray hairs and pluck them carefully. It can be tender there!**

6. **Look along the base of the tail and along the tail itself for any areas that need to be plucked.**

These instructions on hand rolling a coat are simplified. The truth is, finding a pro who can show you how to strip and then roll a coat is the best approach. After you learn how, you'll get into the routine pretty quickly.

Chapter 13

Tidying the Tresses of the Long-Haired Breeds

In This Chapter

▶ Exploring the long-coated breeds

▶ Grooming your long-coated dog

▶ Preparing your long-haired dog for show

*L*ong-coated dogs are among the most beautiful dogs, but they're also some of the most grooming-intensive dogs to care for. Think big hair — like the double coats in Chapter 9 — only with long and luxurious tresses! Long-haired dogs are gorgeous when they're in top form and a nightmare when they're not.

In this chapter, you find out everything you need to do to get your long-coated pooch looking fantastic.

Introducing the Long-Haired Breeds

Many dogs have long hair (see Figure 13-1). If you have one of these breeds, you must be dedicated to working ahead so that you keep your dog's coat in good condition and free of mats. The long-haired breeds include:

▸ Afghan Hound

▸ Bearded Collie

▸ Briard

▸ Chihuahua (Long Coat)

▸ Gordon Setter

▸ Havanese

▸ Irish Setter

▸ Japanese Chin

▸ Lhasa Apso

▸ Longhaired Dachshund

▸ Maltese

▸ Old English Sheepdog

▸ Papillon

▸ Pekingese

- ✔ Polish Lowland Sheepdog
- ✔ Shih Tzu
- ✔ Silky Terrier
- ✔ Skye Terrier
- ✔ Tibetan Terrier
- ✔ Yorkshire Terrier

Many of these dogs differ from their double-coated cousins (see Chapter 9), because they usually don't shed the way a dog with a so-called natural coat does. They do lose hair, yes, but many don't blow their coat — shed profusely — on a seasonal basis.

Figure 13-1:
The Maltese has long hair that requires close grooming attention.

Brushing

Like the double coats, brushing is a big deal with long-haired dogs. They absolutely must be brushed at least three times a week — preferably every day.

No, I'm not kidding about brushing the long-haired dog's coat every day. The best thing you can do for a long-haired dog is to make brushing and combing a daily routine. There's no way around this task when you have a long-haired dog, so it's up to you to make it as enjoyable as possible (see Chapter 5). The coats of these dogs will mat if they aren't groomed properly.

The basics

You can brush most long-haired dogs the same way with a few breed-related differences or exceptions. Some long-haired dogs have *parted coats,* meaning their coats are parted along the back and then brushed accordingly. Others have what are called *topknots* — that is, head hair gathered up in a rubber band or bow. Nevertheless, here are the basics of brushing the long-coated dog:

1. **Check for any tangles or mats and remove them using detangler solution and a medium-toothed comb.**

   If this method doesn't work, try using a mat splitter or mat rake (see Chapter 5 for specific mat removing instructions).

2. **Backbrush, or brush against the lay of the hair, first using a slicker brush and then again with a medium-toothed comb.**

   Some people like to use pin brushes on these types of coats. If your dog is a single-coated breed such as a Yorkshire Terrier or Shih Tzu, a pin brush probably is ideal.

3. **Brush your dog's coat with the lay of the hair.**

   If you have a parted-coat breed — Afghan Hound, Lhasa Apso, Maltese, Skye Terrier, Shih Tzu, Silky Terrier, Tibetan Terrier, or Yorkshire Terrier — you can use a comb (doesn't matter what size) to define and straighten the part in your dog's coat. Slowly run the comb from the top of the nose, between the eyes, over the head, and down the spine to the tail. The part needs to be straight, so if it's crooked, try again to straighten it out. You can also spray a bit of coat dressing on each side of the part to hold it in place.

4. **If you don't plan to show your dog, use electric clippers equipped with a No. 10 blade to shave around the anal area and the abdomen.**

   Be very careful not to touch sensitive areas with the clippers.

   Although this step is optional and depends on the type of dog and whether you're planning to show her, shaving around your dog's anus is a good idea for hygienic reasons.

5. **Check out your dog's feet to see whether they need neatening.**

   You can use your electric clippers (again equipped with a No. 10 blade) to trim any hair growing out from between the pads and neaten the foot so that it's in more of an oval shape.

6. **Go over your dog with a flea comb to remove fleas and any straggling tangles.**

   You can accomplish this task with a long-haired dog by parting the hair and putting the flea comb at the hair roots and putting slowing outward.

If your dog sports a top knot — usually parted-coat toy dogs like the Maltese and Yorkshire Terrier but other breeds like the Old English Sheepdog and the Bearded Collie can have them too, if you want to get hair out of their eyes — you can easily make one by parting the hair from the top of the eyes to the ears diagonally along each side and making a part down the head from ear to ear for the back. Gather up the hair and use a rubber band, ribbon, or barrette (look for ouchless ones so you don't rip the hair) to secure it. You can buy these accoutrements at a pet store, through a grooming supply catalog, or on the Internet (see the Appendix for sources of grooming supplies). In a pinch, you can actually use people hair accessories.

Preventing tangles and mats

Long-haired dogs tend to mat quickly, so the best way to handle tangles and mats is to avoid allowing them form altogether. Consider the following tips to keep your dog free from mats and tangles:

- Brush your dog every day. You can avoid mats if you don't let them form.
- Keep your dog out of thick brush where he can pick up burrs and stickers.
- Always brush out your dog before a bath.
- Keep your dog's coat clean. A clean dog will mat less.
- Always rinse your dog thoroughly after a bath.
- Thoroughly dry your dog after baths.
- If your dog isn't a show dog, keep him in a pet or puppy cut — it's shorter and keeps the hair off the ground (see Chapter 7).

Bathing

Bathing a long-haired dog is essential, especially when he gets dirty. Most long-haired dogs need a bath once or twice a month to keep clean and sweet smelling. More baths are needed when your dog likes to roll around in stinky stuff.

Although once every two weeks sounds a little extreme, it really isn't. Remember many of the long-haired breeds have hair similar to yours. Think about how *you'd* smell if you took a bath only once a month. Every two weeks sounds a little better now, doesn't it?

Dogs luckily don't have sweat glands in their skin, except in their paw pads, so they don't stink after a hard day of work the way humans do. However, they still can get dirty, and a long-haired dog is more likely to pick up icky stuff than a short-haired pooch.

Prebath brushing and clipping

A prebath brushing is absolutely essential. A prebath clipping is up to you, the groomer.

Before bathing your long-haired dog, brush him out no matter how dirty he is. Doing so lessens the chances for tangles and mats to form when you wet down your pooch.

Some groomers prefer to give their dogs a prebath clipping — that's assuming the dog has been thoroughly brushed out. The idea behind a prebath clipping is to get rid of excess hair and any damaged ends before soaking the dog down. A bonus from a prebath clipping is that you have less hair to wash. Other groomers, on the other hand, dislike the idea of giving their dogs a prebath clipping. They cite the potential for bacteria to develop in the just-clipped hair. But this is a matter of opinion, not fact.

The main issues with prebath clipping are that:

- Dirt in the coat can dull clipper blades.
- It can result in an uneven cut, if the hair isn't totally brushed out.

A filthy dog shouldn't be given a prebath clip for those two reasons, but there's no reason not to do so if your dog isn't terribly dirty or just needs a quick touch up.

When you start clipping before the bath, make sure that your dog's coat is free from mats. *Note:* The prebath clip is not the time for trying out new styles or extensive trimming — use the clippers to trim and get rid of split ends or uneven hair. Remember, you'll be giving your dog a full clipping after his bath when he's thoroughly dried.

Bathing basics

It may come as a surprise to you to find out that bathing a long-coated breed isn't much different than bathing any other breed. But it isn't. Here's what it's like to put your long-haired dog through the wash cycle:

1. **Wet down your dog's long hair thoroughly with tepid water in a tub that's an appropriate size for your breed of dog.**

   Using a sprayer attached to the tub faucet or shower is helpful and convenient, especially for larger dogs. If you have a toy dog, like the Maltese or the Yorkshire Terrier, you can use the sprayer attachment at the kitchen sink, provided it's clean (with no dirty dishes) and you use a hair strainer or drain trap.

2. **Soap up your dog thoroughly with a good pH-balanced dog shampoo except around the face and eyes — which you must do separately with a wet cloth.**

3. **Rinse, rinse, and rinse again, sliding your fingers along your dog's skin so that you get all that soap rinsed out.**

4. **Apply a good pH-balanced doggie conditioner that prevents tangles.**

   Using a conditioner that prevents tangles and also keeps the coat from drying out is a good idea. You can find dog conditioner where you purchase your other grooming supplies (or check out the Appendix for other pet-supply resources).

5. **Rinse better than you did in Step 3.**

   No residue is good, but leaving any in your dog's coat can really make it yucky. Feel along the skin, and then rinse some more, just to be sure.

6. **Get out those towels and start drying.**

   As you squeeze the towels into the coat, look for soapy water. If you find any, go back to rinsing.

Drying

Like the really thick-coated breeds, drying your long-coated dog really well is of utmost importance. Otherwise, your dog *will* pick up dirt in his coat, and you *will* have a dirty dog on your hands altogether too soon. Take these steps when drying your long-haired breed:

1. **Use towels first to dry your dog's coat.**

   Wrap the towel around the dog's hair and gently squeeze as much moisture from the hair as the towel will hold. Repeat as needed.

2. **Use a blow-dryer (no heat, of course) to dry your dog's coat.**

   This step both dries your dog and helps fluff his hair.

3. **While using the blow-dryer, use a comb that works for your dog's hair to start combing out the hair.**

If the coat's still too wet, the comb usually sticks and pulls hair, so you may want to start adding leave-in detangler solution and comb with a coarser-toothed comb.

4. **After your dog's coat is dry, brush it out again. Doesn't that look good?**

5. **Clip the coat if required (see the following section).**

If you clip after a bath, be sure the dog's hair is completely dry to ensure a proper cut. Otherwise, you may accidentally take off more than you expected.

Clipping

Some long-haired breeds can be clipped (Yorkshire Terrier and Shih Tzu, for example) while others should not be clipped (like the Afghan Hound and Bearded Collie). If you're worried about having a correct coat going into the show ring, you need to read the breed standard and find out what *is* allowed. A good place to look for breed standards is on the Internet at www.akc.org. Talking to breeders and show people also is helpful.

Neatening the breeds that need it

If you're planning on showing your long-haired pooch, you may decide to keep your dog in a show coat. Clipping is usually not appropriate for these dogs and basically what you do is trim the edges with scissors for an even look.

Even so, many long haired breeds that most folks think of as clipped (the Yorkshire Terrier and the Shih Tzu for example) are actually not really unless you're planning on keeping your dog in a pet cut (see Chapter 7). For example, the Yorkshire Terrier allows trimming of the ears and feet for a neatened appearance, but the rest of the coat is more or less untrimmed. To trim the tips of the ears, you need to use the scissors and put your fingers between the ear leather and the scissors to avoid cutting the dog, and trim along the line of the ear. Likewise, the feet are also trimmed.

The Shih Tzu really doesn't have a lot of trimming, and in fact, excessive trimming is considered a fault. Basically, you follow the bottom line of the hair with scissors to keep a neat appearance. That's pretty much it, unless you're planning to keep your dog in a pet cut (see Chapter 7).

Doing the low-maintenance do: A Puppy cut

Many first-time, long-haired dog owners are surprised by how much work it takes to groom their pups. Not only is brushing a lot of work, but keeping your dog's coat mat-free can be a real headache. Most long-haired dog owners fall into one of these three coat-care camps:

- ✔ They do all the brushing and coat care and don't mind it because they like the look.

- ✔ They like the look, but have no time to do the coat care properly, and the dog ends up looking matted until they can pay a groomer to clean them up once in a while.

- ✔ They like the look, realize their limitations, and keep their dog in a non-standard trim to make life easier.

If you're the first or third type of pet owner, you're doing great. But if you fully recognize yourself as part of the second group, don't despair! There are plenty of reasons why you haven't gotten your dog cleaned up, and I must applaud you for looking for solutions by picking up this book.

However, if you're a member of that second group, you need to be realistic. Do you and your dog a huge favor and accept the fact that your dog just isn't going to get better merely by you expressing your good intentions. Even though it's terribly nonstandard, a clipped dog (and you) can be much happier than one's whose coat is constantly matted and icky.

If your long-haired dog has a severely matted coat, bite the bullet and take him to a professional groomer right away and ask the groomer to remove the mats and give your dog either a Teddy Bear or a Puppy cut. That way, you can either maintain it or have a groomer maintain it for much less hassle and money. Your dog will come out really cute and adorable, and you'll be wondering why you didn't take this step sooner.

Putting your dog in a Teddy Bear or Puppy cut enables you to decide whether it's something you're going to maintain (once a month — at least) or whether you're going to be taking your dog to the groomer thereafter. If grooming your dog is a matter that slips your mind, put your grooming day on the calendar and if you miss it, schedule a spruce-up with the groomer the next day; it'll be much less expensive than the initial session.

Preparing for Show

Prepping your long-coated dog for a conformation show isn't necessarily a big deal if you maintain his coat. But you still need to know some of the tricks of the trade for getting your dog ready to show.

Preparing a long-coated dog for show is time-consuming. The basic things you have to do are

- ✔ Trim toenails.
- ✔ Remove any tangles or mats from your dog's coat.
- ✔ Brush out your dog's coat.
- ✔ Clip your dog's coat prior to a bath (if the breed standard allows).
- ✔ Bathe and dry your dog.
- ✔ Brush out your dog's coat again.
- ✔ Clip your dog's coat (if the breed standard allows).
- ✔ Use coat dressing if appropriate.

The sections that follow look at some of the fine points of getting your long-haired dog's coat ready for the show.

Clip and snip

What about clipping? Well, again, clipping depends on the breed. Some breed standards forbid clipping the hair in any manner. Check the standard to see whether clipping is something you can do. A good place to look for breed standards is on the Internet at www.akc.org.

Even if you can't technically clip your dog's coat, most people like to trim around the feet and the muzzle to provide a smooth appearance or trim the dog's whiskers (see Chapter 18).

Using coat conditioners

Like the double-coated breeds (see Chapter 9), the long-haired breeds sometimes need a little help keeping their coats at their finest. Sometimes these coats can get dry or damaged because of the environment and thus need an occasional spray from an oil-based conditioner.

You can use a coat conditioner to give the coat a proper feel when touched. Of course, coat conditioners won't make an incorrect coat into something wonderful, but they will improve the coat tremendously, especially if you keep your dog otherwise well groomed. Coat conditioners won't necessarily make your dog into a show winner, but they can prevent you from losing badly because your dog's coat looks awful.

Chapter 14

Poodles: A Breed Apart

1 f you own a Poodle, you're probably familiar with the many ways you can clip and cut your Poodle's coat. But there's more to Poodles than just clipping; brushing and bathing also are important.

Poodles receive special treatment because, well, they can be groomed in most styles. Technically these dogs are curly coated canines, meaning their coats are clipped (see Chapter 11). But wow, what choices and what variety! You can find out why the Poodle is a breed apart from other dogs in this chapter.

Brushing

Brushing a Poodle every day is an absolute must, because their coats are incredibly dense and prone to tangling. Loose hair comes out and easily tangles with other hairs. Chapter 5 tells you how to make brushing a fun routine for you and your dog.

When brushing and combing your Poodle, you need to look for mats and for tangles that can quickly turn into mats. The only way to prevent tangles and mats in a Poodle coat is to keep your dog clean and thoroughly brushed out. If you don't, those curly hairs will tangle all by themselves. The instructions that follow explain how to brush out your Poodle properly:

1. **Look for any tangles or mats and remove them using detangler solution and a medium-toothed comb.**

   You can try a slicker brush on the mat, but I've found they don't really do much other than take remarkably longer than a comb to remove the mat (if at all).

If that method doesn't work, consider using a mat splitter or mat rake (see Chapter 5 for specific instructions).

2. **Brush through the coat using a pin brush and then a slicker brush.**

3. **Use a medium-toothed comb to comb through the curls.**

4. **Check for fleas by running a flea comb through your Poodle's coat.**

   You can also use a flea comb to separate small tangles.

Bathing

Poodles need baths about once every two weeks — more often when they get dirty. Because their hair usually acts like a dirt magnet, Poodles can look dingy after only a short time. So give your Poodle a bath at least once every two weeks to be sure he's clean and sweet smelling.

The prebath clip

Many groomers like to give their Poodles a prebath clip right after the pre-bath brushing. Doing so helps you get rid of frizzy hair and split ends, and you end up with less hair to wash when you're done.

If you decide on a prebath clip, make sure your dog is thoroughly brushed out, and then clip only what you need to clip. You can also clip your Poodle's coat after the bath when your dog is clean.

Bathing basics

Bathing a poodle is similar to bathing other clipped-breed dogs (see Chapters 5 and 11). Just be sure to do the following:

1. **Wet down your Poodle thoroughly with tepid water in a tub that's an appropriate size for your dog.**

   Make sure that your dog's coat gets wet all the way down to the skin.

2. **Using a pH-balanced dog shampoo, thoroughly lather up your Poodle's entire coat except around the face and eyes — which you must do separately with a wet cloth.**

   Keep the shampoo out of your dog's eyes — ouch.

Be sure to run your fingers through those dense Poodle curls as you wash them. Doing so is a benefit to the Poodle's coat because it helps break up any straggling tangles as you soap up the hair.

3. Thoroughly rinse your dog's coat.

While rinsing, again run your hands through the thickest parts of the coat, helping to remove the soap residue from those curls and preventing them from tangling.

4. Apply an excellent pH-balanced dog coat conditioner that prevents tangles and keeps the coat from drying out.

Make sure you use a conditioner that doesn't make the Poodle's hair too soft.

5. Repeat Step 3, squeezing out excess water and rinsing again.

When rinsing your Poodle's coat, be sure to remove all soap and conditioner residues. Run your hands through the coat to make sure the water penetrates those areas, and feel for soap or conditioner residue until it's completely rinsed out.

6. Dry your dog's coat thoroughly before clipping.

You can use a doggie hair dryer or one intended for human use that has a "no-heat" setting.

While drying, backbrush the Poodle coat with a comb. As the hair dries, you want to make sure it stands up as much as possible to ensure a good, even clip.

Clipping

Poodles can be kept in all sorts of cuts, including cuts for pets and for show dogs. Most show clips can be used for pets; however, with the exception of the Sporting clip, most show clips are too difficult for the average pet owner to maintain.

When clipping your Poodle, or any dog for that matter, always heed these words of advice:

- Be careful when using clippers around your dog's eyes and other sensitive areas.

- Although scissors may be the best tool to use when trimming your Poodle, be careful when using them on your dog. They can cause severe injuries to you and your dog.

Poodle pet cuts

The many Poodle pet cuts include the Retriever cut (also mentioned in Chapter 11), the Teddy Bear or Puppy cut (also mentioned in Chapter 7), and the Lamb, the Dutch, the Town and Country, the Bikini, the New Yorker, and the Miami cuts. The sections that follow look at each of them.

The Retriever cut

The following instructions explain how to make the Retriever cut (see Figure 14-1):

1. **Select a clipper blade that works well with your dog.**

   Use either a No. 5 or No. 7 blade for the body and a No. 10 or No. 15 blade for close-in trimming around the feet, face, tail, genitals, and anus.

   You can also snap-on a guide comb to help you guide the clippers to a uniform cut. If you do, you need to use a No. 30 blade.

2. **Trim the coat evenly all over your dog's body, but leave the face and ears alone.**

   Run the clipper over the head and down the neck, following the lay of the hair. Clip the entire body following the lay of the hair until it is even.

Figure 14-1:
The
Retriever
cut.

3. **Using a No. 10 or No. 15 blade carefully shave:**

   - The face, following the lay of the hair

   - The feet

   - The tail, from where the base of the tail meets the body (excluding any hair from the rump) to two or three inches below the tip of the tail (to make the pompom)

4. **Trim around the genitals and anus.**

   Use a No. 10 blade, but be careful not to touch any sensitive areas with the clippers.

5. **Finish trimming your Poodle's Retriever cut with scissors.**

   Trim the tail into a rounded pompom.

The Teddy Bear or Puppy cut

The Teddy Bear or Puppy cut is a pet cut that's intended for pet owners who don't have the time to maintain a really awesome clip for their dogs (see Figure 14-2).

Don't confuse the Puppy cut with the (Poodle) Puppy clip that I describe later in this chapter, which applies only to show Poodles.

For the Teddy Bear cut, do the following:

1. **Equip your electric clippers with a No. 30 blade and a snap-on guide comb for the length of coat you desired.**

   You can choose between a 1-inch, 1½-inch, or 2-inch guide comb, depending on how long you want your Poodle's hair.

2. **Starting at the top of the eyebrows, run the clipper over the head and down the neck, following the lay of the hair.**

   Clip the entire body following the lay of the hair until it's even.

   Trim the tail, but leave the face, ears, and jaw alone.

3. **Switch to a No. 10 blade and trim the abdomen around the genitals.**

   Be very careful!

4. **Using scissors, finish trimming the rest of the coat.**

5. **Fluff the coat with a slicker brush or a comb.**

6. **Carefully trim hair around your dog's face.**

   If you want your Poodle to sport a mustache, trim both sides of your dog's face so that the mustache is even.

   If you want your Poodle to sport a beard, shape the hair under the jaw with the scissors into the shape of a *V*.

   Otherwise, use your clippers with a No. 15 blade to trim the jaw.

Figure 14-2:
The Teddy
Bear cut.

7. **Trim the ears so that they hang in the shape of a *U*.**

   Keep your fingers between the skin and the scissors, using them as a guide to prevent you from cutting your dog's ears.

8. **Blend in any transition areas where the hair goes from one length to another.**

   You can use your clippers with a No. 3F blade or thinning scissors.

The Lamb cut

The Lamb cut (see Figure 14-3) is the pet version of the (Poodle) Puppy clip (see the "Poodle show clips" section later on). The face, feet, throat, and base of the tail are shaved, and the rest of the tail is trimmed in a pompom. To groom your Poodle in a Lamb cut, try the following:

1. **Shave your dog's face using a No. 10 or No. 15 blade.**

   Work away from the eyes and down toward the base of the throat.

2. **Clip the abdomen using a No. 10 blade.**

3. **Shave your dog's feet and the base of the tail using a No. 10 or No. 15 blade.**

4. **Shape the dog's body according to Figure 14-3 using a No. 4, No. 5, or No. 7 blade.**

Figure 14-3:
The Lamb
cut.

The Dutch cut

The Dutch cut (see Figure 14-4) is a showy cut with less work than some of the show clips. The feet, face, neck, rib cage and flank, and base of the tail are shaved, and the tail is shaped like a pompom. To groom your Poodle in a Dutch cut, try the following:

1. **Shave your dog's face using a No. 10 or No. 15 blade.**

   Work away from the eyes and down to the base of the throat, continuing to shave the entire neck from the occiput (or the highest point of the dog's skull; see Chapter 2) to the shoulders.

2. **Shave your dog's feet and the base of the tail using a No. 10 or No. 15 blade.**

3. **Shave a straight line along the base of your dog's spine to the base of the tail using a No. ⅝ blade.**

4. **Shave your dog's flanks (loins) from the spine to the abdomen on each side using the No. ⅝ blade.**

5. **Shave your dog's abdomen with a No. 10 or No. 15 blade.**

6. **Shape your dog's fur to blend in so there's a smooth transition between different hair lengths using a No. 30 blade with a one-inch guide comb or a No. 3F blade.**

Figure 14-4:
The Dutch
cut.

Blend in any abrupt transition areas (where the hair goes from one length to another) with the clippers and a No. 3F blade or thinning scissors.

7. **Round off the cap (topknot) — that is, the hair from the occiput to the eyebrows — using scissors.**

8. **Trim the ears with scissors.**

Keep your fingers between the ear flaps and the scissors, using them as a guide to prevent you from cutting your dog's ears.

The Town and Country cut

The Town and Country cut (see Figure 14-5), like the Dutch cut, is a showy cut with less work than some of the show clips. The feet, face, neck, rib cage, and base of the tail are shaved; the tail is shaped in a pompom. To groom your Poodle in a Town and Country cut, try the following:

1. **Shave your dog's face using a No. 10 or No. 15 blade.**

Work away from the eyes down to the base of the throat, and shave the entire neck from the cap (or topknot) to shoulders (the cap is the hair from the occiput to the eyebrows).

2. **Shave your dog's feet and base of the tail using a No. 10 or No. 15 blade.**

Figure 14-5:
The Town
and Country
cut.

3. **Shave a straight line along the base of your dog's withers (or the top point of the shoulders; see Chapter 2) to the base of the tail using a No. ⅝ blade.**

4. **Shave your dog's flanks from about an inch behind your dog's elbow to the hind legs with a No. 10 or No. 15 blade, so your dog's middle is exposed from belly to spine for a clean look.**

   Clip with the grain to avoid digging the clipper into the skin. You need to clip from top to abdomen and from front to back; it will come naturally.

5. **Shave your dog's abdomen with a No. 10 or No. 15 blade.**

6. **Shape your dog's fur to blend in so there's a smooth transition between different hair lengths using a No. 30 blade with a one-inch guide comb or a No. 3F blade.**

   Blend in any abrupt transition areas (where the hair goes from one length to another) with the clippers and a No. 3F blade or thinning scissors.

7. **Round off the cap (or topknot) using scissors.**

8. **Trim the ears with scissors.**

   Keep your fingers between the ear flaps and the scissors, using them as a guide to prevent you from cutting your dog's ears.

The Bikini cut

The Bikini cut (Figure 14-6) is similar to the Retriever cut with a few interesting flourishes that make it look a bit more fancy. To groom your Poodle in a Bikini cut, try the following:

1. **Select a clipper blade that works well with your dog.**

   Use a No. 5 or No. 7 blade for the body and a No. 10 or No. 15 blade for close-in trimming around the feet, face, tail, genitals, and anus.

   You can also use a snap-on guide comb to help you guide the clippers to a uniform cut. If you do, you need to use a No. 30 blade.

2. **Wrap VetWrap — or another kind of self-sticking bandage that won't stick to your dog's coat — loosely around each of your dog's legs just above the feet.**

   Use four two-inch wide pieces.

3. **Trim the coat evenly all over your dog's body, using the body blade you selected or a No. 30 blade with a snap-on guide comb, leaving the face, ears, and of course the covered portions of the legs untouched.**

   Run the clippers over the head, down the neck, and over the entire coat, following the lay of the hair.

Figure 14-6:
The Bikini cut.

4. **Using a No. 10 or No. 15 blade, carefully shave:**

   - The face, following the lay of the hair

   - The feet

   - The tail, from where the base of the tail meets the body (excluding any hair from the rump) to two or three inches below the tip of the tail (to make the pompom)

5. **Trim around the genitals and anus using a No. 10 blade.**

   Be careful not to touch any sensitive areas with the clippers.

6. **Finish trimming your Poodle's Bikini cut with scissors.**

   Trim the tail into a rounded pompom.

7. **Remove the leg wraps so you can fluff and carefully trim the hair underneath into a rounded pompom on each leg.**

8. **Round off the cap (topknot) — that is, the hair from the occiput to the eyebrows — using scissors.**

9. **Trim the ears with scissors.**

   Keep your fingers between the ear flaps and the scissors, using them as a guide to prevent you from cutting your dog's ears.

The New Yorker cut

The New Yorker cut (see Figure 14-7), is another showy cut that is just another pet-cut variation. The feet, face, neck, rib cage, and base of the tail are shaved; the tail is shaped in a pompom. To groom your Poodle in a New Yorker cut, try the following:

1. **Shave your dog's face using a No. 10 or No. 15 blade.**

   Work away from the eyes down to the base of the throat and shave the entire neck from the occiput or (or the highest point of the dog's skull; see Chapter 2) to the shoulders.

2. **Shave your dog's feet and base of the tail using a No. 10 or No. 15 blade.**

3. **Shave your dog's flanks from about an inch behind your dog's elbow to the hind legs with a No. 10 or No. 15 blade.**

   This step exposes your dog's middle from belly to spine for a clean look.

   Clip with the grain to avoid digging the clipper into the skin. You need to clip from top to abdomen and from front to back; it will come naturally.

4. **Shave your dog's abdomen with a No. 10 or No. 15 blade.**

Figure 14-7:
The New
Yorker cut.

5. **Shape your dog's fur to blend in so there's a smooth transition between different hair lengths using a No. 30 blade with a one-inch guide comb or a No. 3F blade.**

   Blend in any abrupt transition areas (where the hair goes from one length to another) with the clippers and a No. 3F blade or thinning scissors.

6. **Round off the cap (topknot) — that is, the hair from the occiput to the eyebrows — using scissors.**

7. **Trim the ears with scissors.**

   Keep your fingers between the ear flaps and the scissors, using them as a guide to prevent you from cutting your dog's ears.

The Miami cut

The Miami cut (see Figure 14-8), is almost identical to the Town and Country cut, except that it doesn't have the line that goes from withers to spine. The feet, face, neck, rib cage, and base of the tail are shaved; the tail is shaped in a pompom. To groom your Poodle in a Miami cut, try the following:

1. **Shave your dog's face using a No. 10 or No. 15 blade.**

   Work away from the eyes down to the base of the throat and shave the entire neck from the cap (or top knot) to shoulders.

2. **Shave your dog's feet and base of the tail using a No. 10 or No. 15 blade.**

3. **Shave your dog's flanks from about an inch behind your dog's elbow to the hind legs with a No. 10 or No. 15 blade, so your dog's middle is exposed from belly to spine for a clean look.**

   Clip with the grain to avoid digging the clipper into the skin. You need to clip from top to abdomen and from front to back; it will come naturally.

4. **Shave your dog's abdomen with a No. 10 or No. 15 blade.**

5. **Shape your dog's fur to blend in so there's a smooth transition between different hair lengths using a No. 30 blade with a one-inch guide comb or a No. 3F blade.**

   Blend in any abrupt transition areas (where the hair goes from one length to another) with the clippers and a No. 3F blade or thinning scissors.

6. **Round off the cap (or topknot) — that is, the hair from the occiput to the eyebrows — using scissors.**

7. **Trim the ears with scissors.**

   Keep your fingers between the ear flaps and the scissors, using them as a guide to prevent you from cutting your dog's ears.

Poodle show clips

Four basic show clips are permitted by the AKC breed standard: the Puppy, English Saddle, the Continental, and the Sporting clips. No other clips are allowed in AKC.

Because these are show clips, they are very difficult to execute. All of them are difficult to achieve because they're time-and labor-intensive and you're working with hair that can be more than a foot — and sometimes even a foot and a half — long.

If you want to learn how to do these clips properly, the best thing you can do is to ask a show person to be your mentor and show you how.

The sections that follow provide more information about each Poodle show clip.

The Puppy clip

The Puppy clip (see Figure 14-9) is the only show clip permitted for dogs who are younger than 12 months old. The Puppy clip needs to leave as much hair as possible on the dog with a shaved face, feet, throat, and base of the tail. The tail is shaped in a pompom. To groom your Poodle in a Puppy clip, try the following:

1. **Shave your dog's face using a No. 10, No. 15, or No. 30 blade (for very close cuts).**

   Work away from the eyes down to the base of the throat. Stop at the point of the throat or Adam's apple.

2. **Clip your dog's abdomen using a No. 10 blade.**

3. **Shave your dog's feet and base of the tail using a No. 10, No. 15, or No. 30 blade (for very close cuts).**

4. **Shape your dog's body coat according to Figure 14-9 using a No. 30 blade with a one-inch guide comb or a No. 3F blade.**

   Note: Scissoring will work better.

Figure 14-9:
The Puppy
clip.

The Continental clip

The Continental clip (see Figure 14-10) is the standard cut that most Poodle people show with. The face, throat, feet, tail, legs, and hindquarters are shaved. Pompoms of fur are shaped on the wrists, ankles, and the tail, and two pompoms around the kidneys are optional. To groom your Poodle in a Continental clip, try the following:

1. **Shave your dog's face using a No. 10, No. 15, or No. 30 blade (for very close cuts).**

   Work away from the eyes down to the base of the throat. Stop at the point of the throat or Adam's apple.

2. **Shave your dog's feet and base of the tail using a No. 10, No. 15, or No. 30 blade (for very close cuts).**

3. **Shave your dog's forelegs from the rounded mane (elbow joint) just about two inches or so using either a No. 10, No. 15, or No. 30 blade.**

   Leave several inches of hair to make the pompoms on the wrists and scissor this hair into an oval.

Figure 14-10:
The
Continental
clip.

4. **Trim two rounded rosettes the size of saucers over your dog's kidneys (just behind the last rib along either side of the spine) using your scissors.**

Some breeders recommend using saucers as models for each one. Simply trim around the saucers with the scissors.

5. **Shave your dog's hindquarters down to the hock and your dog's abdomen from the mane using your clippers with the same blade you used for Step 1.**

6. **Use scissors to round the mane and pompoms.**

7. **Round off the cap (or topknot) — that is, the hair from the occiput to the eyebrows — using scissors.**

8. **Trim the ears with scissors.**

Keep your fingers between the ear flaps and the scissors, using them as a guide to prevent you from cutting your dog's ears.

The English Saddle clip

The English Saddle clip (see Figure 14-11) is an alternative to the Continental clip. The face, throat, feet, tail, and forelegs are shaved, and pompoms are shaped on the wrists and tail. The hindquarters have closer-shaved fur with bracelets (like pompoms) above the knee and below the hock of shaved fur. To groom your Poodle in an English Saddle clip, try the following:

1. **Shave your dog's face using a No. 10, No. 15, or No. 30 blade (for very close cuts).**

   Work away from the eyes down to the base of the throat. Stop at the point of the throat or Adam's apple.

2. **Shave your dog's feet and base of the tail using a No. 10, No. 15, or No. 30 blade (for very close cuts).**

3. **Shave the forelegs from the rounded mane (elbow joint) just about two inches or so, using your No. 10, No. 15, or No. 30 blade (for very close cuts).**

   Leave several inches of hair to make the pompoms on the wrists, and scissor this hair into an oval shape.

4. **Part the coat behind the rib cage and shape the dog's body and hindquarters according to Figure 14-11 using scissors.**

5. **Cut thin bracelets an inch above the hock on the hind legs using a ⅝ blade.**

   Make sure the bracelets match.

6. **Cut thin bracelets just above the knee or stifle on the hind legs using a ⅝ blade.**

   Make sure the bracelets match.

7. **Shape the dog's body according to Figure 14-11 using scissors.**

Figure 14-11:
The English
Saddle clip.

8. **Round off the cap (or topknot) — that is, the hair from the occiput to the eyebrows — using scissors.**

   Note: Scissoring will work better. In fact, you need to scissor and shape the hair so that it's rounded.

9. **Trim the ears with scissors.**

   Keep your fingers between the ear flaps and the scissors, using them as a guide to prevent you from cutting your dog's ears.

The Sporting clip

The Sporting clip (see Figure 14-12) is used for dogs competing in the Stud or Brood Bitch classes and in the Parade of Champions. It's also a nice cut for pets, because it's easy to maintain. The face, feet, throat, and tail are shaved with a pompom on the tail and a smaller cap (or top knot) on the head. To groom your Poodle in a Sporting clip, try the following:

1. **Save your dog's face using a No. 10, No. 15, or No. 30 blade (for very close cuts).**

   Work away from the eyes down to the base of the throat.

2. **Clip your dog's abdomen using a No. 10 blade.**

3. **Shave your dog's feet and base of the tail using a No. 10, No. 15, or No. 30 blade (for very close cuts).**

Figure 14-12:
The Sporting clip.

4. Shape your dog's body according to Figure 14-12 using a No. 5 blade for summer or a No. 4 blade for winter.

5. Trim the pompoms on the tail and legs and the cap (or topknot) in a rounded shape using scissors.

Preparing for Show

As you may have surmised, preparing a Poodle for show is just like everyday grooming times ten.

If you're preparing for a show, you have to begin preparing your Poodle's coat well in advance of the show. In fact, preparing your Poodle for a show takes months, not hours. So if you're planning to enter shows with your Poodle, you're going to have to start planning way ahead.

Much of the show planning is the equivalent of watching grass grow — waiting for the hair to grow. As your Poodle's hair grows out, you have to start shaping it into the eventual show coat. In puppies, that means the Puppy clip, which is just a simplified version of the Continental clip. When your puppy is out of the show Puppy competition and into the Open, Bred-by, American-bred, or other competitions, reshaping the coat into a Continental clip takes less than it would if you started from scratch.

If you're starting from scratch with an adult dog, you have to clip your Poodle in the basic Continental clip, but it won't have the amount of hair that a normal show coat has. From there you need to work on maintaining that style until the coat fills out and becomes more beautiful. Remember that Poodles can have up to a foot and a half of coat on them at show time, and it takes at least six months of constant maintenance to groom the show coat you want. You can count on trimming your dog about once a week to get the shape of the coat just right.

Don't expect to take your Poodle to a professional groomer and thereby get your dog done up into show condition overnight. Remember, these types of coiffures (fancy for hairdos) take considerable time and effort to create.

Although getting a Poodle ready for a show is time-consuming, grooming tasks that you need to do right before the show include:

- Trimming toenails
- Brushing out your dog's coat
- Removing any tangles and mats
- Clipping your dog prior to his bath
- Bathing your dog

 ✔ Drying your dog

 ✔ Brushing out your dog again

 ✔ Trimming your dog

 ✔ Applying a coat dressing whenever appropriate

After you put all that work into getting your Poodle in top shape, you're probably wondering how you move him from home to the show without that gorgeous coat picking up lots of dirt and other debris.

To protect the hair, show people often wrap their dog's ears and manes. You can wrap your dog in a variety of ways, but the main issue is keeping the dog's hair clean. You can use:

 ✔ VetWrap or another type of wrap or bandage that sticks to itself and not your dog's coat, to wrap the ears.

 ✔ An ouchless pony tail holder (sometimes) to hold the topknot.

 ✔ Towels and clips to keep the mane from rubbing against dirty things.

Be forewarned that after you use any of these devices, you have to totally brush out your Poodle once the two of you arrive at the show.

Part IV
Grooming Specialties

The 5th Wave   By Rich Tennant

"Just as I was afraid of—I'm finding a lot of ticks on your dog here, Mr. Grayson."

In this part . . .

You may be wondering how you get gross stuff out of your dog's coat or how certain diseases affect your dog's health. Well, wonder no more, because in this part I cover these ideas and a whole lot more, including grooming first aid, what it takes to become a professional groomer (you may be surprised by the answer!), and how to pre-pare your dog and yourself for the show ring.

Chapter 15

Getting the Sticky and Stinky Stuff Out

....

In This Chapter

▶ Making foxtails and burrs a less prickly problem

▶ Handling really messy problems

▶ Removing sticky stuff from your dog's coat

▶ Stopping the stink — the definitive answer to skunk spray

....

Dogs get into some of the darnedest things. Stickers, burrs, foxtails, tar, and other substances are fairly typical of the stuff that gets caught in dog fur. Even if your dog spends most of his time indoors, he can get into the craziest things around the house, like bubble gum and oil, but don't panic when your dog looks like he rolled in — eww! — What *did* he roll in? Whatever it is, you have to deal with it.

The trick to handling these substances is not to panic and take out the scissors to make an even bigger problem. Don't forget: Clipping can be foul when working with a dog's coat. Instead, take a deep breath, look at the problem, and plan your strategy accordingly. This chapter can help. If the mess your dog gets into is a big hairy one, you may have to call in the pros for help — assuming your pooch hasn't gotten into something at 7 p.m. on a holiday when no vet or groomer is available! Yes, that happens frequently.

The first step to combating the ick that your dog inevitably brings home in his fur coat is to keep on hand a few select items that I like to call my Anti-Stick/Stink Kit:

✔ Baking soda

✔ Medium- and fine-toothed combs

✔ Cornstarch

✔ Paper towels

✔ Detangler solution

✔ pH-balanced dog shampoo and dog conditioner

✔ Electric clippers

✔ Rubber gloves

✔ Grease-cutting dishwashing liquid (like Dawn)

- ✔ Tweezers or forceps
- ✔ Hydrogen peroxide

- ✔ Vegetable oil
- ✔ Mat rake and splitter

Taking a Walk on the Prickly Side

Burrs, stickers, and foxtails abound in all sorts of wild (and not-so-wild) places, from the neighborhood park to an undeveloped lot in the city. These prickly things can be more than just an annoyance — they can be downright dangerous. The following sections explain how to safely remove them from your dog's coat and skin.

Getting rid of burrs and stickers

Sticker burrs tend to collect in a dog's hair faster than anything else I know. They're seeds from various weeds and plants that latch onto an animal's fur (or other means of transportation) so they can be deposited somewhere else as the animal moves from one place to another. Unfortunately, when they get caught up in dog hair, they often cause tangles and make a terrible mess.

The best way to avoid these obnoxious plants is to keep your dog out of dense brush where burrs and stickers get caught in paw pads and fur feathering; otherwise, getting rid of them can be an annoying experience. These areas also are prone to ticks, so keeping your dog out of the thicket makes an infinite amount of sense.

No one ever said, however, that a dog has enough sense to cooperate and stay out of the brush on hikes. So if your dog comes home with stickers in his fur, get them out right away. Working on them section by section is probably the best way, so just follow these steps:

1. **Examine the paw pads.**

   Burrs and stickers are most painful here and can cause your dog to limp. Pick up and inspect each foot and run your fingers between the webbing on the paw pads to feel for anything prickly.

   If you find something prickly, look at it. If it's a burr or prickly foreign matter, use tweezers or forceps to remove it. If it seems to be part of your dog, take your dog to the vet to have it examined.

2. **Check your dog's legs for burrs.**

   If you find one, try separating it from the fur with a medium- or fine-toothed comb.

Sometimes rubbing a little cornstarch through the fur helps smooth out the prickles and loosens the hair. If you use cornstarch, you have to rub it into each of the burrs and then work them out with your fingers.

3. **Check the underside of your dog — the belly, chest, and genital areas — for burrs. Pay particular attention to genital areas, where burrs can be most distressing.**

   Remove burrs from sensitive areas gently with your fingers. Use a comb and cornstarch to work any burrs loose from the chest and belly.

4. **Examine your dog's ears (inside and behind) for burrs.**

   Burrs with minds of their own somehow love to hide in the fluff behind the ears and inside the ears. Use your fingers to remove burrs from these sensitive areas. Don't use cornstarch in the ears because you may leave behind a residue.

5. **Check the rest of your dog's coat and the base of his tail, looking for those darn prickers.**

   Remove them with cornstarch and your fingers or a comb.

If the burrs cause serious mats, don't use scissors to cut them out. Try to loosen them first with cornstarch and your fingers, but if that doesn't work, you may have to get out your electric clippers and gently shave the burrs from your dog's coat. *Note:* Keep your hand between the electric clippers and your dog's skin.

If too many burrs make the task ahead look too big, you may want to seek professional help from either a veterinarian or a professional groomer. They'd rather help you take out the mats than have to suture a cut you inflicted on your dog's skin.

After you get the burrs out, consider bathing your dog because of the greater risk that he's picked up external parasites running around in all that brush. Follow up the bath with a good systemic flea and tick treatment if your dog isn't already using one (see Chapter 16).

No matter how tempted you may be, never bathe a dog with burrs and stickers in his coat. If you don't get them out beforehand, they'll cause mats that are even harder to remove after a bath. And never get cornstarch in your dog's eyes; it can be a real irritant.

Dealing with grass awns (foxtails)

Grass awns (bristle-tips) are much like burrs and sticker-type seeds, with one important difference: These things can be downright dangerous if they're allowed to burrow into a dog's body. Where I live, grasses produce awns that look sort of like a fox's tail (hence the name foxtail); see Figure 15-1a. Bushy on one end and pointed on the other, the pointed end has small barbs that enable the foxtail to work its way deep into hair and eventually into skin and muscle (see Figure 15-1b).

Left alone, foxtails can cause severe damage to a dog's body. They burrow into a dog's coat with every movement. They've also been known to get inside paws, noses, eyes, and even internal organs. Because they're a foreign body, they eventually cause abscesses and require your veterinarian to remove them surgically. I've heard of dogs that have lost their eyesight or had to have surgery to remove foxtails from their nasal cavities.

Figure 15-1: Keep an eye out for foxtail barbs in your dog's coat and skin.

If these tales of horror aren't enough to scare you into thinking these seeds are bad news, nothing can. If your dog gets into a field of foxtail, get out your brush and comb immediately and start going through his coat, following these steps:

1. **Brush off any loose foxtails from your dog's coat.**

   Remove the stuff that you can easily see.

2. **Check your dog's feet and paw pads for sticking awns.**

   Make sure you check paw pads, between toes, and in fur feathering.

3. **Check for foxtails or barbs around your dog's face and ears.**

   If foxtails burrow into these areas, you can run into many problems. For extra safety, look around the flews (lips) and gums to make sure your dog hasn't gotten any in his mouth.

4. **Check your dog's belly and underside for foxtails, and brush them out or otherwise remove them.**

If you find an embedded foxtail that can be easily removed with a forceps or tweezers, by all means, remove it. If, however, the foxtail is severely embedded and you'd risk leaving part of it under the skin when you try to remove it, seek veterinary attention to have the awn removed.

Watch for signs of infection — redness, swelling — around areas you know were affected. If your dog shows any hint of infection, seek veterinary attention immediately.

Shedding the Slick and Sticky Stuff

The following sections tell you how to remove gunk like petroleum-based products, tarry substances, gum, glue, or sticky and sugary stuff from your dog's fur.

Always remember to bathe your dog in a pH-balanced dog shampoo and to apply a good dog-fur conditioner after you've removed the problem substances. And don't forget to thoroughly rinse all soapy residues from your dog's coat.

If the problem substances are overwhelming and you don't think the methods for removing them outlined in the sections that follow will get the job done, you may want to resort to using electric clippers to remove the matted fur or even ask your vet or a pet groomer to do it for you. There's no shame in that.

Never use scissors to cut any of these substances from your dog's fur coat, because you risk cutting his skin and a bloody trip to the emergency vet for sutures. Furthermore, never use the electric clippers while your dog is in the wash tub. You and your dog risk electrocution.

For more about bathing your dog, see Chapter 5, and for more about using electric clippers, see Chapter 7.

Oil slick (petroleum-based chemicals)

Greasy stuff — motor oil, grease, and other petroleum products — can become sticky nightmares for pet owners and pets. Licking off a bit of oil can upset your dog's digestive tract, so don't allow such substances to stay on your dog's coat for any extended period of time. Besides petroleum products, dogs can get into other dangerous fluids. Antifreeze is one such culprit that can be lethal. The more quickly you get this stuff off your dog, the safer she is.

For almost all types of oils, an emulsifying, hand dishwashing soap like Dawn is your best bet. Environmentalists who clean up oil-covered birds and other marine wildlife use Dawn to break down and get rid of the oil. Besides, it's an extremely safe soap, provided you don't get any in your dog's eyes.

Here are the steps for cleaning off an oily dog:

1. **Using paper towels, blot or wipe off as much excess oil from your dog as you can.**

2. **Draw a tub of tepid water, add emulsifying (grease-cutting) dishwashing soap, and then put your dog in the tub.**

3. **Apply the dish soap solution liberally throughout your dog's coat, lathering her up well.**

   Be sure to work the soapy solution all the way to her skin.

4. **Thoroughly rinse the soap from your dog's coat.**

   You may need to drain the tub and rinse well a second time to make sure that the soap residue is removed.

5. **Check your dog's coat for any oily residues; repeat Steps 2 through 4, lathering and rinsing your dog as necessary until the oil is gone.**

While lathering and rinsing, be careful around your dog's eyes. You don't want to get any soap or chemicals in them.

Why can't I use scissors? (Or lessons learned the hard way)

Throughout *Dog Grooming For Dummies,* I repeatedly warn you about not using scissors on your dog's fur coat, and you may be wondering why. Many well-meaning pet owners accidentally cut their dog's skin while trying to get a foreign substance out of the coat, and they then have to rush the pooch to the emergency room for sutures. Even I've had an accident with scissors, which proves that even the pros screw up. No matter how careful and well-meaning you

are, if your dog is struggling or you get in a hurry (or even if you don't), you can really botch a good grooming session with one accident.

I've asked vets about scissors, and almost all of them agree that using scissors on a dog's coat is a common problem. Well-meaning owners with scissors should stay far away from their dogs. Use electric clippers instead, or have a professional groomer handle the situation.

Tar babies

Actual tar from roads and other tarry substances, like tree sap and creosote, can be a nightmare to get out of a dog's fur. If the stuff is still soft and warm, you may be able to use a grease-cutting, emulsifying dish soap, especially if the tarry substance is petroleum-based.

Never ever use solvents or chemicals to remove the tar. They can be caustic and burn your dog.

Try one or both of the following methods for getting the tar out:

- ✔ Soak the affected areas in a mixture of warm water and emulsifying dish soap for 10 minutes to find out whether the soap will loosen the substance. Then use a medium-toothed comb to remove the tar if you can.

- ✔ Blot the area dry first. Then keep the substance warm with a warm, wet dishrag, or use the body heat from your fingers while working vegetable oil into the tarry substance. This method sometimes enables you to remove the tar.

If neither of these methods works or the tarry substance is too widespread, you may have to use electric clippers or consult with a professional groomer or veterinarian to help you get the tar out of your dog's coat.

Gummy pups

Chewing gum is one of my least favorite things to find in a dog's hair. It usually happens because some kid left a wad of chewed gum on the blacktop outside, and it became a gooey concoction that sticks to your dog's hair, to shoe bottoms, and just about anything else.

You'll probably have better luck getting most of it out while it's still warm. Use warm water to loosen the gum and help get rid of most of it. Then try working in vegetable oil to break down the gum. Some people recommend peanut butter, but that's about the same as using vegetable oil — instead of the oil from the peanuts.

Remove gum by following these steps:

1. **Soak the gummed up areas in warm water to loosen the gum.**

2. **Pick out what gum you can with a medium- to fine-toothed comb.**

3. **Blot the area dry, and rub vegetable oil into the remaining warm gum.**

   The oil should help break down the sticky properties of the gum so you can remove it carefully with your fingers.

4. **Use electric clippers to remove any remaining gum.**

   When the gummy area is widespread, you may need to seek the help of a veterinarian or professional groomer.

Glue

Glue can create a pretty sticky situation when it comes to dog hair, because so many different adhesives are on the market. Some are dangerous; others aren't a big deal. Household or craft glues like Elmer's School Glue are usually water soluble, nontoxic, and fairly easy to remove. (Remember the kids who used to eat the stuff? Yuck!)

However, if your dog gets into something serious like superglue or some type of ultra-strong bonding agent, you'd better read the labels to get a better idea what you're up against. The really toxic stuff needs to be treated like poisonous chemicals (see the section on "Dealing with Downright Dangerous Chemical Poisons" later in this chapter).

Try the following for removing various types of glue:

- **Water-based glue:** If the glue is water-based, use warm, soapy water (with a dishwashing soap like Dawn) to clean the area, and then follow up with a bath (see Chapter 5).

✔ **Contact cement:** If the glue is a type of contact cement, read the label to determine the best way to remove it and follow the directions. If the directions require some pretty hazardous chemicals, seek professional advice from a veterinarian or poison-control hotline.

Corn syrup and sugary problems

Corn syrup, honey, molasses, and other sticky sweet stuff become a nightmare in a dog's hair. The combination of sugar and dog hair pits the good news against the bad news.

First the good news: Almost all sugar problems can be remedied with warm water and an emulsifying dish soap. After all, sugar dissolves well in warm water, and the gunk breaks down when confronted with an emulsifier (Dawn works well), which helps substances mix with water. The bad news: If you don't get the entire sugary mess out on the first try, you'll probably have a real mess on your hands, because sticky sugar attracts dirt and causes nasty mats.

To remove sugary substances from your dog's coat, do the following:

1. **Pour a tepid bath, add an emulsifying dish soap, and put your dog in the tub.**

2. **Apply the soapy solution liberally throughout your dog's coat, and soap her up well.**

   Be sure to work it in all the way to her skin.

   If you find hardened lumps of sugar, dissolve them and work them loose with warm water and soap by rubbing them between your fingers.

3. **Rinse well, drain the tub, and rinse well again.**

4. **Check the coat for any sugary residues and repeat Steps 1 through 3 until the sugar is gone.**

Surviving Stinky Skunk Odor

The worst thing that a dog can get into is skunk odor. I've never known anything as unpleasant or as stinky as a dog who's been skunked. Skunks seem to find dogs even when the dogs aren't looking for them. One time, my dog was in my own fenced-in backyard and was sprayed through the fence when a skunk took a disliking to him.

Smelling a skunk is all in your mind: Yeah, right!

Why do people think that some skunk remedies work when they really don't? The truth is, at some point, your olfactory senses just get overloaded with the smell and seem to shut down. Basically, you get used to the smell, and after a bit, it may not smell as bad as it really is. The bad news: The smell still exists despite your body's best attempts to deal with it.

A skunk's spray is made up of a number of stinky compounds called thiols. *Thiols* are the same things that make decomposing flesh and dog poop stink, but the ones in skunk spray aren't quite the same. Skunks usually produce about two tablespoons of the spray — enough for six quick shots. When a skunk actually dumps all of it, the animal needs a week to two weeks to recharge. All this is small consolation when your dog gets skunked.

But don't be fooled by some of the popular remedies. Here are reasons why they *don't* really work:

- ✔ **Tomato juice:** An old standby, tomato juice does darn near nothing. It may cut through the oils in the thiols, but you still end up with a stinky dog — and a pinkish colored one at that.

- ✔ **Vinegar and water douche:** Here's another home remedy that really doesn't do much. Yes, it may mask the thiols a bit, but it doesn't do much else.

- ✔ **Professional odor removers:** These substances work okay on a variety of levels, but you'll still know that your dog has been skunked.

So what can you do? You can use the only remedy that I know of that actually works and works well. It requires baking soda, hydrogen peroxide, and dishwashing soap. Always keep these ingredients on hand in case your dog runs into a skunk. When I used this solution on my own dog, he ended up smelling much better than he did even before he was skunked. So I can state from experience that this stuff really works.

Here are the amounts you need for any-sized dog:

- ✔ One pint hydrogen peroxide
- ✔ ⅛ cup baking soda
- ✔ 1 teaspoon hand dishwashing soap

Using these ingredients, follow these steps:

1. **Combine all ingredients in an open container.**

2. **Draw a tepid bath and put your dog in it.**

3. **Apply the deskunking solution liberally throughout your dog's coat, and soap him up well.**

   Be sure to cover every inch of his body, all the way to the skin.

   Don't get any of the solution in his eyes.

4. **Rinse your dog well, drain the tub, and rinse well again.**

5. **Smell for any spots you've missed and repeat Steps 1 through 4 if necessary.**

6. **Follow up with a good pH-balanced shampoo and a good conditioner for dogs, and as always, rinse well to remove all residues.**

You can't make the deskunking solution ahead of time and store it for future use. The gases aren't poisonous, but they can build up and cause an explosion if contained.

Dealing with Downright Dangerous Chemical Poisons

Dogs can get into plenty of icky substances, and unfortunately, many of them aren't just a nuisance; they can be downright deadly. Lawn chemicals, insecticides, de-icers, antifreeze, and other hazardous chemicals abound out there. Some chemicals are quite caustic and can burn.

When something gets on your dog's coat, the natural reaction is for your dog to lick off the offending substance. The problem with your dog's reaction is that the offending substance can become even worse after it's swallowed. For that reason, you should *always* have the number to a poison-control hotline on speed dial or posted close to your phone. If possible, have the substance your dog has ingested on hand, and try to be able to readily identify it.

National Animal Poison Control Center hotline

The American Society for the Prevention of Cruelty to Animals (ASPCA) has a nationwide Animal Poison Control Center hotline set up exclusively for pets. The number is 1-888-426-4435. The center has veterinary toxicologists available 24 hours a day, 365 days a year. A $50 consultation fee may apply per incident, but that fee covers as many calls about the same incident as are necessary.

You can find out more about the ASPCA/APCC hotline by visiting its Web site at www.apcc.aspca.org.

Here's how to get rid of chemical poisons on your dog:

1. **Identify the poison if you can.**

2. **Contact a local poison-control hotline or the national ASPCA Animal Poison Control Center hotline at 1-888-426-4435 for help; proceed as follows:**

   If possible, try to provide your name, address, and phone number; the name of the poison, amount, and time since exposure; your dog's symptoms; and your dog's age, sex, breed, and weight.

   - If you know what the poison is and have the label available, read the precautions and find out whether an antidote is recommended; then follow the instructions for safe removal.

   Although many chemicals require you to flush the skin with water and then follow up with a mild soap-and-water bath, some poisons don't react well when combined with water, so don't use water unless you're sure the chemical won't react with it.

   - If you don't know what the poison is, remove as much of it as you can from your dog while wearing rubber gloves.

3. **Take your dog to the veterinarian for a thorough exam and further possible treatment.**

   This step is important, especially when your dog has accidentally ingested something.

Chapter 16

The Skinny on Hairy Health Issues

*N*ot all problems with your dog's skin and coat can be fixed with a quick brushing or a bath. If your dog's coat is dry or brittle, for example, you may be reaching for coat conditioners and bodifiers to fix the problem when the real issue is with his health. Your dog's bad hair day may be more than skin deep.

In this chapter, I focus on common health problems with symptoms that appear in the skin and hair and how you can cope with them.

Canine Cuteness More Than Just Skin Deep

You've probably heard the adage that beauty is only skin deep. Well, that isn't necessarily true when it comes to dogs. If your dog appears unhealthy outside, the chances are good that she's also unhealthy inside. Although the skin and coat aren't the first to show signs that a problem exists, an unhealthy fur coat or skin is probably the first sign that you actually see.

The problem with these kinds of symptoms and conditions is that they develop without your being aware of them. It isn't as if one day your dog looks fantastic and the next day she looks awful — if that happens, get your dog to the vet immediately! You're more likely to notice changes that occur over time — your dog's hair growing dull, thin, or brittle or her weight fluctuating to extremes — and for the most part, you won't see the problem until a month goes by, and you wonder what happened to your beautiful dog.

Now you can understand why keeping a grooming diary or log is so important (see Chapter 1). The memory of what you saw three weeks ago while brushing your dog may not be very clear, but a notation in a log or diary can help you recall that you took out a bit more fur than usual during your last grooming session, or a lump that you felt was a half-inch smaller a couple of weeks ago.

Whenever you notice a condition growing worse, go back through your grooming diary or log to find out when it started. In most cases, you need to take that kind of information to your dog's vet, because you want to give the vet an estimate of when your dog began showing signs of a problem.

Whenever you're unsure about your dog's symptoms, take her to a veterinarian. Doing so is important because you may not be able to cure or treat many of the conditions that your dog can contract. In fact, in some instances, these conditions can be life-threatening.

Allergies

Allergies are on the rise in dogs, just as they are in humans. Many allergies manifest themselves as skin and coat issues with dogs. That's why they're so important to understand.

Allergies are reactions of a dog's fur or skin to certain substances either through contact, ingestion, or inhalation. When exposed to an *allergen* (the substance that causes the allergy), a dog's body produces an immune-system response to it. Because I deal primarily with problems of the skin and coat in the sections that follow, I talk about allergies and how they relate to skin problems.

Contact allergies

Contact allergies cause a dog's skin or fur to react in an adverse manner because the dog has touched something to which he's allergic. The reaction can be hives-like (immediate) or delayed, which involves itching later.

Hives

If your dog has hives, his face may swell up, he may have raised bumps, and he may be very itchy — scratching profusely. Dogs can get hives from insect bites or as allergic reactions to vaccinations, certain antibiotics, chemicals, shampoos, or insecticides. Your dog's reaction may be immediate when exposed to substances to which he's particularly allergic or susceptible.

If you notice hives symptoms, take your dog to the vet for treatment right away. Hives can be a precursor to anaphylactic shock, which is a serious condition that leads to death if untreated.

Your vet will likely suggest removing the dog from as much exposure to the offending substance as possible and medicating with an antihistamine — usually Benadryl (diphenhydramine). If treated, hives usually disappear within 24 hours.

Atopic dermatitis

A type of contact (and sometimes inhalation) allergy, *atopic dermatitis* is usually associated with environmental factors such as pollen and grasses. Dogs are itchy and usually scratch or lick their paws when they're affected. You can see where your dog has licked her paws because of the brown saliva stains on them.

Dogs can experience worse symptoms of atopic dermatitis, such as redness in the skin, hair loss, skin infections, and even ear infections. Although this allergy is common, it's difficult to diagnose, requiring expensive testing. Most dogs need to be treated either with corticosteroids or antihistamines. Some dogs do well with Omega-3 fish oils.

Omega-3 fish oils are supplements that you can buy at a grocery store, but your dog *can* overdose on these oils. A better way to give your dog a good balance of Omega-3 fatty acids is to buy dog food that contains the right balance (many dog foods now do).

Your veterinarian can usually prescribe the dosages of these medications and supplements. In the case of coritsteriods or antihistamines, some are over-the-counter; others require a veterinary prescription. Regardless of which treatment you use, talk to your vet about proper administration and dosages first.

Food allergies

Food allergies are a big problem because dogs can be allergic to many things, including chicken, beef, various poultry, corn, rice, wheat, milk, soy, or other foods in their diets.

The tough part about food allergies is that they can show up weeks, months, or even years after the dog has been eating the same food (or food with some of the same ingredients). So your dog may look a mess, but there's no apparent cause for it.

Don't confuse a food allergy with a food intolerance. With a food allergy, the symptoms tend to manifest themselves in the skin and coat. In a *food intolerance,* the dog can't digest the food properly and has diarrhea or vomiting as a result. Think of people who are lactose intolerant (in fact, dogs can be lactose intolerant, too) — they're not allergic to milk; they just can't digest the milk sugars.

So, how do you find out whether your dog is allergic to his food? Contact your veterinarian first for help determining what your dog may be allergic to. Your vet will probably suggest that you stop feeding your dog his normal diet and switch to a *hypoallergenic diet* (that is, a diet that's unlikely to cause an allergic reaction with your dog) with a *novel protein source* (a meat your dog hasn't eaten) and an *uncommon carbohydrate source* (a grain that your dog hasn't eaten). On that diet, the dog is fed the new food at normal mealtimes until the symptoms completely disappear (usually six to eight weeks or more). After that, the veterinarian returns the dog to his regular diet, one ingredient at a time, until the problem resurfaces. When you know the culprit (or culprits), you can steer your dog away from food with those ingredients.

Many people feed their dogs lamb-and-rice dog food, thinking that it's a hypoallergenic diet. The truth: It used to be considered a hypoallergenic diet because it wasn't routinely fed to dogs; however, because lamb and rice have been introduced into commercial feeds, dogs now are showing allergies to those ingredients.

Many people recommend going to a raw diet when a dog shows symptoms of food allergies. Feeding raw or homemade food does nothing to fix an allergy if you end up using the ingredients to which your dog is allergic. For example, if your dog is allergic to beef and chicken, feeding your dog raw hamburger and chicken backs isn't going to stop his allergy. In most cases, your dog's allergy is probably caused by the big ingredients (the protein or carbohydrate sources) in the dog food. Although some dogs are allergic to preservatives, the amounts of preservatives used in dog food are miniscule, and your dog is less likely to show sensitivity to them than he is to the main ingredients in the dog food.

Flea allergy dermatitis

Flea allergy dermatitis (FAD) is a condition caused by a hypersensitivity to flea bites. A dog with FAD is allergic to flea saliva, so a flea bite becomes sheer torture. Itching is immediate and can last even after you get rid of the fleas. FAD is the number one allergy in dogs.

Preventing FAD is as easy as preventing fleas. (See the "Fleas, Ticks, Lice, and Mites" section later in this chapter.) Get rid of the fleas, and you'll have a much happier dog. Occasionally, your vet may recommend treating your dog with antibiotics or antihistamines and steroids.

Coat Funk

Coat funk, which is believed to be a hereditary condition and is sometimes called *alopecia X,* affects a number of breeds, mostly those of Spitz origin, Poodles, and Cocker Spaniels. Affected dogs start out with healthy, beautiful coats, and then sometime during their lives, guard hairs (or top coat) become brittle and break off, leaving only the undercoat.

Dogs with coat funk look awful. Without the protection provided by guard hairs, the undercoat becomes tangled, and the tail thins out. The coat is a nightmare to work on. Nothing you do seems to fix it, either.

Breeders have called this condition coat funk for years. I first heard about it in connection with my own breed — Alaskan Malamutes — but I figured it was just some version of hypothyroidism that's prevalent within the breed. The Alaskan Malamute Club of America and other Alaskan Malamute breed clubs, however, have financed studies that suggest that coat funk is a separate genetic disease. If you do suspect your dog has coat funk, have her tested for hypothyroidism, Cushing's disease, and other problems that can cause her coat to look bad (see the respective sections in this chapter). If no cause is apparent, you may have to consider that coat funk is to blame.

Spaying or neutering causes a dog to shed out the old coat and regrow a new one. This regrowth can improve your dog's coat for a while (sometimes permanently), but it doesn't address the underlying cause of coat funk. Some owners have reported having success using various nutritional supplements, but whether they're truly effective is hard to say.

Experimental treatments for coat funk are available, but in most cases, they're prohibitively expensive or have a certain amount of risk associated with them. Dogs who suffer from coat funk shouldn't be bred, making spaying or neutering a viable option.

Collar Rot

Collar rot is a term that I've heard used for dogs who have sores under their collars. The dog usually ends up wearing his collar all the time, and the collar rubs off the hair and may produce sores. If the collar is never removed or the hair under the collar is never brushed, that hair can become matted and harbor bacteria, which, in turn, can cause sores and infections.

Collar rot is unusual for pets whose owners usually groom their dogs. But if the dog is a long- or double-coated breed, it can suffer collar rot if the owner hasn't maintained the coat.

Collar rot requires dogs to have their necks shaved, and the affected area must be cleaned with a 10-percent Betadine antiseptic and water solution, followed by a good antibiotic ointment. In severe cases, you may need to have your veterinarian clean and bandage the neck and perhaps prescribe oral antibiotics. The best way to prevent collar rot is to keep the hair around the neck combed out and to occasionally wash your dog's collar to keep dirt and bacteria from building up.

Cushing's Disease

Cushing's disease is a serious condition in which a dog is exposed to cortico-steroids for a long period of time either as a result of long-term medications or as a result of a tumor on the adrenal or pituitary glands. (Corticosteroids affect metabolism, responses to inflammation, and reactions to stress.) Dogs who have Cushing's usually have hair loss, excessive thirst and urination, brittle and dry hair, a tragic-looking expression, a pot-bellied abdomen, weakness, and loss of muscle mass.

If your dog has any of these symptoms, he needs to be taken to the vet as soon as possible. Treatments are available to help suppress the cortico-steroid production, and in some cases, surgery may be an option.

I once had a dog with Cushing's that showed signs of adrenal involvement. At the time, I was able to give him a bit over a year of life with treatment, but he had other complications caused by a damaged immune system. Better treat-ments are available nowadays for Cushing's, which is why you must talk with your veterinarian if your dog is symptomatic.

If your dog develops Cushing's-like symptoms because he's taking cortico-steroids, don't take him off the medication without first consulting a veterinar-ian. Your vet needs to check whether your dog has Addison's disease, a dangerous illness that can cause a dog to go into shock and circulatory col-lapse when abruptly taken off corticosteroids. Dogs with Addison's must be taken off them gradually.

Fleas, Ticks, Lice, and Mites

External parasites, such as fleas, ticks, lice, and mites, can make your dog miserable. But they're more than just pests; they're health hazards for you and your pet. These bugs can ruin your day, too. Nothing is worse than getting these pests yourself.

In the sections that follow, I tell you about each of these parasites and how to take care of them.

Cats and pets other than dogs also may be affected by fleas, ticks, lice, and mites and therefore need to be treated; however, they need their own types of treatment. Never use any type of dog products on cats or other animals, because they can harm or even kill your other pets.

Fleas

Fleas are the worst when it comes to dogs. They thrive in virtually all climates, except in extremely cold and extremely dry conditions and at high altitudes. I live in an extremely cold, dry, high-altitude area, but even we have fleas here, and ours tend to carry wonderful diseases like bubonic plague (you remember — the Black Death. Charming, isn't it?)

Some people don't take fleas seriously. However, a quick surf through the Centers for Disease Control and Prevention (CDC) Web site (www.cdc.gov) reveals that fleas can spread other diseases besides bubonic plague *(Yersinia pestis)*, including typhus *(Rickettsia typhi* — an oldie but a goodie), Brazilian Spotted Fever, *Rickettsia felis* (causes fever, headache, and rash), and *Bartonella henselae* and *Bartonella clarridgeiae* (cat scratch disease). Dogs also can get tapeworms from fleas.

As if diseases and parasite transmission aren't enough, many dogs are allergic to flea saliva, which can cause flea-allergy dermatitis. If your dog has fleas, she's probably pretty miserable scratching all the time. Check out the previous section on "Flea allergy dermatitis."

Fleas can transmit other diseases, too, but you've probably read enough to know that fleas are more than just an inconvenience. So how can you declare war on the bugs without collateral damage to namely you and your pets? In an earlier time, you had to flea bomb your house, flea dip your dogs, and spray wildly. You don't have to do that anymore, thankfully, except in the most extreme conditions.

Discovering some amazing flea facts

Here are some exciting (or not-so-exciting) facts about fleas. Keep these in mind whenever you want to impress your friends or win a trivia-based board game.

✔ Fleas are wingless creatures. They don't fly; they jump.

✔ Fleas jump great distances to their targets. They can jump as high as 8 inches and as far as 15 inches.

✔ An adult flea is only as big as $\frac{1}{25}$ to $\frac{1}{4}$ of an inch long.

✔ The most common species of flea is the cat flea.

✔ Fleas feed off of birds and mammals, including humans.

✔ Fleas are dark brown or black.

✔ An adult flea can live up to 115 days on a dog but dies within one to two days if it can't find a host.

✔ Fleas mate within 24 to 48 hours after feeding. A female flea can lay up to 2,000 eggs.

Before you get started with your dog's flea control, make a note to be extra careful if you also have cats. Flea control products that are meant only for dogs can harm or even kill cats.

Finding the fickle flea

First you need to determine whether your dog has fleas. Fleas love warm areas, so places around your dog's belly and groin are prime flea stomping grounds. Around the base of the tail is also a place to look for fleas. Of course, if you see an adult flea hopping around, it's a good bet that fleas are present.

Use a flea comb (see Chapter 3) to look for fleas. If you see blackish or reddish grains that turn red when wet, you're looking at flea feces (yes, flea poop), and you can bet fleas are on your dog.

Getting fleas to flee

Fleas don't go away with only a bath, but bathing your dog may help. If your dog has fleas or if you live in a flea-prone area, talk with your vet about a good systemic flea-control product. These products are so good that they effectively break the flea life cycle, ending the suffering of countless dogs (and their owners). What's more, using these systemics means that you apply the flea control products (in most cases) only once each month to rid your dog of fleas.

Most of these products are available through your veterinarian. They're not super cheap, but then neither is using all the older remedies to get rid of fleas. Here are some of the top systemic flea-control products and what they do:

- **Advantage (imidacloprid):** Kills both adult fleas and larvae within 48 hours. It's a topical, spot-on systemic that works for six weeks and is available through a veterinarian.

- **Bio Spot (pyrethrins and fenoxycarb):** Kills fleas and ticks for one month. I've seen it repel flies, too. It contains an insect growth regulator that prevents immature fleas from reproducing. It's a topical, spot-on systemic and is available at pet supply stores.

- **Frontline Top Spot (fipronil) and Frontline Plus (fipronil and methoprene):** Kill fleas within 24 to 48 hours. Frontline Plus contains an insect growth regulator that keeps immature fleas from reproducing. It's is a topical, spot-on systemic that works for three months on fleas and one month on ticks and is available through a veterinarian.

- **K9 Advantix (imidacloprid and permethrin):** Kills fleas, ticks, and mosquitoes and prevents them from biting within one to two hours of application. It's a topical, spot-on systemic that you apply once a month. It's also effective when your dog gets wet or even after a once-a-month bath. It's available through a veterinarian.

- **Program (lufenuron):** An insect growth inhibitor that prevents eggs from hatching and immature fleas from maturing into adults. Administered once a month in pill form, it's available through a veterinarian.

Most of these flea medications are available only through a veterinarian or supply chain (with the exception of Bio Spot). It's important to note that with the exception of Program and K9 Advantix, spot-on topicals tend to wash off, so you need to reapply them after bathing your dog.

Where you purchase your flea-control products is important. Some veterinarian-only supplied flea products have been sold through pet supply catalogs and some have been counterfeited. If you want to be sure that you get the right medication, see your veterinarian.

Fighting fleas around the house

When you have one pet with fleas, you pretty much guarantee that all your pets have fleas, so you need to treat them all at the same time. Otherwise, leaving one or more pets untreated gives fleas a safe haven to go to when other pets are treated. Spend the money and make sure all your pets are treated.

Don't use flea products intended for dogs on any other species in your house. That includes cats, rabbits, birds, ferrets, and rodents. A flea product intended for a dog can kill other animals.

Be careful not to get the topicals on you when you first apply them, and be mindful of where they are until they dry. Although I've suffered no ill effects from getting the treatment on my hands, some people have experienced bad reactions to it. When in doubt, wear rubber or latex gloves when applying the treatment and wait for it to dry before petting your dog along her back. If you've experienced an adverse reaction to the treatment in the past, ask your vet about flea treatments that come in pill form (such as Program).

Flea dips and insecticides can react with some canine medications, other flea products, and dewormers, so make sure that what you're using won't interact with other pesticides or medications. Ask your veterinarian or poison control center before mixing any such products.

When cleaning your house, you need to vacuum all the carpets, furniture, and drapes and wash all the sheets and blankets. When you're done vacuuming, get rid of the vacuum cleaner bag or empty the container in a dumpster pronto! Otherwise, fleas can find their way back into your house and onto your dog.

Some pet owners slip a piece of flea collar into a vacuum cleaner bag to kill any fleas sucked up by the vacuum, but that's about the only good use I can find for them. Flea collars are mostly ineffective and contain poisons that can make your dog sick if chewed and swallowed.

When making your house flea-free, avoid using insecticides whenever possible, because they're poisons that can harm your pets if used improperly. Ask your veterinarian what insecticides are safe to use around the house and the lawn with your current flea products.

Keeping a well-maintained lawn helps limit the number of hiding places for fleas. Although it won't eliminate flea nesting places entirely, it does help reduce them. Likewise, reducing the amount of vegetation also helps. After all, fleas don't live on rock or paving stones.

Ticks

Ticks are nasty, bloodsucking relatives of the spider. I've known a few people who were so used to having ticks around that they didn't think twice about seeing a tick or two on their dogs. However, ticks carry dangerous diseases that are contagious to humans and dogs.

If you find a tick on you or your dog, you need to remove the tick immediately. The longer that a tick is on you or your dog, the longer it has to transmit diseases.

Tick-borne diseases

You or your dog can get numerous diseases from ticks, and more potential illnesses are being discovered every year. You can find out more about tick-borne diseases through the CDC's Web site (www.cdc.gov) by searching for "tick-borne diseases."

Major dangerous tick-borne diseases that can infect both humans and dogs include

- **Babesiosis:** This disease, which can be fatal, is caused by a parasite that's transmitted through the bite of a tick. Babesiosis may be asymptomatic (without apparent symptoms), or it may include symptoms such as fever, chills, muscle pain, fatigue, and sweating. It also may result in hemolytic anemia (the lack of blood cells) and enlargement of the liver and spleen.

- **Ehrlichiosis:** This illness is caused by several types of bacterial species called *Ehrlichia,* which are transmitted through tick bites. Early symptoms may include fever, malaise, headache, nausea, vomiting, muscle aches, rash, cough, and joint pains. As the disease progresses, it affects the blood, lowering white blood cell and platelet counts and elevating liver enzymes. In severe cases, it results in prolonged fever, *meningoencephalitis* (brain and spinal cord swelling), uncontrolled bleeding, coma, respiratory distress, and even death.

- **Lyme disease:** A highly publicized disease since its outbreak in the 1970s, Lyme disease is transmitted through tick bites. It's caused by the bacterium *Borrelia burgdorferi.* Symptoms usually (but don't always) start with a circular rash and may proceed to fever, chills, fatigue, headaches, swollen lymph nodes, and muscle and joint aches. Left untreated, it can cause shooting pains, loss of muscle tone in the face, arthritis, joint swelling, meningitis, and other neurological problems.

- **Rocky Mountain spotted fever (RMSF):** This disease is caused by the bacterium *Rickettsia rickettsii* and is one of the most severe diseases transmitted through a tick bite. Contrary to what its name implies, RMSF has been reported in every state except Alaska, Maine, Vermont, and Hawaii. Initial symptoms are fever, rash, headache, muscle pain, nausea, vomiting, and a lack of appetite. The disease, which can be fatal, lowers the white blood cell count and reduces the amount of sodium in the blood. As it progresses, the rash takes on the characteristic mottled rash from which the disease gets its name. It can affect the kidneys, lungs, nervous system, or gastrointestinal system.

As you can see, ticks are no fun. They can also transmit a number of other diseases, including typhus.

Removing ticks

Knowing how to remove a tick is important. Do it wrong, and you can leave part of the tick embedded in your dog and cause a serious infection. When I was a kid growing up in Virginia, I had a tick on my back that didn't come completely out. The site was infected for weeks, and it finally took a shot of something from a second doctor (the first doctor was worthless) to cure me of the inflammation.

You may have heard of dousing a tick in alcohol or nail polish or of using a match or a lit cigarette on the tick to get it to retract. Don't do it. You can either injure your dog or cause the tick to burrow deeper. And believe me, you don't want an unnecessary vet bill associated with tick removal.

To properly remove a tick, you need a forceps (tweezers), a jar with rubbing alcohol and a lid, latex gloves, and a powder specifically made for killing fleas/ticks that's safe to use with dogs (available at a pet supply store). After gathering your equipment, follow these steps:

1. **Wearing the latex gloves, sprinkle some flea/tick powder on the tick.**

   Let the powder sit for a few minutes to work on the tick. It should at least make the tick loosen its grip if not actually kill it.

2. **Using the forceps, grasp the tick as close to the dog's skin as possible, and try to remove it by pulling it straight out to ensure you don't leave behind its head or legs.**

   If the tick doesn't easily release, wait a moment for the powder to do its work, and try again. Don't squeeze the tick, and pull steadily.

3. **After you remove the tick, drop it into the jar of rubbing alcohol to kill it.**

   Wait an hour to make sure the tick is dead, and then dispose if it by flushing it and the alcohol down the toilet. Or you can save the tick and take it to the vet for identification.

4. **Thoroughly wash the affected area of your dog's skin, and watch for signs of an infection or rash.**

   If you see signs such as reddened or oozing skin or skin that looks swollen, take your dog to the veterinarian immediately.

5. **Thoroughly clean your forceps with soap and water followed by rubbing alcohol.**

   Never handle ticks or anything that comes into contact with one with your bare hands. And don't crush a tick! They can transmit diseases to you.

Understanding Lyme disease

Lyme disease was discovered in 1975 in Lyme, Connecticut. The bacterium *Borrelia burgdorferi* causes Lyme disease, and it's carried by ticks and transmitted through an infected tick's bite. The deer tick *(Ixodes dammini)* is the most notable of the ticks that carry Lyme disease, but the black-legged tick *(Ixodes scapularis)* and the western black-legged tick *(Ixodes pacificus)* also carry the bacterium.

Unlike the common dog tick, the deer tick and its relations are small. A normal-sized adult deer tick is not much bigger than the head of a straight pin. Deer tick larvae and nymphs are much smaller than the ticks in their adult stage and can carry Lyme disease to their hosts. Sixty percent of Lyme disease sufferers were not aware of their deer tick bites.

Lyme disease affects humans, dogs, cattle, horses, and wild animals, and it may start with a noticeable red rash around the bite. Many sufferers, however, never develop the rash. In dogs, the most common signs are arthritis, anorexia, lethargy, and weight loss. Lyme disease can usually be treated with a combination of multispectrum antibiotics.

Left untreated, Lyme disease can affect nerves, joints, and heart tissue, and in some cases may be accompanied by post-Lyme disease syndrome, which includes arthritis-like symptoms. As of 2003, every state in the United States with the exception of Montana has reported some incidence of Lyme disease, according to the Centers for Disease Control and Prevention (CDC).

Take precautions against picking up any ticks. A vaccine against Lyme disease is available for dogs, but it may not provide full protection for your pet. Avoid tick-infested areas, such as heavy brush, woods, or tall grasses. Use tick repellents, and brush your dog whenever she enters tick habitats. Remove any ticks you find, and put them in a glass jar for identification by your vet.

For more information about Lyme disease, visit the CDC's Lyme disease Web page at www.cdc.gov/ncidod/dvbid/lyme/, the Lyme Disease Association's Web page at www.lymediseaseassociation.org, or the Lyme Disease Foundation's Web site at www.lyme.org.

Lice

Although pretty unusual for dogs, lice infestations can happen. They usually occur in dogs who come from bad situations, such as living in rundown puppy mills or experiencing abandonment or neglect. As a result, dogs who have lice are usually physically run-down. So after you get the lice under control, having your vet check the dog over for other problems is probably a good idea.

Lice are light-colored insects that don't fly (they're wingless) and are only 2 or 3 millimeters long. You can identify them visually by seeing either the lice on the dog or the eggs, which are known as *nits.*

A good flea dip usually kills lice and their eggs. (Use the same precautions you'd use with any insecticides.) You can also try Nix, which is the human version of anti-lice soap. Keeping some on hand may not be a bad idea, because humans can get lice from a dog and you may have to treat yourself.

If your dog has lice, you must bag and throw away all bedding and any material your dog has slept in. Other pets that have come into contact with the affected dog also need to be treated. You need to wash and disinfect all areas where the dog has been and any place your other pets have been.

Mites (or mite not)

"A mite is a very small spider," or so the joke goes. Actually, the joke isn't far off; mites are related to spiders, and they can cause a host of problems. Several types of mites can infect your dog — none of them is pleasant!

Some mites cause a condition known as *mange,* which is characterized by intense itching, lesions and scabs, and hair loss. (Doesn't sound pleasant, does it?) When people say "mangy dog," they're really talking about a mite-infested dog, even if they don't know it.

Mites like cheyletiella mites and chiggers usually don't show up if you've been treating your dog faithfully to prevent fleas, even if you're in a flea area. The mites don't like systemic flea control, so it's less likely your dog is going to get them.

I describe five types of mites and four types of mange they can cause in the sections that follow.

Cheyletiella mange

Cheyletiella mange, or walking dandruff, usually affects puppies. (Dog dandruff is white and flaky just like human dandruff.) Although this type of mange is contagious, it's also fairly rare, typically affecting dogs in large breeding kennels or pet shops. It's caused by a red mite that can infect humans. You usually see these mites along the back with a considerable amount of dandruff.

If you suspect your dog has cheyletiella mites, take him to the veterinarian. Your vet will need to make a diagnosis by examining the dandruff for mites or eggs. He or she can then recommend an appropriate treatment (usually a flea shampoo). Other pets in your household also need to be treated, and you have to disinfect areas where your dog routinely lounges. You may also want to wash or throw out any bedding.

Chiggers

Chiggers are a type of mite called the trombiculid mite. These mites are really nasty creatures that cause itching. They live in high grasses in very warm areas. I remember camping out in Texas and getting chiggers. They itch like the dickens. And yes, you can get them, too, although you're not likely to get them from your dog but rather from grasses in which you've been stomping around.

The chiggers you and your dog get are actually mite larvae. They love to start munching as soon as you come into contact with them. They're red or orange and burrow under the skin, making little red or orange bumps under the skin. After you've had a chigger infestation, you won't soon forget it.

The best way to treat chiggers is to avoid getting them in the first place. That means not allowing your dog to roam through high grasses and keeping him on a good systemic flea control product.

If those efforts fail and your dog is infested by chiggers, use a good flea shampoo that's recommended by your veterinarian. Make sure that it doesn't interact with anything your dog is already using for flea control. In severe cases of chiggers, your veterinarian may prescribe corticosteroids to control the itching.

If you have chiggers on you, take a hot bath or shower with lots of soap, and follow it up with an antiseptic. That's the consensus of Phillip J. Hamman, area extension entomologist for the Texas Agricultural Extension Service of Texas A&M University (insects.tamu.edu/extension/bulletins/L-1223.html), and William F. Lyon, professor of entomology at Ohio State University (ohioline.osu.edu/hyg-fact/2000/2100.html). After that, you need to use some sort of anti-itch medication with a mild anesthetic, like benzocaine. You also need to wash your clothes in hot, soapy water for a half an hour or more to kill any chiggers on them and to prevent them from reinfesting you or your dog.

Never use benzocaine on a dog. It's extremely poisonous to them.

Another way to treat chiggers that get on you (but not your dog): Try the old standby of painting over the chiggers with clear nail polish on your skin. I used this method when I was a kid, and it seemed to be pretty effective. You'll probably want to use some anti-itch cream while you wait for it to work.

Demodectic mange

Yet another skin mite infestation is *demodectic mange,* which is caused by *Demodex canis.* This mite normally exists on a dog's skin and presents no problems, unless something goes awry with the dog's immune system and the mange mites take over. Two types of demodectic mange are

- ✔ **Localized demodectic mange:** This infestation occurs in puppies under a year old. It's usually localized (hence the name) and may occur around the face or legs. In 90 percent of the cases, the dog's immune system kicks in, and eventually the mange clears up. Your veterinarian also can provide a topical ointment to treat this type of mange.

- ✔ **Generalized demodectic mange:** This mange usually occurs in dogs who have compromised immune systems. The mange is widespread, much more difficult to clear up, and requires veterinary intervention.

In all cases of demodectic mange, you need to have your veterinarian diagnose it and treat it (most likely with prescription medication). It can't be treated with any over-the-counter remedies.

Otodectic mange (ear mites)

If your dog scratches or shakes his head incessantly and has dark brown, waxy, coffee-ground–like stuff in his ears, he probably has ear mites. Ear mites can easily spread from dogs to cats and other pets, so if you have one pet with ear mites, be sure to check them all.

Although plenty of over-the-counter remedies are available for ear mites, most ear mite infections are accompanied by a secondary bacterial infection that needs to be treated by a veterinarian. Your vet can recommend an over-the-counter mitacide or (more likely) a prescription mitacide that contains a topical antibiotic and/or something to relieve the itching.

Sarcoptic mange (scabies)

A particularly nasty form of mange, sarcoptic mange is caused by the *Sarcoptes scabiei canis,* an itchy mite that can make your dog miserable. Sarcoptic mange is highly contagious and can transfer from dog to dog or even through contact with contaminated grooming equipment. These mites love the ears, face, elbows, hocks, and belly. What's more, this mange is contagious to humans, too.

Scabies, another name for sarcoptic mange, causes hair loss and crusty, itchy skin. If you suspect scabies, take your dog to a vet immediately. Your vet will prescribe a specialized dip for scabies and perhaps an oral medication.

Don't use over-the-counter products to treat scabies unless your vet recommends them. Scabies mites have become resistant to a number of dips, including many over-the-counter brands.

Cooling Down Those Hot Spots

Hot spots are a form of moist dermatitis that's red and can be extremely painful. The symptoms are reddening and oozing skin and hair loss. Hot spots can occur because of allergies, mats (one more reason to keep your dog combed out and clean!), external parasites, and anything that can cause moisture and dirt to get trapped near the skin.

If hot spots aren't too painful, you can use a guarded clipper to clip around the hot spot, but you need to be extremely careful to not nick the tender area. Then you can clean the hot spot with a 10-percent mixture of Betadine antiseptic and water twice daily. If the hot spot is too painful, your vet will have to anesthetize your dog, clip away the hair, clean the hot spot, and prescribe corticosteroids and antibiotics.

Hypothyroidism and Hyperthyroidism

Hypothyroidism and hyperthyroidism are conditions of the thyroid, a gland that controls the metabolism. *Hypothyroidism* is a deficiency in the functioning of the thyroid, while *hyperthyroidism* is excessive functioning of that gland. These conditions can affect a dog's coat and grooming.

Hypothyroidism

By far, hypothyroidism is the most common thyroid disease in dogs. It occurs when the thyroid gland produces too little *thyroxine,* or thyroid hormone. Certain breeds of dogs tend to have a predisposition to hypothyroidism, and in some breeds, the condition may have a genetic component.

Symptoms of hypothyroidism include hair loss, poor haircoat, obesity, excessive shedding, intolerance to cold, aggression, and energy loss. A reliable signal of hypothyroidism is poor hair growth after your dog has been clipped.

If you suspect your dog is suffering from hypothyroidism, have your veterinarian test your dog for the disease. If your dog has hypothyroidism, your vet can prescribe thyroid pills.

Hyperthyroidism

A rather unusual condition in dogs, hyperthyroidism is the opposite of hypothyroidism; namely, the thyroid gland produces too much thyroid hormone. Thyroid cancer is the usual cause of hyperthyroidism in dogs.

Symptoms include a greasy haircoat, weight loss, hyperactivity, increased thirst, increased urination, and occasionally, vomiting and diarrhea. You also may see lethargy and depression.

You must have your veterinarian diagnose and treat hyperthyroidism. If your dog has it, your vet will have to address the cancer or (if not cancer) the overproduction of thyroid hormones either with radioactive iodine (which destroys thyroid tissue) or antithyroid medications.

Internal Parasites

You may be surprised to find something about internal parasites in a grooming book, but internal parasites can ruin a dog's skin and hair. The reason's quite simple: A dog can't be beautiful outside if something inside is ruining his health.

Internal parasites often result in a haircoat that becomes dingy and lackluster, especially when there's a worm infestation. Roundworms most often are the culprit, but I've seen hookworms and tapeworms take their toll on a dog's coat, too. Mishka, a dog I adopted, had tapeworms when she was taken in by the shelter. The shelter dewormed her, but as a result of her parasites, she had a horrible coat and was terribly thin. (She may have had more parasites other than just tapeworms.) After being worm-free for a while and on a diet of good food, Mishka shed out her old, sickly coat, and a beautiful new coat grew back in its place. She gained weight, too, looking much better than she did when I adopted her.

Some worm infestations can actually kill a dog. Whipworms and hookworms, for example, can cause severe anemia. Roundworms can take away enough nutrition to actually kill a puppy.

Worms aren't a health hazard only for your dog. Certain worms, like roundworms, hookworms, and even tapeworms can be transmitted to people (especially children) who come into contact with infected soil or feces and don't wash their hands before eating.

In all cases of worms, take your dog to the veterinarian. Don't try to treat your dog with over-the-counter dewormers — many don't work on all worms. Many dewormers are poisonous, especially when used improperly. Your vet can diagnose what kind of infestation your dog has and prescribe the best method of treating it.

Some heartworm medications now contain dewormers that control various internal parasites (see the upcoming section about "Heartworms"). Ask your veterinarian about them.

In the sections that follow, I discuss the different types of worm infestations that can affect dogs.

Hookworms

Hookworms *(Ancylostoma caninum)* feed off of blood in the small intestine of your dog. These thin worms are ¼- to ½-inch long. Infestations of these worms come from a mother's milk or from worms that penetrate the skin. Because these worms drink blood, think of them as vampire worms that can be a terrible health hazard for your dog.

Your dog may show no outward signs of a hookworm infestation, but these worms can cause weight loss, bloody diarrhea, anemia, and weakness.

Roundworms

Roundworms *(Toxocara canis)* are the most common form of worm infestation in dogs. Infestations usually occur in the intestines, but these worms can live in the lungs, stomach, and intestines, and they can migrate among those organs. Roundworms can grow to several inches in length, and they love to live off the vital nutrients your dog needs to live.

During a roundworm infestation, you're feeding the roundworms but not necessarily your dog. Puppies often get roundworms even before they're born, because if the mother has had an infestation at any time during her life, the roundworms lie dormant and then migrate to the unborn puppies or travel through her milk to the nursing puppies. Roundworms also can be picked up through the soil. Roundworm eggs can live for years in the soil and thus can be transmitted through virtually anything a dog eats off the ground.

Symptoms of severe roundworm infestations, especially in puppies, can include a poor haircoat, weight loss, vomiting, diarrhea, a potbelly, and sometimes a garlic odor on the dog's breath. Dogs sometimes pass roundworms either by vomiting or through their stool. I always suspect roundworms whenever a dog of mine loses weight or doesn't gain weight even with more food.

Tapeworms

Tapeworms *(Dipylidium caninum)* live in your dog's intestines and may grow from a few inches to several feet in length. The common method of infestation is through fleas. The dog bites at a flea and swallows it along with the tapeworm. Other types of tapeworms can be found in dogs who eat rodents or raw game meat.

You can usually tell whether your dog has tapeworms by seeing body segments (of the worm) crawling near your dog's anus. They sometimes look like grains of rice. Although tapeworms don't usually cause many health problems, they still can result in a bigger appetite, weight loss, poor coat, diarrhea, and other symptoms.

Whipworms

Whipworms *(Trichuris vulpis)* are 2 to 3 inches long and reside in a dog's intestines. They latch onto the intestine and feed off the blood. Whipworm infestations can be tough to diagnose, because light infections seldom show symptoms and the worms don't always produce eggs in fecal matter. Dogs become infested with whipworms by eating something off of soil that's contaminated with whipworm eggs.

Symptoms of whipworms include bloody diarrhea, weight loss, dull coat, and anemia. Whipworm infestations can be quite serious.

Heartworms

Heartworm infestations are more difficult to detect because they don't always affect your dog's coat; however, they are life-threatening. Unlike other internal parasites described in this chapter, your dog doesn't ingest heartworms; they're spread by the bite of an infected mosquito.

Mosquitoes transmit heartworm after feeding on an infected dog. The mosquito picks up the *microfilariae,* or heartworm larvae, which then incubate in the mosquito for several days. When the mosquito feeds on another dog, the microfilariae infect that dog. Heartworm larvae eventually move into the dog's heart, lungs, and even the veins in the liver. Left untreated, the dog will die from heartworm.

Preventive and treatment measures have been developed for heartworm, but treating it is somewhat risky and very expensive. The safer, more cost-effective, and certainly healthier route is heartworm prevention prescribed by your vet. Almost every state has some incidence of heartworm, and the latest guideline suggests that dogs need to stay on heartworm preventives year-round and be tested annually.

Several preventive heartworm medications are available, including

- **Heartgard and Heartgard Plus (ivermectin):** These heartworm medicines are extremely effective at preventing heartworm, but on rare occasions, some dogs can be sensitive to them and should not be put on either one. Heartgard Plus also controls roundworms and hookworms.

- **Interceptor (milnemycin):** Milnemycin is effective at controlling heartworm and can be used as an alternative to ivermectin. Interceptor also controls roundworms, hookworms, and whipworms.

- **Sentinel (Milbemycin and Lufenuron):** Like Interceptor, Sentinel controls not only heartworm but also fleas.

- **Revolution (selamectin):** Selamectin is a monthly systemic heartworm control product that prevents heartworms and fleas.

Lick Granulomas

Lick granulomas are open sores that a dog continuously licks. They usually start out as an irritation from allergies, mange mites, or other infections. If your dog has lick granulomas, you need to take her to the vet for treatment of the sore and the underlying cause.

Sebaceous Adentitis

A hereditary skin disease, *sabaceous adentitis* destroys the sebaceous (oil) glands in the skin, especially in Standard Poodles. It can also appear in Akitas and Samoyeds. Dogs who have this disease lose hair symmetrically, along both sides of the face, ears, neck, body, and tail. The dog's skin becomes flaky with seborrhea (see later section by the same name). Your veterinarian needs to test your dog for sebaceous adentitis and can treat it with various medications, including corticosteroids, antiseborrhea medications and shampoos, and Accutane (isotretinoin).

Ringworm

Ringworm isn't a worm at all; rather, it's a fungal infection that causes hair loss and gets its name from the red rings it causes on people. This same fungus leaves round, hairless, scaly patches of skin on your dog. Ringworm is contagious to other animals and to humans, especially children and cats, so be sure to use latex gloves and wash your hands thoroughly after treating it. Most adults (people and animals) have adequate immune systems to fight off ringworm, but if your immune system has been compromised (cancer, HIV, diabetes), you definitely need to use latex gloves or have someone else treat your dog to avoid infection yourself.

You can treat localized ringworm with a 10-percent Betadine antiseptic and water solution. Rinse the area several times each day. Antifungal shampoos and soaps containing iodine also work.

If you have a cat or kitten with ringworm, take her to the vet. Don't use iodine, or you may risk iodine poisoning.

Dogs can get ringworm from physical contact with other infected animals or from the soil, and that makes it difficult to eradicate. Your veterinarian can prescribe oral medicine or topical creams for chronic or widespread ringworm.

Seborrhea

Seborrhea is a disease of the sebaceous glands where there are oily or dry flakes of skin. The two types of seborrhea are

- ✔ **Primary:** Primary seborrhea seems to have a genetic component; it affects many breeds, including American Cocker Spaniels, English Springer Spaniels, Basset Hounds, Chinese Shar-Pei, West Highland White Terriers, Dachshunds, Labrador and Golden Retrievers, and German Shepherds. It causes oily or flaky skin, or a combination of both, all over the body. Primary seborrhea can be controlled with antiseborrhea shampoos and rinses. Consult your vet for the one that works best for your dog.

- ✔ **Secondary:** Secondary seborrhea is the result of another disease that causes hair loss and inflamed skin. You first need to have your vet examine your dog to diagnose the underlying cause of the seborrhea, and then treat that disease accordingly. You can then treat the symptoms of seborrhea the same way primary seborrhea is treated.

Tumors and Cysts

A dog can get a tumor or cyst just about any time during his life, but the likelihood increases with age. If you feel a lump or bump on your dog, check the opposite side to see whether the bump is *bilateral,* meaning that you find the same bump in the same location on both sides of the dog. If it is, the bump's probably normal. If it isn't, you need to have your veterinarian examine it immediately.

If you still aren't sure whether the bump is normal (that is, part of the dog's anatomy), go ahead and take your dog to the vet for a quick check. Better to be safe than sorry.

In most cases, the vet will want to remove the tumor and do a biopsy on it to make sure that it isn't malignant. That means shaving around the area, surgically removing all or part of the tumor, performing a lab test, and giving the dog sutures. Although not aesthetically pleasing, the procedure's certainly better than the alternative (possible death).

If the tumor is benign (and many of them are), you then have a choice whether to have the tumor removed. If you decide not to have it removed, you must remember to be careful when grooming around it. Tumors tend to bleed profusely when nicked with a comb or clipper, and if they continue to grow, you may want to have it removed for aesthetic reasons or for the comfort of your dog.

Zinc Responsive Dermatosis

Zinc responsive dermatosis is a hereditary disease in which a dog fails to adequately absorb enough zinc in his diet. The result is a scaly and crusty nose, paw pads, and belly. This condition may be mistaken for other autoimmune diseases, like Collie nose (an autoimmune disease that looks like a sunburnt nose, common to Collies), so it needs to be diagnosed through a skin biopsy in which the vet removes and tests a small piece of the nose.

Zinc responsive dermatosis is prevalent among northern breeds such as Siberian Huskies, Alaskan Huskies, Malamutes, and Samoyeds. Dogs that have this condition need zinc supplements included in their diets.

Chapter 17

Grooming Emergencies: Knowing Doggie First Aid

*E*mergencies can and do happen, even when you're grooming your dog. I'm not talking about the horrible trim that the so-called professional groomer gave your dog; I'm talking about serious injuries. Although you never like to think about them, being prepared for such eventualities is important. So in this chapter, I tell you about being ready for most emergencies you'll face as a groomer and how to deal with major and minor problems that you may encounter.

Preparing for a Grooming Emergency

Humans have an innate ability to foresee the future. No, I don't mean psychics here; I mean your normal cognitive abilities, thinking your actions through and pondering the possible consequences they may have. For example, you know that when you leave a burning candle or other open flame unattended, something may catch fire. You're able to foresee this terrible outcome because you've either been down that fiery path before, heard about it from someone else, or simply considered what can happen if you don't extinguish the flame.

You can use the same approach when making sure that you're prepared for grooming-related emergencies. When you're prepared for the worst possible circumstances, you can turn those emergencies into less terrible and more manageable situations.

Preventing an emergency

The best way to handle a grooming emergency is to prevent it from happening in the first place. If you look around your grooming room, I'm sure you'll see plenty of "lighted candles" that need to be put out, especially the ones that flare up into, well, emergencies when you add a dog to the mix. Here are some items that can cause problems in your grooming area:

- **Electrical cords:** Dogs love to chew them, and the results can be shocking (no pun intended) and devastating. Keep cords unplugged and/or out of the way when they're not in use.

- **Electrical devices near sinks or tubs:** You know that electricity and water don't mix, right? Keep all electrical devices unplugged and safely away from water.

- **Grooming nooses (neck and body):** Use these restraints only when you're attending to your dog's grooming needs. Otherwise, store them away from your dog to prevent strangulation and injury. Never leave your dog unsupervised in a noose.

- **Scissors (or shears) and other sharp objects:** Sharp tools and objects need to be stored in a drawer or other dog-proof container when not in use. If left on the counter or in a bin and they get knocked off or upset, they can stab you or an unfortunate dog.

- **Other dogs:** Keep other dogs crated or out of the room. Groom only one dog at a time.

- **Cage dryers:** Cage dryers can seriously overheat your dog, and for that reason, I don't recommend them. If you use a cage dryer, you simply can't leave the dog unattended.

  Make sure your entire grooming area has proper ventilation, because without it, dogs can become overheated in hot, stuffy areas.

- **Shampoos, conditioners, and other sweet-smelling items:** Dogs are tempted to eat these substances. Keeping them away from your dog takes away that temptation.

- **Grooming tables and other equipment:** Make sure your grooming table is sturdy and that all your equipment is in working order. Be aware of what can happen if your dog jumps off the table or your equipment malfunctions.

You can prepare for emergencies by anticipating what can happen. Looking at a tray full of scissors on the counter probably has you wondering, "What if my dog were to knock that over?" Or seeing your best friend bring in her princess for a quick brush-out while you're bathing your own dog, you definitely need to think about how the two dogs are going to react. Even if they're just friendly, they'll probably be excitable when they spot each other. An excitable dog in the tub may try to jump out with the noose attached. Foreseeing problems before they happen can prevent many emergencies.

Always have your veterinarian's phone number and the numbers for an alternate veterinarian and a 24-hour emergency number posted, taped onto, or otherwise inscribed next to your telephone. (Put it on speed dial, too!) That way, if a problem occurs, the number's handy. You also need to have the national Animal Poison Control Center hotline number available (see Chapter 15). That number is 1-888-426-4435.

Assembling a first-aid kit

One preventative measure that helps during emergencies is having a well-stocked first-aid kit. You need to assemble this first-aid kit for your dog and have it available in your grooming room in case a real problem crops up. Having a first-aid kit can't prevent an emergency, but you'll be better prepared for dealing with one.

When you use any of the supplies from your first-aid kit, don't forget to restock. If you don't, you may not have what you need when the next emergency occurs. Likewise, check expiration dates on medications and throw them out if they've expired. If something's close to expiration but the first-aid kit item is something you use regularly, replace it in your first-aid kit before using it. In other words, buy fresh supplies to replace the old ones.

Your groomer's first-aid kit needs to include the following items, most of which you can purchase at your neighborhood drugstore unless otherwise noted:

- ✔ **A muzzle:** To prevent your dog from biting you. It's available online, in pet supply catalog, or from your vet. The "Muzzling a dog" section later in this chapter explains how to make a makeshift muzzle in a pinch, but it's best to have an actual muzzle on hand.

- ✔ **Aspirin (not ibuprofen or acetaminophen):** For pain; ask your vet about the proper dosage.

- ✔ **Large and small nonstick bandages plus bandage scissors and tape:** You can also buy self-adhesive elastic pet bandage online or in pet supply catalogs. (Elastoplast for humans works well, too; it's available at supermarkets and drugstores.)

- ✔ **Pressure bandages:** To stop bleeding.

- ✔ **Sterile gauze wrappings and sponges:** For bandaging.

- ✔ **Forceps or tweezers:** Available online, in pet supply catalogs, or from your vet.

- ✔ **Betadine antiseptic solution:** For cleaning wounds and preventing infection.

- ✔ **Blood-clotting gel or powder (cut-stop gel) or styptic power:** To stop bleeding. It's available online, in pet supply catalogs, or from your vet.

- ✔ **Hydrogen peroxide:** For cleaning wounds and inducing vomiting.

- ✔ **Triple antibiotic ointment (without benzocaine or lidocaine):** To prevent infection.

- ✔ **Electronic ear thermometer made for dogs, or an electronic rectal thermometer:** Available online, in pet supply catalogs, or from your vet.

- ✔ **Petroleum jelly (Vaseline):** To use when taking temperatures with a rectal thermometer.

- ✔ **Cortisone cream:** To help sooth itching.

- ✔ **Disposable latex gloves:** To keep substances off of you.

- ✔ **Isopropyl alcohol:** To sterilize stuff.

- ✔ **Syrup of ipecac:** For inducing vomiting.

- ✔ **Kaolin product for dogs:** To stop diarrhea. It's available online, in pet supply catalogs, or from your vet.

- ✔ **Mineral oil or activated charcoal:** To use for poisonings. Mineral oil acts as a laxative, and activated charcoal absorbs some toxins.

- ✔ **Unflavored pediatric electrolyte (Pedialyte):** To treat dehydration and heatstroke.

Talk to your vet to see whether he or she has any other recommendations for first-aid supplies. Put these items in one place, preferably in a container marked "FIRST-AID KIT" with a permanent marker.

Emergency know-how

Knowing what to do in case of an emergency is just as important as having the right stuff on hand. You need to find out how to use a muzzle, and you have to be able to administer mouth-to-mouth resuscitation and cardio-pulmonary resuscitation (CPR) on a dog. Showing you the correct way to resuscitate a dog in a book like this is pretty difficult, so ask your vet to show you how to do it properly before a problem arises.

Muzzling a dog

No matter how sweet and gentle your dog is, I can guarantee that she'll bite if she's fearful or in pain. That reaction isn't a question of good temperament; it's a question of instinct. Before you treat a dog for any emergency, you have to muzzle her to keep her from biting you. Protecting yourself is important.

Muzzle a dog only if the following conditions are met. Your dog

- ✔ Is conscious
- ✔ Does not have an obstructed airway
- ✔ Isn't having trouble breathing
- ✔ Isn't suffering from heatstroke
- ✔ Doesn't have a fractured skull
- ✔ Isn't suffering from a sucking chest wound

You will aggravate any injury and possibly kill your dog if you muzzle her under these circumstances.

I don't know whether you've ever been bitten by a dog. If you haven't, make sure the situation stays that way. If you have been bitten, you know what I'm talking about when I say that dogs can bite down with a bone-crushing pressure as high as 400 pounds per square inch. Even a minor bite can be pretty serious, because a dog's saliva starts breaking down your skin right away. Even a small bite can become severely infected and may require medical attention. Assuming your dog hasn't broken any (of your) bones, you'll still feel the bite and have a lot of bruising and pain for days afterward. Trust me, I speak from experience. Dog bites are no fun.

If you already have a muzzle in your first-aid kit, that's great. But if you don't, you still can muzzle a dog with a makeshift muzzle made from a belt, a long piece of sturdy fabric or cloth (that doesn't have much stretch to it), a necktie, or a rope.

Here's how to make a makeshift muzzle from a belt, tie, or rope (I use a lead/leash for this example; see Figure 17-1):

1. **Put the lead beneath your dog's chin.**

   Be sure to place your dog's chin in the middle of the lead so that both sides are equal in length.

2. **Wrap the two ends of the lead upward and tie once at the top of the dog's muzzle (foreface).**

Figure 17-1:
Muzzling a
dog in pain
(even with
a belt, tie,
or rope in
a pinch)
can prevent
her from
biting you.

3. **Wrap two ends of the lead downward and tie once under the chin.**

4. **Bring the two ends of the lead under the ears toward the back of the head, and tie them there securely.**

Performing mouth-to-mouth resuscitation

I hope you never have to use this advice, but I'd nevertheless encourage you to ask your veterinarian to show you how to administer mouth-to-mouth resuscitation and CPR for a canine. Here's a checklist that you need to review before you start any type of resuscitation. *Note:* These techniques should never be used with or performed on a healthy or conscious dog.

1. **Find out whether the dog has a pulse.**

   You can feel your dog's pulse on the inside of her back leg. Try feeling it when she's healthy and uninjured so you know where it is.

2. **If the dog has no pulse, perform canine CPR as instructed by a veterinarian.**

   If you don't know how to do canine CPR, contact an emergency veterinarian as soon as possible.

3. **If the dog has a pulse but is not breathing, remove the collar and all other constricting items.**

4. **Check the dog's airway to find out whether anything is blocking it.**

   Use forceps to remove any small item, or try performing a doggie-modified Heimlich maneuver by pushing or squeezing the dog just below the ribcage to cause her to expel the foreign object.

   Don't practice the doggie Heimlich maneuver on a healthy dog, but when you must use it on an unhealthy one, don't press too hard, because you can injure your dog. Have your vet show you how to do the doggie Heimlich.

5. **Begin mouth-to-mouth resuscitation the way your vet showed you.**

   Make sure the dog's tongue is in the proper position, and hold her mouth closed as you blow air into her nose. (On larger dogs, you may have to hold your hands around the nose.) Blow air *in only* so that it just inflates the lungs.

   Don't overinflate, or you can rupture your dog's lungs. Let the dog breathe the air out. Do CPR/mouth-to-mouth at a rate of 20 breaths per minute.

Handling Minor Grooming Snafus

Occasionally, you're going to encounter some minor accidents while grooming your dog. They usually occur because you've either shaved your dog too closely or you've cut or nicked your dog. When the wounds or cuts aren't too bad, you can use your first-aid kit. Check out two of the less-serious problems.

Cuts and nicks

Maybe you were using scissors when you shouldn't have been, or maybe your dog squirmed a bit — they have been known to do that. Whatever the reason, you've somehow cut or nicked your dog, and he's pretty unhappy with you, I'm sure. So you need to be sure to treat the nicks carefully. Anything that *looks* like it needs to be sutured probably does, and you need to take your dog to the vet to get him stitched up immediately.

If there's still a fair amount of hair, use a guarded clipper to remove as much of it as you can from around the cut. If it's bleeding, use some cut-stop gel or styptic powder to clot the blood. Then you need to clean the cuts with a solution of 10 percent Betadine antiseptic and 90 percent water and follow that up with an antibiotic ointment. If the cut is in a place where you can bandage it with a sterile pad and self-adhesive bandages — on the leg or any place that you can wrap the bandage around — do so. Don't use tape to keep the pad on unless you wrap the tape only around the bandage and not the fur. In other words, don't apply tape directly to the fur. Removing a bandage that's been taped directly onto a dog's hair is far worse than pulling off any bandage that's ever been taped onto you — so be careful! Change the bandage every day, and watch for infection (redness, pus). If your dog shows any sign of infection, take him to the veterinarian immediately.

Skin irritation

Your dog can suffer skin irritation from the clippers or from virtually any of the products you're using. If your dog suffers clipper burn, you can apply some aloe vera on the irritated areas. To prevent clipper burn, you can use a clipper coolant, which cools off the clipper blades fast, before working on your dog's coat (see Chapter 7).

If you suspect your dog has irritation caused by a particular product, try washing your dog again, this time with a hypoallergenic shampoo and conditioner and then rinsing really well to remove all the residue. You can use an over-the-counter cortisone-type cream on the rash. If the irritated area doesn't get better, or if it gets worse, take your dog to a vet.

Doggie 911

Whenever things go wrong in a serious and big way, it's up to you to help your injured pet. One thing to keep in mind: Don't panic. Your dog is relying on you to help her.

Serious cuts

Serious cuts are the ones that may require sutures and usually have a fair amount of blood associated with them. If the blood is bright red and spurting, you must apply pressure to the wound to stop the bleeding, except when it's a severe crushing injury. Apply a bandage on the wound (that's not a severe crushing injury) and use a self-adhesive elastic pet bandage to apply pressure to the wound. When you apply the bandage, don't cut off the circulation, because applying too tight of a bandage can do more damage than good. If your dog experiences any type of severe injury, get her to a veterinarian as soon as possible.

For a deep puncture wound, try to determine how deep it goes. If the object is still embedded, leave it in the wound until you can get your dog veterinary attention, because pulling it out can cause more bleeding. Seek immediate veterinary attention for all puncture wounds.

Allergic reaction

The most serious allergic response is an *anaphylactic reaction,* in which the dog stops breathing. The other, more common type of allergic reaction involves simple redness and itching.

Luckily, anaphylactic reaction is a rare condition that you're unlikely to see. Unfortunately, its beginning symptoms are virtually the same as for the simpler reaction. If your dog is suffering from anaphylactic reaction, time is of the essence! Take your dog to a veterinary emergency room immediately, because you can't treat a dog with anaphylactic shock. The first signs may be hives or swelling of the face, or the reaction may start with itching and redness of the skin and progress to agitation, diarrhea, vomiting, and difficulty breathing.

In the more common, less serious type of allergic reaction, you'll see redness of the skin, hives, and itching, and the face may swell up; however, you won't see the respiratory (breathing) distress.

Whenever your dog suffers from an allergic reaction, remove as much of the offending substance as you can from the dog — if she hasn't experienced any respiratory distress. Contact a veterinarian to find out how much antihistamine to administer. Benadryl is a common one used for less serious reactions. In any event, you need to seek immediate veterinary attention for your dog.

Knowing reactions are nothing to sneeze at

You may be wondering how serious an allergic reaction can be for a dog. In some cases, it can be so severe and so immediate that it can cause death in a matter of only seconds. The problem is that dogs (and people, too, for that matter) can become allergic to something after they've been exposed to the substance several times with no ill effects.

Always watch for signs of an allergic reaction when you're using grooming products. Even hypoallergenic products sometimes can cause reactions, but only in rare circumstances.

Taking your dog's temperature

Taking a dog's temperature isn't easy, but knowing how to do it is a necessity. Normal temperature for a dog is 100.5°F (38°C) to 102°F (38.9°C). You need to take your dog's temperature to find out whether he has a fever or is overheated or hypothermic. You can do so one of two ways. One way is to use an ear thermometer, though ear thermometers are rather expensive and are sometimes hard to get. A friend of mine bought one and discovered that her dog had a type of ear canal in which the ear thermometer wouldn't work. So even if you get an ear thermometer, you may still have to do it the old-fashioned way:

1. **Purchase an electronic thermometer that can be used rectally.**

2. **Wash it with warm soapy water (not hot), and disinfect it with isopropyl alcohol.**

3. **Lubricate it with petroleum jelly (Vaseline), and turn it on.**

4. **Lift your dog's tail and gently insert it in your dog's anus about an inch (more if your dog is large; less if your dog is a toy breed).**

   Make sure that you hold your dog still and keep him quiet until the thermometer signals that the temperature has been taken.

5. **Remove the thermometer and wipe it clean with a paper towel.**

6. **Read the temperature.**

Always wash the thermometer after each use with warm soapy water and then disinfect it with isopropyl alcohol.

Overheating

Overheating, or heatstroke, is a serious condition in dogs that can rapidly lead to coma and death. Symptoms of overheating include high temperature (above 103°F — 39.4°C), extreme thirst, watery diarrhea, vomiting, seizures, lethargy, pale gums, difficulty breathing, weakness, and eventually, coma and death. In most cases, the dog is also suffering from dehydration. See the next section for more about dehydration. Check out the "Taking your dog's temperature" sidebar in this chapter for directions to help you do just that.

Dogs are more susceptible to heatstroke than humans, partly because of their origins — coming from Asiatic wolves some 20,000 or so years ago. Dogs with a double coat are better suited for colder weather than for warmer temperatures. Dogs don't perspire the way humans do. Instead, they rely on panting to cool their bodies, so whenever airflow's restricted, a dog isn't able to cool herself off fast enough and becomes overheated or suffers heatstroke. Remember, dogs can't take off their fur coats when it's hot.

When talking about heatstroke, most people know they should never leave their dogs in a parked car in the sun, even with the windows down. Temperatures inside the car can rise quickly, and a dog can become distressed in only a short time. However, dogs also can suffer heatstroke in other ways. Your dog can suffer heatstroke with too much exercise in warm weather, not enough water, or confinement in small spaces where no cool air flows. So in a grooming area, you need to be careful with cages and cage dryers, hot-water baths, and leaving your dog out in the sun.

You can prevent your dog from getting heatstroke simply by following a few guidelines. Keep her in cool and shady places when the temperatures soar, and turn a cooling fan toward her and give her fresh water. Don't use cage dryers when drying her. Also, keep her bath-water temperature tepid or slightly on the cool side.

Here's what to do if you suspect your dog is suffering from heatstroke:

1. **Remove collars or anything else that can restrict the dog's breathing.**

   If the dog has no pulse and/or isn't breathing, perform CPR or mouth-to-mouth resuscitation.

   Never put a muzzle on a dog that's suffering from heatstroke.

2. **Move the dog into a shady area that has good airflow; start giving her fluids.**

   If the dog is conscious, give her cool water or unflavored pediatric electrolyte beverages, such as Pedialyte, to drink.

   You can add broth to make the liquids more appealing if you have to.

3. **If you can, cool the dog in tepid or cool water.**

   Don't use cold water to cool down an overheated dog; otherwise, you may cause the dog's capillaries to constrict and thus retain heat.

4. **Seek immediate veterinary attention.**

Knowing where your dog can overheat

Here's a list of some of the places in which dogs can become overheated:

- Inside cars, even with the air conditioner running
- Inside trailers that have dog compartments
- Inside recreational vehicles
- Inside tents
- Inside un–air-conditioned shops and buildings
- In cages with crate dryers
- In crates in the car or in the sun
- On the back porch in the sun
- On walks or while hiking
- In sports competitions

Dehydration

Dehydration can be a serious condition, occurring alone or in conjunction with overheating (see the preceding section for more about overheating). Dehydration can result from overheating, a serious medical condition, diarrhea and vomiting, or an inadequate water supply.

Dogs who are dehydrated may vomit or have watery diarrhea, and they're often weak and lethargic.

To find out whether your dog is dehydrated, check the look and feel of her gums. If they're dry and sticky (not wet), your dog is dehydrated. Another test you can perform is the *skin-snap test;* however, for this test to work appropriately, you need to have performed it while your dog was healthy so you can tell when she isn't. Age, diseases, and breed all play a factor in how the skin-snap test looks. Here's how you do it:

1. **Look for the loose skin along the nape (back) of the neck, just in front of your dog's shoulders.**

2. **Grasping the loose skin gently, pull up and then release (see Figure 17-2).**

3. **Observe how it springs back.**

   If the dog is healthy, the skin springs back quickly.

   If the dog is dehydrated, it springs back slowly.

   If the dog is severely dehydrated, it may melt back slowly or even stay up. When that happens, you have an emergency on your hands and need to get your dog to a vet!

With mild forms of dehydration, giving your dog water or pediatric electrolyte beverage is probably all you need to do. You can mix it with broth to make it palatable. In severe forms of dehydration or in cases where your dog won't drink water, you need to take her to the veterinarian as quickly as possible for intravenous fluids and care.

Dehydration can kill a dog. When in doubt, get that dog to a veterinarian.

Strangulation

If your dog is somehow strangled, remove grooming or bathing nooses or whatever is constricting your dog's breathing (such as collars or harnesses). If your dog is unconscious, follow the steps under the "Performing mouth-to-mouth resuscitation" section earlier in this chapter. Get your dog to a veterinarian as soon as possible even if she is conscious.

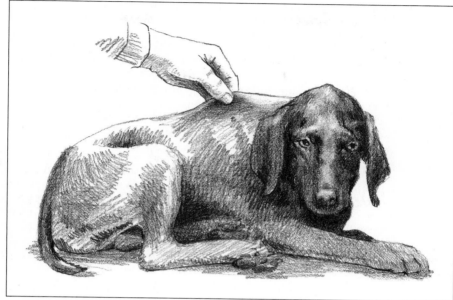

Figure 17-2:
Check your
dog for
dehydration
by
performing
the skin-
snap test.

Electric shock

A dog can be electrocuted by chewing an electric cord or when electrical
equipment (like your clippers) falls into the bathtub. If your dog receives a
shock from either from chewing a cord or having an appliance fall into the
tub, don't touch the dog. Use a wooden broom handle or other nonmetal,
nonconductive item to unplug the cord.

After you get your dog out of the tub, if she's unconscious, follow the steps
in the "Performing mouth-to-mouth resuscitation" section earlier in this
chapter, and take your dog to a veterinarian as soon as possible (even if she's
conscious).

Hypothermia

Hypothermia is a life-threatening condition in which a dog's temperature drops
dangerously below normal. Toy breeds, puppies, older dogs, and dogs with
short coats are more likely to become hypothermic than dogs with long and
double coats. A dog can quickly become hypothermic in the wintertime if
washed and left outside or in a drafty area.

You can prevent hypothermia by drying the dog quickly and not allowing him outside until his coat is thoroughly dry. Signs of hypothermia include shivering and listlessness, followed by unconsciousness, coma, and death. A low body temperature (below 99°F — 37.2°C) is a possible sign of hypothermia (see the "Taking your dog's temperature" sidebar in this chapter).

Whenever you find a dog shivering, move him to someplace warm and wrap him with a blanket. If he's conscious, give him warm broth to drink. If unconscious, follow the steps in the "Performing mouth-to-mouth resuscitation" section earlier in this chapter. Get your dog to a veterinarian as soon as possible, even if he is conscious.

Dog bites

If you have more than one dog present while grooming, you may have to deal with dog fights and therefore, dog bites.

In any dog fight, you're likely to be bitten if you get between two battling dogs. On the other hand, allowing two dogs to continue to fight can result in a dead dog. You can usually separate dogs by throwing water on them or by forcing something (other than you) between them. If you can, get help so that you and the other person can grasp the each dog by the hind legs and pull the two animals apart. If you're alone, try separating the dogs by herding them into a doorway and shutting the door between them. In extreme instances, a couple of blasts from a fire extinguisher can work.

After you separate the dogs, be sure to keep them separated, preferably in crates. Dogs will go back to fighting even after an initial cool-down, especially if they've drawn blood. When you take your dogs to the vet, make sure that you have at least one of them in a crate to prevent a fight in the car.

Anything you do to separate dogs in a dog fight can result in your being bitten.

Again, after you separate the dogs, examine them carefully for wounds. Some wounds won't show up right away. With bad injuries, treat as for serious cuts and take the dogs to the veterinarian immediately. Any puncture wounds need to be cleaned by a veterinarian.

Chapter 18

It's Showtime! Grooming a Dog for the Ring

In This Chapter

▶ Exploring what a dog show is all about

▶ Understanding how dog show preparations differ from pet grooming

▶ Discovering what grooming needs to happen at the show

Grooming a dog for a dog show is a little like grooming your pet — but just a little. You have to know how to groom your dog as a pet, but then you must go one step further and groom him for inspection by a judge who's well-versed in the standards for your dog's breed. Part of that standard is his coat. So in this chapter, I give you the scoop on grooming and how it pertains to the show ring.

Note: This chapter is for the owner-handler, as most people who start showing their dogs are owner-handlers, meaning that they own, groom, and handle their own dogs in the show ring.

Brushing Up on Dog Show Basics

So what, exactly, is a dog show, and why is it so important for your dog to look pretty in one? When dog people talk about dog shows, they're usually talking about conformation dog shows and not necessarily a performance event, such as obedience or agility trials. *Conformation shows* are the typical dog shows most people think about and see on television, in which the dog is judged on how he looks and how he *conforms* to the standard. (Performance events usually are called *trials* to make a distinction.) The two types of conformation dog shows are all-breed and specialty.

✔ *All-breed shows* are just as the name implies — all breeds compete in the show. If your dog does well and wins Best of Breed, he goes on to compete against other dogs of different breeds in a group setting and then on to the Best-in-Show setting. All-breed shows are usually sanctioned by a national or international kennel club, such as the American Kennel Club (AKC) or the United Kennel Club (UKC).

✔ A *specialty show* is for one particular breed — meaning your dog competes only against dogs of the same breed. Specialty shows are usually put on by a breed club and may be regional or national in scope.

Dogs in all-breed and specialty shows are both judged according to their respective *breed standards,* which are blueprints for how each dog breed should look and act.

Breed standards go into such excruciating detail that no dog can ever match up to all the standards. Dogs who come close, however, are said to be of show quality, and dogs that have serious faults or even disqualifications when measured up against the breed standard are said to be pet-quality dogs. The faults or disqualifications usually are cosmetic, such as a splash of color where it shouldn't be, the wrong type of bite, or even a missing tooth or two. Of course, pet-quality dogs are not inferior to show-quality dogs when it comes to having them as a pet, but you need to understand the standard for your dog's breed and whether your dog is truly cut out to be a show dog before you start grooming him for and dishing out the money to enter him in shows, because showing a dog can be expensive.

You can find your dog's breed standard online at the AKC Web site (www.akc.org), or you can check out the various breed club Web sites.

Just because your dog is cute or smart or even a purebred doesn't mean that he's ready to hit the conformation dog shows. First, you must determine whether your dog is of show quality. Because AKC is the main kennel club that plays host to shows in the United States, I talk exclusively about its rules; UKC has a similar set of rules. If you decide to go the UKC route, you need to determine what the UKC rules are and how they differ from AKC rules. AKC requirements for showing indicate that your dog must

✔ Be registered with the American Kennel Club with a full (not limited) registration.

✔ Have parents who either have or were working toward conformation titles. This requirement establishes that your dog is from show lines.

✔ Come from a breeder who thinks your dog is show quality and knows you're going to show him.

✔ Conform to the individual breed standard with no disqualifications and few flaws.

- Be intact — not neutered or spayed. You may be surprised that you have to have an intact dog, but AKC rules require that the dog be breeding stock, so dog shows are not simply beauty pageants.

- Be six months or older.

- Be trained to stack and to gait properly around the ring.

Earning a championship title

The two reasons for showing dogs are to obtain championship points and to campaign a dog who has already earned champion status (that is, show the dog off as a champion and let him or her compete against other champions). Dogs must obtain 15 championship points to earn a championship title. When campaigning a champion, breeders are showing their dog against other dogs who are champions; the more a dog wins, the closer he or she gets to being a top-ranked dog. (AKC and the breed clubs keep track of who's ahead.) But the situation gets much more complicated than that.

Dogs who are not yet champions must win best dog of their sex — that is, either Winners Dog or Winners Bitch of their particular breed. If they win over all other untitled dogs in their breed, they earn points. The number of points awarded depends on the breed, the region of the country, and the number of dogs competing at a given show. If the dog wins over a small number of dogs, for example, the award is considered a *minor* and earns the dog one or two points. The maximum number of minor points that can apply toward a dog's championship title is nine points. If a dog wins against many other dogs, the award is considered a *major.* A major win is worth three, four, or five points. Any dog that wins points goes up against the champions for the Best of Breed competition.

When your dog goes up against other dogs in the ring, you can win various ribbons. In the competition for dogs who aren't yet champions, your dog can win a fourth-place through first-place ribbon. The dogs who win first place go on to the Winners Dog and Winners Bitch competitions. A dog who's runner-up to the Winners Dog or Winners Bitch wins Reserve Winners Dog or Reserve Winners Bitch.

The Winners Dog and Winners Bitch go into the Best of Breed Competition. The dog can win Best of Breed, Best of Winners, or Best of Opposite Sex. (Best of Opposite Sex is the best dog who's the sex opposite that of the Best of Breed winner. So if a male wins Best of Breed, the very best female dog will be picked as Best of Opposite Sex, and vice versa.) The Best of Breed advances to the Group competition, where the dog can win Best of Group. In turn, the dogs who win Best of Group advance to the Best in Show competition.

After a dog earns a championship, a *CH* is placed in front of his or her AKC name, such as *CH* Skywarrior's Mishka Ice Dragon. But that isn't the end of the road. After a dog achieves championship status, he or she can enter competitions only for Best of Breed or for any higher competitions, such as Best in Group and Best in Show. But those kinds of shows are where the fun begins, because competition advances a whole other level.

Showing dogs can be a costly endeavor not only in terms of show fees but also in terms of time, fuel, food, and lodging expenses. People caught up with the show bug often pay thousands of dollars each year to earn champion status for their dogs and then campaign them afterward. If you live in an area where shows are infrequent, you may have to travel great distances to earn majors.

Wow! That sounds like a lot, doesn't it? So much, in fact, that you may be wondering why dog owners even bother. That's easy — dog shows are to show off a breeder's stock and to judge the best of the best. The dog may even win points toward being a champion (check out the "Earning a championship title" sidebar for more information about dog show prizes). What do you get as a groomer? The satisfaction of a dog who wins, of course.

Going to the show is more that just showing up. Your dog needs to be trained to gait, stand, and stack, and the best way to develop these skills is to take a conformation class at a professional trainer's facility or to have a breeder or handler teach you how to handle the dog. Here's what those three skills entail:

- ✔ **Gaiting:** This is the way your dog moves beside you. In most cases, the correct gait is a trot (see Figure 18-1), but occasionally, certain breed standards require a different gait.

- ✔ **Standing:** Standing a dog is just as it sounds — getting a dog to stand in one place.

- ✔ **Stacking:** Stacking a dog is a type of pose that has the dog stand straight with his legs positioned so that he looks solid. A well-stacked dog stands straight with all four paws facing straight ahead, positioned directly under the shoulders, and a body that looks more or less square. Good handlers can stack their dogs (literally manipulating the dog into position) to minimize the dogs' respective flaws (too long or short of a back, cow hocks, or whatever).

You train a dog how to stack by *baiting* him, or by using yummy treats so he looks attentive and alert (think about the look your dog gives you when he's begging for food). You give the treat when your dog is in the proper position.

Most dog-show handlers stack their dogs, but some dogs *free stack;* that is, they stack themselves whenever the owner or handler shows them food.

If you think your dog has what it takes to show well, sign up for a show in your area. You must sign up for AKC shows months in advance, and the cost can be anywhere from $20 to $30 per class per show (usually one show per day). You need to have your dog's registered name, AKC number, breeder info, and other pertinent information on your dog's AKC registration.

Then you can let the grooming begin! If your dog isn't clean, the judge is unlikely to pick him, because he doesn't look presentable. Likewise, certain approved appearances, or looks, are set for each dog. For example, some dog breeds call for no scissoring or trimming the coat; others require certain cuts as being acceptable for show. The following sections help prepare you and your dog for the exciting experience of participating in a show.

Figure 18-1:
Show dogs strut their stuff as they gait around the ring.

Grooming for the Show

So, you've decided that your dog is show quality, you understand what's required to win those points, you've registered for the show, and you've received your dog's confirmation (the dog show organizers send you a card that confirms you're registered). Now you need to figure out just how to properly prepare your dog for the big show. Quite honestly, you're going to brush, comb, bathe, and blow-dry your dog exactly the way you would a pet, but you're going to be using more coat conditioners, and if you clip your dog, the style is going to be one that's allowable by the breed standard. That usually means maintaining a show clip year-round or at least before and while the dog is showing.

You'd think that in the conformation ring, having better conformation is the most important. Well, that's true, but how well-groomed your dog looks is crucial, too. So do yourself and your dog a favor: Show a clean and sweet-smelling pooch.

Successfully grooming your dog for a show requires planning well in advance of the show so you don't run into any surprises the day of the show. The following sections help you prepare for the big day.

Trimming whiskers

Some show people like to trim whiskers. I don't, because I think they're an important part of the dog, and besides, they're very sensitive. Trimming whiskers is more of an option than anything, and most standards don't call for it. The point of trimming the whiskers is creating the type of look that the show person wants to convey. For example, trimming whiskers (or not) can soften or harden the look of the dog, depending on the shape of the head. In a small or long-muzzled dog, clipping the whiskers emphasizes the shape and makes it look smaller. So if your dog happens to have a nose that's a bit snippy (where the muzzle is pointed or weak), trimming the whiskers overemphasizes that point, which isn't desirable. However, on a dog whose muzzle is blocky, trimming the whiskers can make it look a little less rough.

Use scissors to trim whiskers, but be careful — one slip can send your dog to the emergency vet.

In the weeks leading up to the show

Getting a show coat in optimum condition can take months if your dog's coat isn't ready. If you're planning on showing, start shaping the dog's coat at least six months in advance of the show. Check out your particular dog's breed standard and clipping requirements. For example, if you have a dog with a clipped or stripped coat, you must start preparing the coat for show months or weeks in advance. That means that each week, you either clip or roll the coat (see Chapters 11 and 12).

Although grooming can't fix a real fault, good, focused grooming well in advance can, on occasion, diminish a flaw to the point to where it isn't quite as noticeable. This tactic is helpful when showing, because dogs don't spend much time in front of a judge in the ring to begin with, and if your dog truly is a good specimen with the exception of that one flaw, the judge may decide the flaw really isn't that important, if you've done everything you can to minimize it.

The night before the big event

On the night before you show your dog, you probably don't want to wait up just to hear David Letterman's Top Ten, so in its place, I give you the top ten steps you need to follow the night before the big show:

1. **Brush out your dog's coat.**

2. **Do any prebath clipping as required.**

3. Trim toenails.

4. Clean ears.

5. Express anal sacs if needed.

6. Bathe your dog.

7. Blow-dry your dog.

8. Brush out your dog's coat.

9. Do any postbath clipping.

10. Keep your dog clean.

    That means crating him when it's bedtime and walking him on a leash when outside.

Now that your dog is taken care of, what about you? Yes, you, too, are going to have to look smart for the show. That means a suit if you're a guy and a dress or pantsuit if you're a woman. (Occasionally, you can get by without suit coats and jackets.) No jeans or grubbies. You're supposed to look as good as your dog!

One change to the dressed-up ensemble is that you have to have really good shoes for running about and moving. That means no high heels and no dress shoes. Sneakers or shoes with good support and good tread are a must.

People usually bring two outfits to the show: One comfortable outfit to groom in and one outfit to show in. If you're worried you won't be able to find a place to change, simply wear your showing outfit and bring a groomer's apron to keep most of the hair off you.

The morning of the show

The day of the big show has arrived, and you need to put your dog through a normal routine so the both of you are ready for the show ring. Here are the steps you need to take the morning of the show:

1. Keep your dog clean by using a *snood* or other ear/hair covering, and always walk your dog on a leash.

2. Brush out your dog's coat and check for areas that may need touch-up clipping.

3. Use leave-in coat conditioners if your breed and/or dog requires them (for example, your dog may need coat dressings, bodifiers, and texturizers to help make the coat look and feel the way it's supposed to).

4. **Prepare your dog's crate and get your equipment ready for the show. Here are some items you need to have:**

   - Bait pouch
   - Battery-operated portable fans (for summertime or warmer environs)
   - Bed and blankets for the dog in wintertime
   - Combs and brushes
   - Coverings like snoods to keep hair from dragging
   - Crate for your dog
   - Cut-up liver, meats, cheeses, or compressed meat rolls in tiny portions
   - Dog food
   - Electric clippers
   - Folding grooming table
   - Grooming apron
   - Leave-in coat conditioners and bodifiers
   - Mat (for shows on dirt)
   - No-rinse shampoo (blue groomer's soap)
   - Paper towels
   - Pet bowls (for food and water)
   - Plastic bags for trash and wrapping up dirty towels
   - Plastic basin (for keeping chalk off floors or for using no-rinse shampoo)
   - Poop cleanup bags or scoops
   - Rugged tack box (for all the stuff you're hauling around)
   - Show slip-collar and leash (preferably close to your dog's color) or show martingale (standard show collars and leads that are available online and through catalog supply retailers)
   - Spray bottles with water and other coat products
   - Toenail trimmers or grinders
   - Traveling dryer
   - Water jugs (with water), as most show sites don't have a good and easy access to water
   - Washcloths and towels
   - X-pens or exercise pens

Petiquette

Most people don't think about etiquette when it comes to their dogs, but good manners really are a necessity. Rude dog owners have made bad impressions, so much so that many hotel people don't want to play host to any traveling pets. That's a shame, because so many conscientious pet owners are out there. I'm sure you're one of them!

But (lest you forget) here are some tips for taking your dog out in public:

- Make sure your dog has basic obedience training and basic housetraining.

- Keep your dog on a leash at all times.

- Never yell or punish your dog in public — it really looks bad.

- Don't try to sneak your dog into a hotel or other place that doesn't allow dogs. They'll know, trust me.

- Always crate your dog when you can't watch him.

- Don't leave your dog alone so he can bark in the room (or anyplace else, for that matter) and disturb other guests.

- Room service is your friend. Use it.

- If your dog must sleep on the bed, put your own blanket or towel where your dog sleeps to keep hair off the bed.

- Place your dog's food and water bowls in the bathroom so it's easy to clean up if anything spills.

- Don't let your dog run loose.

- Don't bathe your dog in the tub, and don't groom your dog in the room. Bathe your dog at home, and groom your dog at the show site.

Without a doubt, you'll think of other things to add to this list as you gain more show experience. The main thing to remember is that you want to keep your dog looking good and feeling healthy and comfortable — cool in the summer and warm in the winter. Depending on how far you travel to shows, you want to have enough gear to handle any grooming that you need to do while on the road.

Putting on the Finishing Touches at the Show

When you arrive on the show grounds, you're likely to see a lot of confusing activity. There'll be people rushing about with their dogs on leads, people trying to do some last-minute grooming, and people just taking in the sights.

Arrive early at the dog show site. Finding the ring you're in (which should be printed on the judging schedule you should've received in the mail before the show), getting your armband for identification, and checking in with the *ring steward* (the person in charge of checking everyone in and making sure each round goes as scheduled) take a lot of time.

If you have enough time, you can stake out a place to groom your dog in the designated grooming area. Sometimes — but not always — these areas are assigned to certain breeds, so look for a place where your breed may be. If there's a space where you can set up your table and finish grooming, great! Otherwise, use any place you can find (even out in the parking lot, as long as it's not raining or too cold).

Touching up before entering the ring

Even if you make it through the morning routine with flying colors and you arrive at the show thinking your dog's ready to score some points toward a championship title, make sure that you take the time to go through these four steps:

1. **Brush out your dog's coat and check for any areas that need touch-up clipping.**

2. **Touch up any place that needs to be touched up.**

3. **Keep your dog clean until it's time to get in the ring.**

4. **Relax and have fun!**

When it's ring time, give your dog one last spritz and use your comb to fluff her coat if you have to.

Although you may be ready to carry a whole bunch of spray bottles full of bodifier and conditioners and a comb and brush with you while you wait, resist the temptation. Don't do it, unless you have a friend handy to help you. After all, where are you going to put the stuff when the ring steward calls your dog's number? If you have to bring something, take along a comb that you can slip in your pocket or on your armband before you head into the ring.

You'll probably have butterflies in your stomach. That's natural. But relax — you'll do fine. If you're nervous, your dog will most likely be nervous, too. The following section prepares you for your moment in the spotlight.

With everything going on at a show, it's easy to get distracted and forget to watch the time. Showing up late to your ring is bad news — the judge may not even let you show your dog if you're late, and it's doubtful you'll win, so be early just to be safe. You may have to wait for your turn, but being early and prepared is always better than being late.

Chalking it up

Chalking is a bit of a controversial topic.

Chalking is the addition of a substance like chalk, talcum powder, or cornstarch to a dog's legs to make the fur look whiter. Chalking adds body to the leg hairs, and in breeds where a larger-boned appearance is preferred, chalking can actually help you make your dog's legs look bigger. But when you groom your dog for a show, nothing that makes the dog's fur whiter or fuller than normal is supposed to be left over.

Chalking technically is against American Kennel Club rules, but the truth is, show people do it all the time, and nobody talks much about it. Of course, if your dog is walking around in a powdery cloud like the *Peanuts* character Pigpen, the judge may not be so understanding — your dog can be dismissed from the ring and disqualified. If you get caught chalking and are disqualified, don't blame me. Just, ahem, chalk it up to the fact that there are rules and then there are *rules*. And if you get a judge who goes by the letter of the law, then yeah, you're in deep trouble.

But like anything, you can chalk in a way that improves the appearance of your dog's legs but still removes most of the residue (the following steps tell you how). If you chalk your dog and do it right, not much of the powder will be left over in the fur. (Your dog won't walk in a cloud of white when you do.) The point is to get rid of as much of the substance as possible but still keep the look. Technically, you've brushed nearly all of the powder out. But there's still going to be some left in the coat; that can't be helped.

1. **Rub a product that's a little sticky all over the dog's legs, front and back.**

   I've found that Kolesterol (by Wella), a product found in the women's hair-care department, works really well for chalking. It's greasy enough to be sticky but goes on clear. Or you can use human hair mousse or gel.

2. **Apply the chalk powder (cornstarch or chalk) through your dog's legs, back and front.**

   You can buy chalk (and colored chalk) through grooming supply catalogs and online Internet retailers. I use cornstarch because it neither cuts the hairs on the legs nor results in the glittery appearance that real chalk or talcum powder sometimes can.

3. **Use a small slicker brush to brush the coat upward against the lay of the hair.**

   The leg hairs will puff out and become white (or whatever color you're using). Keep brushing upward until no more powder puffs into the air and the legs look white and pretty. Don't brush the hair back down along the lay or you defeat the purpose.

Because your dog has sticky stuff on his legs (with the chalk, of course), getting them dirty becomes easier. If you can, wait until you're at the show site before chalking your dog if you choose to do so.

Handling your dog in the show ring

The big moment has arrived. You've managed to keep your dog's coat clean and presentable, and you've found your way to the proper place in line for the show. The following sequence of events is what you can expect to take place next as you show your dog:

1. **When you get into the ring, you line up according to armband number and do a full circle around the ring when prompted by the judge.**

2. **Line up your dog in the stacked position in relationship to the other dogs (for more on stacking, see "Brushing Up on Dog Show Basics" at the beginning of the chapter).**

3. **The judge looks at all the dogs, one at a time, from the first through the last positions in the line, checking each dog's head, bite (the way the teeth are set), body, and rear, feeling the testicles on male dogs to determine whether the dog's intact and both testicles have descended properly.**

Now isn't really the time to adjust anything on your dog. Some show people may take a quick brush, but other than that, you pretty much have to leave your dog's coat be. The ring is not a grooming place.

Buying stuff at the dog show

One of the fun things about going to a dog show is visiting the vendors. Depending on the show, the vendors' booths may be many or few. You can often see and touch grooming equipment and other items at a dog show and buy things you normally wouldn't get at your pet supply store.

Dog shows are great for finding odd and different grooming items, such as special scissors (or shears) or things like snoods — devices that keep a dogs' hair from dragging. Because your dog is present at the show, you can often try these items on your dog to see whether they're really going to work.

Although you can find interesting and unusual items at a dog show, they can have extravagant or even out-of-reach prices, or they may be on sale as part of a show special. The best bargains usually happen on the last day of the show — if there are going to be any sales.

When you look for grooming supplies (like shampoo and conditioner), look for them in bulk, and look for items you can't just order from a catalog. Sometimes a dealer has an item on hand that you can otherwise order for less from the catalog. You can decide whether such items are something you want or need right away or whether you can wait until later to order. If the price at the show is close to the mail-order price, you may have to factor in how much shipping would cost or whether being able to immediately buy the items at the show is worthwhile.

If you decide to go shopping, try to do so only *after* you've shown your dog. That way, you won't get your dog dirty before entering the ring.

4. **After the judge finishes the individual examinations, he or she directs you to gait your dog, either in an up and back (diagonal) or triangle shape.**

   You may get away with running a comb through your dog's coat before you begin walking, but be careful. Often, grooming in the ring can annoy the judge, and you really don't want to do anything to annoy the judge.

   Be sure to stop your dog in front of the judge and stack her again before taking her around the ring and back into the lineup. When you return to the lineup, keep your dog stacked and looking good, but don't fuss too much (if at all) with combing (see Figure 18-2).

5. **After all the dogs have taken an individual turn, the judge asks the handlers to circle the dogs around the ring one more time together as he or she chooses (usually) the top four. Good luck!**

   If the judge doesn't choose the winners at this point in the competition, he or she may ask to look at two or three dogs again or may ask for the handlers to gait their dogs again. At large shows, the group may be split up, and the judge may choose several from each group to compete for placement.

Figure 18-2:
A little sprucing up in the ring is allowed to keep your dog looking great.

Chapter 19

Going Pro: Starting a Dog Grooming Business

*Y*ou've been grooming your dog for some time and find that you really enjoy doing it. And while helping your friends groom their dogs, too, maybe they've handed you $20 or so to keep Fifi looking great. Everyone says you ought to turn pro, but should you?

Then again, maybe you're looking for a career move. You like working with dogs, and you've heard that you can earn a pretty decent wage grooming them. Maybe the idea of being your own boss sounds appealing, but how do you go about it?

In this chapter, I tell you what it's like to turn pro and to start your own business in the field of dog grooming. You'll find out various pitfalls of working for yourself, and I help you determine whether you really can do it.

Deciding Whether Professional Grooming Is Right for You

Now that you've honed your dog grooming skills, you're finding that the oohs and ahhs recognizing your beautiful dog are turning to dollars and cents. The word is spreading, and those neighbors who once slipped you some cash for doing a good job taking care of their pooches now are telling all their friends about you. You're almost there, right? You're almost in business for yourself.

Tallying up how much groomers make

Arguably, you can make pretty good money as a pet groomer. In a 2004 survey of more than 3,000 respondents, PetGroomer.com found that 31 percent of respondents made $30,000 to $50,000 a year, and 40 percent made $50,000 to $75,000 a year. Twelve percent made less than $30,000, and 17 percent made more than that in gross business earnings. These amounts don't account for business expenses, but 60 percent of the groomers who were self-employed said they made between $20,000 and $40,000 before taxes and after business expenses.

Well, almost. However, running a business is a bit more than hanging out a shingle and setting up shop. You must deal with customers, marketing, and with rules and regulations governing businesses. And, of course, you need to know about the liabilities associated with opening your own business. But first, you need to check out all the pros and cons of owning your own business.

Weighing the pros and cons of starting a grooming business

Owning your own business can be a dream come true or a nightmare, depending on your willingness to work and your entrepreneurial spirit. Here are some valid reasons for wanting to own your own grooming business:

✔ You like being your own boss.

✔ You like setting your own hours.

✔ You hate having your paycheck limited by a boss or a company.

✔ You want to have control over your success (and failure).

✔ You want the freedom to work when you choose and where you choose.

✔ You can choose who you work with.

✔ You enjoy challenges.

✔ You love working with and meeting people and dogs.

Many other reasons exist for becoming a business owner, but the ones in this list are the main ones.

Just as there are positives for becoming a business owner, here also are some of the negatives to owning a business:

- Cash flow typically is uncertain and can be unsteady.

- Someone (you or someone you hire) needs to do the bookkeeping chores and pay taxes.

- Your income must be reported to the IRS, and you're double-taxed for Social Security.

- You need to work long hours, lift heavy objects (dogs included), and risk possible injury.

- You run the risk of being bitten — not all dogs are nice.

- You may have to deal with snarky or downright rude pet owners.

- If you're sick or take a vacation, nobody is paying you.

- You must have investment or start-up capital (money) to get your business off the ground. Depending on the type of business, it can run a few thousand to several thousand dollars.

- Bad things happen to businesses all the time, which are not your fault: burglaries, disasters, or other problems can mean lost money and time.

- You have to maintain insurance coverage and pay proper bonding fees because you may be sued for injuring a dog or for other business practices.

- You have to work not just with dogs but also with their owners — and that isn't always pleasant.

- The first year is often low pay or no pay, so you have to stay motivated, even during lousy times when the business isn't doing so well.

- You have no safety net — you either sink or swim.

You may be thinking, "Wow, that sure is a bunch of negatives," and you'd be right. That's why not everyone owns their own business, but instead some choose to work for someone else or another company.

Considering whether you're ready to be the boss

Before you get too embroiled with the thought of having your own business, you need to find out whether you have the time, money, and ability needed to start a business.

If you're currently unemployed, time isn't so much a factor, but if you have a full-time day job, planning to start a grooming business on the side may take up what little time you have left.

Money is a requirement, too. Can you get the loans necessary to start your business from a bank? Or do you have enough cash stockpiled? Or maybe you have friends or family willing to invest in your business? In most cases, you'll need thousands of dollars to get started.

Where are you planning to work in your grooming business? Out of your home? In a separate shop someplace? Or are you going to be a mobile groomer? The cheapest (and most inconvenient) is to work from home, but doing so can have drawbacks, such as obtaining the proper zoning and deciding whether your neighborhood permits home-based businesses. A separate shop costs quite a bit in rent and refurbishing, and a mobile salon requires at least a van or an SUV with enough room to carry all your supplies.

Foremost, starting a business and working for yourself take a mind-boggling amount of effort. Taking a day off here and there is fine, provided you have the money to carry you through. However, when you own your own business, you can't just call in sick on a day when your schedule is filled with customers. And don't forget the paperwork, the taxes, and of course, dealing with clients. When you're the boss you have to wear many different hats.

Evaluating the need in your area

This question may seem a little strange, but even if you have the ability and the money to start a new business, should you? Part of being successful in a business is fulfilling a need. First you need to assess where you intend to operate your business to find out whether a market exists for your services and whether much competition already exists there. If several groomers are in your area, you need to determine whether there's room for another one.

Check out the Yellow Pages or an online directory to search for dog groomers and see who is working in your area. If you find fewer groomers than you'd expect, then perhaps the time is right to start a business in the area. If not, perhaps you need to look for a business owner nearby who is looking for help.

The other problem is if there are lots of groomers in your area, you may be forced into a price structure that is comparable or at least competitive with what is out there. If fact, you may have to offer lower rates to entice pet owners to use your business when there are established businesses in your area.

Sometimes pairing yourself with a veterinarian or a pet supply store can help get your business off the ground. Although you may have to sacrifice some money that you'd normally make, you nevertheless develop a clientele that you may be able to take with you if you choose to open up your own shop.

A perceived lack of groomers may signal another problem. In some places, dog owners may consider that grooming is just for froufrou dogs or a luxury they can't afford. Do your research and find out before investing time and money in a business that no one wants to patronize.

Training

You may have heard that you need to be certified to groom dogs professionally. Actually, you don't have to be certified to be a groomer or open a grooming business, but certification looks good to savvy customers and ensures that you're up-to-date with the latest techniques.

But to be able to consider yourself a professional groomer, regardless of whether you're certified, you need to hone your skills through training that you can get nearly anywhere. You can be self-taught, learning grooming skills by working on your own, your friends' and other people's dogs; you can be hired on with another groomer who's interested in getting some help in exchange for teaching you how to groom; or you can attend a formal grooming school or take correspondence courses. The sections that follow weigh the pros and cons of each training option.

No training method alone is better than another. How you develop your skills depends on how much time and effort you put into improving your skills *and* your willingness to learn the trade.

Heading back to school

If you're serious about diving headlong into becoming a professional groomer, you can take grooming classes at a grooming school. Grooming schools provide major advantages, but they also have some disadvantages. The advantages are that you can

- ✔ Learn grooming in a hands-on, structured environment.
- ✔ Learn the trade from the pros who are intent on teaching you how to groom a pet properly and safely.
- ✔ Focus on classes you want to take in addition to the basic instruction.

✔ Receive feedback. You know how well you're doing or whether you need to work harder.

✔ Earn certifications from some of the schools, or you can at least earn a diploma.

✔ Discover how to be a pro groomer in a definitive amount of time.

The disadvantages of grooming school are that they're

✔ Costly. Most schools are pretty expensive. Some have financial aid for students.

✔ Not always conveniently located. If one isn't close by, you have to either move or at least spend some time at the school, thus uprooting your household.

✔ Not always easy to attend while working a second job.

✔ Schools. Remember tests? Lectures? More tests? Long hours of studying?

✔ Competitive. You may be surprised to know there's a fair amount of pressure to do well.

Okay, so you're convinced school is the way for you to go. Now, where do you find good grooming schools? You can contact:

✔ The National Dog Groomers Association of America (NDGAA), www. nationaldoggroomers.com, 724-962-2711.

✔ International Professional Groomers (IPG), www.nanhall.com/ grmipg.htm, 847-758-1938.

✔ International Society of Canine Cosmetologists (ISCC), www.pet stylist.com/ISCC/ISCCMain.htm, 972-414-9715.

✔ PetGroomer.com, www.petgroomer.com.

If you want your schooling to include certification of your grooming skills, check out the first three Web sites in the previous list. They explain what certification is, offer programs aimed at certification, and tell you where and when you can take grooming certification exams.

Another way you can find a grooming school online is to use DexOnline.com or search for "schools" on a favorite Web search engine.

Going to school isn't a picnic, so if you decide to follow this route, be sure the school you attend is the right one for you. Here are some questions to ask:

✔ Is the school licensed and accredited? If so, by whom? Schools that are licensed and accredited are likely to give you good training and not be a rip off.

✔ Do graduates of the program receive certification or diplomas after successfully completing the course?

✔ Does the school teach grooming only for dogs or does it incorporate the grooming needs of other pets?

✔ How long does it take to complete the coursework?

✔ How long has the school been in existence?

✔ Who teaches the classes? What credentials do they have? Can you talk to the teachers?

✔ How much is tuition? What other purchases do you have to make?

✔ Can the school provide any references (graduates, groomers, teachers, and so on)?

Ask other groomers you know whether they've heard of the school and what its reputation is like. You don't want to spend a lot of money only to find out that your diploma isn't worth the paper it's printed on.

Taking correspondence courses

Correspondence courses are another way to get training. They are much like teaching yourself, except that you usually have a mentor or someone whom you can ask questions and give you appropriate feedback. You've probably seen commercials on TV for courses such as Thomson Education Direct (www.educationdirect.com, 800-275-4410). I actually wrote a couple of course books on its Dog Trainer/Obedience Instructor courses, so I know a little bit about them. Other correspondence schools are out there, but before you choose one, make sure that it's licensed and accredited.

Many correspondence courses make use of booklets, tests, and videos. The downside to these courses, however, is that you don't get the hands-on training that a regular school environment provides. By the same token, correspondence courses enable you to learn at your own pace.

Taking a correspondence course has its own distinct pros and cons. The positive sides are

- Taking the course in your spare time, without quitting your current job or leaving home.

- Getting feedback through tests and other evaluations (you usually send in videos and photos for evaluation).

- Avoiding travel to faraway grooming schools.

- Learning at your own pace.

- Receiving a certification and sometimes accreditation when you complete the course.

- Having someone to ask questions, get advice from, and in general, serve as your mentor while taking the course. In many correspondence courses, some schools have on-staff experts who are available via phone and e-mail for consultation.

The downsides of correspondence courses are that they:

- Lack a teacher. Not having anyone to actually teach you can be rough.

- Can be expensive.

- Take longer than if you were trained at a school.

- May let you fall through the cracks; your mistakes may not be caught.

- Rely on testing that can put (undo) pressure on you.

- May not be reputable nor prestigious.

The biggest downside to correspondence courses is finding out whether they're truly reputable and legitimate. After all, you don't want to spend a boatload of money and have nothing to show for it. Ask around.

One place to look for correspondence courses is on PetGroomer.com (www.petgroomer.com).

After you compile a list of correspondence courses, call them up and ask questions. Here are some questions you may want to ask:

- Are the courses licensed and accredited? If so, by whom?

- Do you receive certification or diplomas after successfully completing the course?

- Do the courses apply only to dog grooming or do they incorporate grooming needs of other pets?

- How long does it take to complete the coursework?

- How long has this correspondence course existed? How long has the school been in existence?

✔ Is the school a member of the Better Business Bureau? (If so, contact the BBB and ask about complaints.)

✔ Who wrote the courses (what are their credentials)? Were they written by one or several professionals?

✔ Can the school provide any references (graduates, groomers, teachers, and so on)?

You may also want to ask any professional groomers you know whether they've heard of the correspondence course and what their opinions of it are.

Working for an established groomer

Nothing is like hands-on experience when it comes to learning how to do something. What better way to find out about grooming than to work for a professional groomer who can show you the ropes?

Finding a groomer who's willing to take you on may be as easy as walking into a grooming shop or answering a want ad. If you currently have a groomer, she may be a good place to start. Otherwise, you may have to get a little more creative. Asking veterinarians or dog trainers in your area may turn up something.

Working for a groomer has its benefits and pitfalls. Some of the benefits are:

✔ Getting to watch a professional groomer at work using all the techniques that you're hoping to learn.

✔ Having someone watch over you and show you new skills and point out when you're doing something wrong.

✔ Earning money while you learn.

✔ No real studying; just hands-on experience.

✔ Having someone to ask questions and get advice.

The downsides to working for a groomer are:

✔ Low pay. Need I say more?

✔ Scut work. You may be relegated to cleaning floors and tubs and other dirty jobs.

✔ Poor or inflexible hours. You're working according to a schedule someone else has dictated. It's a job, and you have to treat it as such.

✔ More scrutiny. When you mess up, the groomer may not look so kindly on you. After all, you're affecting *her* business!

✔ Less of an opportunity to do actual grooming than you expect. You may not get to watch the groomer groom dogs because you're so busy cleaning crates or mopping the floors. Granted you'll see the whole side of grooming, but you may not learn as much as you'd hoped.

✔ You can have personality clashes with the groomer.

Quitting a high-paying position to go to work for a groomer in an entry-level, minimum wage job can be devastating, especially if you find out that you're not really cut out for grooming. Also, be aware that if you do work, you *must* be paid. That's an employment law in the United States. You must be paid at least minimum wage for each hour you work. Don't let anyone trick you into thinking that this kind of work is an internship for which you don't get paid. If you work, you get paid.

Home-schooling yourself

One of the ways you can learn about dog grooming is to teach yourself. It's a fairly inexpensive method. You buy some books, and you practice on your dog and your friends' dogs to find out how to do some techniques.

The positives of home schooling are that you:

✔ Teach yourself in your spare time without quitting your current job or leaving home.

✔ Don't have to take any tests and have no real pressure.

✔ Don't have the expenses associated with attending school or taking a correspondence course. You learn by reading books, watching videos, and trying the techniques out on your dog.

✔ Avoid travel to faraway grooming schools. Home schooling is good for folks who live in the country where groomers may be rare.

✔ Learn at your own pace.

✔ Create your own well-blended education by being able to learn from many different books and methods.

The downsides of teaching yourself are that you:

✔ Have no one to show you whether you're doing something wrong.

✔ Won't have the opportunity to work on as many different breeds and different dogs as you would in a school environment.

✔ Can't rely on an expert being close at hand to answer your questions.

✔ Won't receive any accreditation or certification.

✔ Take more time than if you trained with a school.

Getting Down to Business

Opening a dog-grooming business, regardless of whether it's in your home or in a shop at one of the local strip malls, means that you must take care of some legal matters, such as choosing just how you want to operate your business.

Choosing how to set up your business

You must choose between three ways that you can operate as a professional groomer. You can do business as a sole proprietor, as an incorporated entity, or as a limited liability company. All three have advantages and disadvantages.

Before you embark on any business endeavor, however, you need to seek the advice of an accountant or perhaps even an attorney who is familiar with setting up businesses.

Stepping out on your own as a sole proprietor

A sole proprietorship is the easiest way to start a business, but it's also the most risky. In essence, you hang out your shingle and get paid by customers. The money you make is yours to keep, and you don't have to mess with separate tax identification numbers and whatnot. What could be easier? Well, read on.

The downside to opening for business as a sole proprietorship is that anything that you do wrong can make your personal assets (the house, the car) vulnerable. Lawsuits will be aimed directly at you and not against an entity like a corporation.

Big business: Incorporating

The second way you can operate your grooming business is as a corporation. Various types of corporations exist, but for the moment, I'll discuss the *S* Corporation. Many small businesses are *S* Corporations, because operating as one provides good protection, and the business entity can be sold, if need be.

The downside to incorporating is contending with the paperwork and the number of hoops you must jump through to get one started. Keep in mind that some types of corporations can be taxed more than individuals, so be sure that you talk to your accountant before deciding whether and how to incorporate.

The limited liability company

A fairly new way of doing business, the limited liability company (LLC) blends together parts of doing business as a corporation and as a sole proprietor. An LLC enables one or two people to operate a business like a sole proprietorship in some ways and like a corporation in others. However, because not all states recognize LLCs and not all LLCs are the same, be sure to talk to someone who's experienced at setting one up before you decide to take this route with your grooming business.

Creating a business plan

When you start thinking about operating a business, you need to put together a business plan. All successful businesses have one, and even a vague plan is better than no plan at all. By putting down where you want to go and choosing the methods you'll use to get there, you'll be ahead of your competition.

For example, your business plan needs to specify what type of grooming business you want to open. It needs to say whether you're operating:

- ✔ A home-based business where you groom out of your home.
- ✔ A standalone grooming business usually with only one groomer.
- ✔ A small to medium business with employees who groom.
- ✔ A mobile grooming business.
- ✔ A business adjacent to a veterinarian, training facility, boarding kennels, or pet supply store.

Think about which type of grooming business you'd like and determine whether you'd like to offer other services, such as training, boarding, or supplies. The clearer you are about what your business will be, the more successful you're likely to be.

An accountant can help you formulate a business plan, or check out *Business Plans For Dummies* by Paul Tiffany and Steven D. Peterson (Wiley) for more information.

Securing licensing

Currently none of the 50 states in the United States require groomers to be licensed. In fact, anyone can become a professional groomer as long as he or she fills out the right forms. It's as simple as opening up a shop and hanging out a sign.

Depending on the type of business you choose to operate (see the earlier section on "Choosing how to set up your business"), you'll have to fill out the appropriate business forms, and if your state requires service and sales-tax licenses, you'll have to apply for them. Beyond that, you may want to check with your state government to find out about any requirements to which professionals who work with animal professionals must adhere.

Paying taxes

One downside of working for yourself is that you must pay your own taxes rather than having your employer withhold them for you. So you need to get in touch with an accountant who can explain quarterly tax filings and payments and provide other information about dealing with the IRS.

Now that you're self-employed, your social security tax (FICA) is twice the amount you paid before. Why is that? Because before you were self-employed, your employer paid the same amount you did. When you become self-employed, you get hit with the entire tax.

Setting Up Shop

You have your training, applied for your business and sales licenses, checked with your accountant and attorney, and now you're ready to set up shop. What next? Read on!

Finding a workspace

Where you plan to operate your grooming business is the most important decision you need to make as you set up shop. You have a few choices, including in your home, as a standalone shop, or in conjunction with another business?

Working at home alone

Many first-time groomers set up shop right out of their homes, but before you hang out your sign, you need to understand the zoning of your home and how local ordinances affect a home-based business in a residential area. No matter how good of a neighbor you are, some nosy busybody neighbor is going to take an interest in the customers showing up at your doorstep. And if you're violating any covenants or ordinances, you're bound to have your homeowners' association or the county zoning officer show up at your front door.

Ordinances and covenants are enacted for specific reasons. The most obvious reason is traffic and congestion. Although you may have only a client or two show up every day, think of what would happen to your street if everyone was running businesses out of their homes. Your quiet, sleepy suburban neighborhood would quickly devolve into a busy thoroughfare. Well, maybe not. But that's how the zoning commissions and homeowners' associations see it.

Assuming that you can get around the zoning and covenant problems, working out of your home can be a hassle unless you have a separate shop. Do you have enough parking for customers? What about access for folks with disabilities? Yes, the Americans with Disabilities Act applies to your business, too.

Although working from home can be wonderful, it can also be terribly distracting. Your family and friends can pop in and make demands on the time you'd otherwise be devoting to working on a customer's dog — you know, making money. Then there's the TV and the gallon of ice cream in the fridge . . .

And don't forget about the client who's late picking up the dog while you're left waiting with the pooch until the owner shows up. However, by the same token, you can also throw in a load of laundry or start dinner, if a client turns out to be a no show — and believe me that will happen.

If you become successful as a groomer, at some point, you'll be looking either to expand your shop inside your home or have to find another place to work.

A shop of your own

In most cases, situating business where your homeowners' association and zoning officers won't nag you — someplace where it's allowed — is best. Your kids will just have to make a special trip (or call you) when you have your own shop, and there's no ice cream in the fridge unless you really want it there.

Another great reason for having a separate shop is for tax purposes. By having a place of business outside of your home, you can deduct all operating expenses and prove to the IRS that you're truly operating a business — something that's pretty hard to do working from home.

Where you put your separate shop is important. You need to look for a place that's in a busy area (like a strip mall) where no other groomers are present. A veterinarian's or a pet-supply store, on the other hand, is a bonus. Although the areas I mentioned are prime locations, they're often accompanied by prime costs. The point is you need to be in an area where people can see your business.

Be careful about getting a bargain location that's out of the way and off the beaten path. A place that doesn't get much traffic can spell disaster for a new business. You can choose to move to a less trafficked site after you've established a good client base.

Sharing the load

What if you just don't have the investment capital for opening your own shop? Believe it or not, you still have options that will allow you to remain self-employed, including:

- ✔ **A mutual arrangement:** Having a standalone business can be costly, so if you don't have the investment capital to open your own business or rent a shop, try asking a veterinarian, a pet-supply store, or other pet-oriented business whether you can rent space from them to do grooming. Such an arrangement can be mutually beneficial to both parties. You benefit by having a place to do your work and from customers you gain through the regular patronage of the business, and the business benefits from the rent you pay and from being able to provide yet another added service to its customers.

    This type of arrangement is wonderful for a startup groomer, because it provides an instant client base. Anyone who walks into the business is automatically a potential customer for you.

- ✔ **Contract grooming:** Another possibility is freelance work in someone else's grooming shop. Instead of being a direct employee of the groomer, you work on a contractual basis, meaning the shop owner gets a cut out of what you get paid. Say, for example, that the shop owner takes 20 percent of your earnings. If you charge clients $30 for bathing their dogs, you get $24, and the shop owner gets $6. Just make sure that when you enter this type of arrangement that you have all of details worked out in writing.

On the go: Mobile grooming

Like setting up a grooming shop, mobile grooming is a big investment. You need a van, RV, or SUV that's been converted to handle grooming. On the low end, a grooming van carries your equipment and maybe a portable tub and water heater. On the high end, your grooming vehicle can be a retrofitted van or RV complete with a grooming tub and all the accoutrements you need. The latter can cost anywhere from $30,000 to $75,000.

The biggest advantage of mobile grooming is that you go where your customers are, which is ideal for people who can't get out, people who lead busy lives, and people who live in areas where groomers are few and far between. What's more, you can charge premium prices because of the service factor.

Be aware that gasoline prices can severely affect your bottom line. Although other groomers may charge $35 to $50 for a complete grooming session, you may have to price your services from $40 to $70 or more to cover your traveling expenses, including gas. And while you may not have rent or utilities to pay, you may have a big truck finance and insurance payment every month.

Obtaining insurance and bonding

Making sure your new business is properly insured and that you're adequately bonded are a couple of the first things you need to do before you open your shop. Not only do you need insurance on your property for fire, theft, and other catastrophes, but also for liability. What if Fluffy bites Mrs. Smith? What if she then slips and falls in your shop and breaks a hip? Having enough liability insurance to cover you, your workers, and your customers is vitally important.

Bonding, or the monetary guarantee that you're a trustworthy individual and won't steal or damage something important to the client like a pet or other property, is another assurance you may want to obtain. You'll probably want to consider being bonded, especially if you're going to other people's homes to groom their dogs.

Ask an insurance representative for an evaluation of what your business needs in terms of insurance and bonding.

Be aware that if you have a home-based business, it won't be covered by your homeowner's policy if something happens. Get business insurance. It's worth it.

Purchasing supplies and equipment

If you're wondering what to do after you open your business, consider that money probably will be pretty tight, especially after you just laid down a huge chunk of change to rent a building or buy a mobile grooming salon. You're not going to feel like paying those high retail prices for supplies that you use everyday, so . . .

The good news is that you don't have to spend a lot. Now that you're a business, you can buy supplies and equipment wholesale from distributors. Just look for pet-supply distributors in the Yellow Pages, hop online and purchase your supplies from places like PetEdge (www.petedge.com), or look through groomer trade magazines like *Groomer-to-Groomer* (www.groomer togroomer.com).

There are also grooming seminars and trade shows around the country that offer hands-on demos and display every imaginable piece of grooming equipment known or sold to professional groomers. You can ask vendors and company reps all the questions you want. Plus the prices are reasonable. One place to find show listings is at the GroomTeam USA Web site (GroomTeamUSA.com).

You should probably buy the best equipment and supplies you can afford now to avoid problems in the future. But high cost doesn't always equal high quality. Shop around!

When mail-ordering supplies either from catalogs or off the Internet, be careful. The savings you get on the price may be eaten up by shipping costs. Likewise, be sure that the company you're buying from is reputable.

You can buy your business supplies at places like Office Depot, Office Max and other big box stores that now cater to businesses. Take a look at Costco and Sam's Club, too. Although you won't find many grooming supplies there, you can find other essentials like cleaners, mops, and containers at cheaper prices than you'd normally buy them.

Getting the word out: Marketing

In the business of dog grooming, marketing is everything. Your customers won't be your customers unless they can find you.

Word-of-mouth is the best kind of marketing to which any business can aspire, but until you actually attract customers who can rave about your work, you're pretty much stuck with marketing yourself.

An excellent book to consider when you're looking for extra help with promoting your new business is *Small Business Marketing For Dummies* by Barbara Schenck (Wiley). Another series worth looking into is the *Guerilla Marketing* series by Jay Conrad Levinson (Houghton Mifflin).

The sections that follow look at some of the ways that you can attract customers.

No matter which advertising strategy you decide to use, always ask your newfound customers how they heard about you and your business. In fact, you need to keep a log of how successful your marketing strategy has been. After a few months, you'll begin to see a pattern that tells you what's working and what isn't.

'Let your fingers do the walking'

Yes, the Yellow Pages are expensive, but where's the first place you turn to when you look for something — anything? If I'm looking for a specific business (especially something that's local), I either reach for the Yellow Pages or check DexOnline.com (dexonline.com), which is an online type of Yellow Pages. Anymore, it's almost as if I've been programmed to use these tools.

I bet you do that, too. The ubiquitous Yellow Pages have been part of society for a long time. It's a marketing tool, albeit an expensive one to advertise in. If you can at least get your business *listed* in the Yellow Pages under pet groomers and afford to buy a small box ad, many people will look at it. Having an ad in the Yellow Pages also makes you look more established than just someone with a single line.

Placing ads in local newspapers and circulars

Another way to attract attention is to place ads in local newspapers and circulars. Doing so has pluses and minuses that you need to consider. On one hand, your ad reaches the number of people that make up the publication's circulation, but on the other hand, whether you reach the right customers is debatable. Sure, the circular says it reaches 55,000 homes, but how many people actually open it up and read your ad as opposed to just tossing it away as a bit of junk mail? And, for that matter, how many people have pets who need grooming.

Other than the cost, there's no real harm in trying one or more of these ads. Some local newspapers are read voraciously by consumers. Others are simply ignored. In the town where I live, people always look at freebie ads in a newspaper format. If you want to find a local business, that's where you look.

Direct-mail advertising

Direct mail probably is the least effective form of advertising — somewhere between 0.5 percent to 2 percent of business is generated by direct-mail marketing. It's also somewhat costly — printing, postage, and mailing can amount to quite a sum. So if you mail your ad to 5,000 households, the best you can expect is 25 to 100 inquires. Obviously, the more households to which you send direct mail, the more customers you're likely to snag — but watch that postage meter.

Internet advertising

In this day and age, businesses without Web sites are left in the dust. Posting a Web page or at least a personalized URL is dirt cheap. In fact, if you have access to the Internet, your Internet service provider (ISP) may already provide a free Web page for you.

Having a Web site is a great way to attract customers and to announce coupons and specials. If you have a flair for writing articles and providing information (or you know someone else who does), you can direct your customers to read this free information (known as content). If they enjoy it, they'll pass along the information and links to your Web site to their friends. It's an easy way to get customers.

You can also create e-mail lists of your current customers, so you can keep in touch with them and let them know about current promotions. Plenty of e-mail list services can assist you. Yahoo! Groups (www.groups.yahoo.com) provide free LISTSERVs, that is list services that provide e-mail groups.

Never send out unsolicited advertising e-mail (Spam) hoping to attract clients. Not only will you tick off your potential clients by spamming them, you're also likely to be marked as a spammer, which may cause you to lose your Web site and e-mail privileges if it's reported to your ISP.

Posting flyers

Another way to attract attention to your new grooming business is to print flyers and post them on bulletin boards at pet-related businesses and grocery stores. Some places to consider might be vet offices, boarding kennels, training facilities, and anywhere dog owners might frequent.

Satisfying Your First Customers

Your first customers are often your most special customers. They're the folks who took a chance to hire you to take care of their pups, so you need to start making a good first impression with them right off the bat.

Exhibiting professionalism

Your sense of professionalism is the first thing that impresses new clients, so make sure it's well honed by:

- ✔ Answering the phone in a professional manner
- ✔ Setting up a schedule and reminding clients of their dogs' appointments
- ✔ Always treating clients courteously

Good business practices like these go a long way toward making new clients feel more comfortable about taking a chance with a new groomer — someone who looks and acts professionally. Keeping your shop clean and your attitude upbeat and courteous will make all the difference in the world.

When I was growing up, kids were told to address adults either by Mr. and Mrs. or Ms. Sadly, many people don't extend that courtesy anymore. If you want to amaze people with your politeness, try addressing Connie Smith as Ms. Smith, rather than Connie, for example. You'll be surprised at how they react to you.

You've probably heard the adage that "the customer is always right." For the most part, that's true. If your customers aren't happy, they'll be sure to tell the people they know just how unhappy they are, and that will hurt *your* reputation. Always try to fix a problem, even if it wasn't your fault.

You're in a service position. Although you shouldn't necessarily be a doormat, you also shouldn't be looking to argue with your customers. If you have an angry customer, your attitude never should be one of "get off my back." Instead, your attitude needs to be one of "How can I fix this?"

Dealing with difficult clients/difficult dogs

At some point, you're going to encounter difficult clients and difficult dogs. It's inevitable; there's no way around it.

It is your right to say no to anyone with a difficult dog. Getting bit isn't worth the amount you're going to make from this customer.

Unless the dog truly is aggressive, moving slowly, talking or singing to him nicely, or giving him treats should calm his fears. If you fear that a dog may bite, using a muzzle may be an option. But be aware that doing so does look bad in front of other clients, so you may want to use the muzzle away from where other clients can see. Remember that you should never leave a muzzle on a dog any longer than you absolutely have to.

More often, a difficult dog is one that hasn't been groomed for a long time and probably is a terrible mess. When that's the case, if the dog is so matted that you can't do anything, talk to the owner and explain that the best thing to do may be to shave the mats off and start working to maintain a good coat as it grows back in. Leave that decision, however, to the owner.

Unlike the difficult dog, the difficult client is hard to deal with. Be diplomatic and polite with these clients. The more professional you can be, the better.

You can always refuse to work on a difficult dog or with a difficult client. In most cases, that refusal means some revenue lost. But if you can, resolving those problems always is better.

Some tips to keep customers coming back

You've just started your shop. Congratulations! But now you need to know how to keep happy clients coming back again and again. Here are some suggestions:

✔ Greet both the customers and their dogs by their names.

✔ Have a bowl of biscuits ready as treats.

✔ Offer a referral bonus. Give clients who help you sign someone else up a discount. Take a certain percentage off their dog's next grooming session.

✔ Offer a discount near certain holidays.

✔ Offer a frequent groomer card (for example, with ten full grooms, you give the client something free).

✔ Be sure to know if your client's dog is a he or she. Owners hate it when you get it wrong!

✔ Make your clients and their dogs more comfortable while they're waiting, especially if the dog is in a crate — perhaps provide blankets to nap on and a toy.

✔ Make the waiting areas inviting. For example, provide free coffee.

✔ Keep grooming areas clean.

✔ Always return phone calls in a timely manner.

✔ Send thank-you cards to new customers.

Part V
The Part of Tens

The 5th Wave   By Rich Tennant

"We try to pay personal attention to the dog's grooming but it's time consuming and lately Agnes has been hacking up hair balls."

In this part . . .

In this part, I debunk ten myths about grooming dogs, share ten time-saving grooming tips, and provide expert advice for making grooming a pleasant experience for you and your pup. Enjoy!

Chapter 20

Ten Popular Myths About Grooming Dogs

*E*veryone's heard the urban legends about dogs. Unfortunately, you've probably heard so many strange stories through the years that you're likely to take some of them as fact even though they're fiction.

In this chapter, I bust a few of those myths about dogs. You may have heard these stories as truth, or you may have told them yourself. Now it's time to find out which ones are works of overactive imaginations.

Never Bathe Your Dog Unless He Is Really Dirty

A myth that I hear all the time is that you shouldn't bathe your dog unless he's dirty, because you'll dry out his coat or his coat needs those vital oils, or something to that effect.

If you show dogs, you know that claim just isn't true. But when you delve deeper into this myth, you find that at one time, it was true, primarily because shampoos weren't formulated to be pH-balanced with a dog's skin. Today's shampoos and conditioners for dogs are so well formulated that you can wash your dog every day without problems. You just have to make sure the shampoo you're using is pH-balanced.

At one time, everyone believed that taking baths or showers every day was bad. It isn't — we got over it and moved on. You can wash your dog whenever you want to now and not dry out his coat.

Certain Breeds Are Hypoallergenic

The popular myth that only certain dogs' coats are hypoallergenic and won't affect human allergies to dogs only recently started its rounds. This myth has become quite popular with the advent of *designer dogs,* that is crossbred dogs that come from two different breeds — Poodle + Labrador = Labradoodle.

The reasoning behind claims that dogs sport hypoallergenic coats is pretty simple. Poodles and other single-coated dogs don't shed as much as dogs with double coats do. So if you breed a Poodle with another breed, you'll have a shed-free dog — or so logic goes.

So is this one truly a myth or is it factual? Well, yes and no, but peoples' allergies are far more complex than that. Here's why hypoallergenic coats are a fallacy:

- ✔ People who are allergic to dogs aren't necessarily allergic to dog hair or even the dander produced by the dog's skin. They're often allergic to a protein the dog carries around, and thus they're often allergic to the dog's saliva.

- ✔ Because people with dog allergies react differently to different dogs, those people may be allergic to certain dogs and not allergic to other types of dogs. No one breed of dog, however, is hypoallergenic.

- ✔ Single-coated dog breeds tend to shed less, but they still lose hair and produce dander.

- ✔ A crossbred dog like a Labradoodle may not be shed free — genetics can produce a full range from dogs that don't shed much to dogs that shed a bundle.

If you find that you have dog allergies, you need to work with an allergist, so that you're better able to cope with the grooming tasks you need to perform on your dog. If the allergist says that you shouldn't have a dog, you can always argue that he doesn't tell people not to have trees or grass in their yards when they're allergic to them, so why can't he work toward making you more comfortable around your dog?

That said, some types of dogs seem to be more easily tolerated by people with allergies. If you're allergic and trying to find the type of dog your allergies can tolerate, your best bet before purchasing one is to visit the home of someone who has the kind of dog you're considering to find out whether you can tolerate it at home.

Lamb and Rice Is a Good Food for Coats

The lamb-and-rice/good coat myth is interesting in that it started when vets prescribed lamb-and-rice–based dog foods for dogs whose owners were looking for relief from skin allergies for their pooches. At the time, the lamb-and-rice diet was a novel protein and carbohydrate source to which dogs were not allergic. Suddenly hot spots disappeared, and all the skin conditions went away. So, breeders and pet owners began believing the lamb-and-rice combination was the miracle dog food for coats. Dog food companies naturally complied with the demand, providing lamb-and-rice dog food for consumers.

A lamb-and-rice diet isn't any better for your dog than any other dog food. The reason it worked so well at the beginning was because the ingredients were novel; dogs never had eaten the lamb and rice in tandem before and therefore hadn't had a chance to develop any allergies to it. Guess what happened when lamb and rice went mainstream? Dogs were fed the lamb-and-rice diet for generations, and they developed allergies to it. So the magic that was in lamb and rice is no more. It no longer is a hypoallergenic diet.

Tomato Juice Gets Rid of Skunk Odor

If you've checked out Chapter 15, you know the answer to this one. If you wash a skunked dog in tomato juice, you get a stinky pink dog!

A skunk's spray is made up of a number of stinky compounds called thiols. *Thiols* are the same things that make decomposing flesh and dog poop stink, but those thiols aren't necessarily the same ones that are in skunk spray. Skunks usually produce about two tablespoons of the stuff — enough for six quick shots. If a skunk actually dumps all of it, the skunk needs a week or two to recharge.

Most people think the tomato juice bath works because eventually the stench assaults your nostrils so badly that your brain actually starts getting used to it. So after several minutes of stink, the skunk smell really won't smell as bad as it does to someone who has just been exposed to it.

You can successfully handle skunk spray only in a handful of ways, and they're covered in Chapter 15.

Dogs Naturally Have Bad Breath

Your dog doesn't have to have bad breath. The myth that surrounds doggie breath stems from people who think that dogs are naturally supposed to have bad breath — and that just isn't true. Your dog's breath needs to be kissably sweet, except, of course, when he's been eating something vile or disgusting.

If your dog's breath constantly stinks like a sewer, it can be a more serious problem — tooth and gum troubles. It may be that your dog has an even more serious problem — like oral cancer. So when you detect a constant odor, it's time for a trip to the vet for a checkup.

Raw Egg Is Good for Your Dog's Coat

Here's another old wives' tale: Giving your dog a raw egg is good for his coat. Yes, eggs are great protein sources and full of vitamins and minerals, so nothing is wrong with treating your dog to an egg from time to time, but raw egg contains raw egg whites, which can cause a biotin deficiency, which, in turn, can cause hair loss, among other things.

When you cook an egg, you make the egg white safe for doggie consumption, and it no longer binds with biotin. You can give your dog a cooked egg as a wonderful treat anytime, but saying that it's better than having a balanced diet is ridiculous. You can do more for your dog's coat by feeding him a balanced diet.

Never, Ever Shave Your Dog's Coat

This myth is one of the partially true ones. When you shave a dog, you expose the skin to the elements and leave it unprotected. For example, for long-coated and double-coated dogs, shaving your dog's coat in the summer isn't a great idea. Those dogs normally shed out their undercoats, leaving the top coat for protection against the sun's rays, and besides, the area from which the undercoat is missing actually helps cool the dog against the hot sun.

However, shaving a dog's coat sometimes is warranted — no way around it. These times include:

> ✔ If the breed standard calls for shaving the dog. Poodles and other breeds fall into this category. The types of coats they have require such grooming.

> ✔ When dreadful mats occur throughout the dog's hair. In some cases, the dog has to be shaved to enable a healthy new coat to grow in.

> ✔ Skin conditions or other problems arise. You may be forced to shave your dog's coat so you can treat these problems.

When you do have to shave a dog, you need to realize that what you're doing is taking away his natural protection. As a result, you'll have to add back that protection in the form of something like a T-shirt or sweater depending on the climate. *Note:* Dogs can get sunburned, so if you have a bare dog, you're going to have to use a good quality sunscreen (either one intended for humans or one developed for dogs, which you can find online).

Shaving a dog isn't the best thing in the world for the dog, but with a little care you can make it work.

Garlic and Brewer's Yeast Get Rid of Fleas

A myth out there that purports that garlic and brewer's yeast get rid of fleas is so wrong, it's almost funny. Brewer's yeast has plenty of B-vitamins and other good things for your dog, but it's completely wrong when it comes to controlling fleas. Oddly enough, when companies that make flea and tick products want to grow fleas, they do it in brewer's yeast — so brewer's yeast doesn't kill fleas at all.

What about garlic? Well, when it comes to blood suckers, garlic may keep away vampires (the science is inconclusive), but it won't do much for fleas. A proven systemic flea-control product (either topical or oral) works much better and more efficiently than these old wives' tale cures.

Never Use Human Shampoo on Dogs

This myth also is another of the partially true ones. Using human shampoos on dogs isn't a great idea, because they're not formulated for a dog's coat. However, in a pinch when you have nothing else, you can use human shampoo on a dog's coat. Just make sure that it isn't medicated and that you rinse it really well. Using a human shampoo all the time can dry out a dog's coat, but once in a while isn't going to hurt anything. If you're faced with a dirty dog and no doggie shampoo, go ahead and use your own. Just don't get in the habit of using it all the time.

A Dog's Saliva Has Fewer Germs than a Human's

You probably heard that dogs' mouths are cleaner than human mouths a million times while growing up — I know I did. The myth generally goes something like this: A dog's saliva somehow has healing properties and has fewer germs than a human mouth. I remember people sagely claiming this one while a dog was licking a wound on his leg or maybe licking a kid's face.

Well, I have news for you. It isn't true.

Now before all you dog lovers throw rocks at my house and flood my mailbox with hate mail, let me explain. In most cases, dogs don't carry the same diseases that humans do, so in that respect, their saliva is somewhat safer. But dogs have plenty of bacteria and other germs in their mouths that can cause an infection as bad as anything else. In fact, dogs have an enzyme in their mouths that actually breaks down skin tissue. I've been bitten enough times to know that the first thing the doctor worries about in a dog bite is infection. Left untreated, a dog bite can cause a serious infection called *cellulitis*. One untreated bite I suffered caused my finger to swell up twice its normal size, and I needed serious treatment that included antibiotics and painful hydrogen peroxide soaks.

Veterinarians who treat cuts on any dog will tell you to prevent your dog from licking his wounds. In fact, the vet will put an Elizabethan collar (E-collar) on your dog to prevent him from licking his wounds and keep him from getting infected.

You may wonder where the dog saliva myth came from. I do, too. I'm guessing that in the old days before pet owners understood about keeping wounds clean, they watched dogs clean their wounds. The dogs probably did a better job of cleaning their wounds than their human counterparts, who perhaps didn't clean their wounds, which then became infected. So somebody decided that dogs just naturally did better because of their saliva. When faced with a dirty wound or at least one with no dirt in it, the saliva probably was better than nothing, and the enzyme within the dog's mouth probably helped get rid of the bad stuff in the wound. But in a modern age of veterinary medicine, leave the licking to face washes and not to trying to heal a wound or skin condition.

Chapter 21

Ten Timesaving Grooming Tips

In This Chapter

▶ Making grooming easy for you

▶ Getting around certain grooming problems

Grooming is time-consuming — there's no doubt about it. Lucky for you, I've got some handy tricks you can use to speed up the time you spend on grooming your dog.

The tips that I give you in this chapter are little tricks of the grooming trade that I've picked up through the years that I love being able to share with you. The tips focus on grooming your pet; if you want tips for grooming your dog especially for the show ring, check out Chapter 18.

Use No-Rinse Shampoo for Touchups

You've groomed your dog to perfection, but now your dog has pooped and left something hanging around behind. Or maybe he's gone through the mud or picked up some dirt — from where, you don't know. What to do? What to do?

Someone must've had this problem right before his or her in-laws arrived for a visit, because plenty of no-rinse shampoos (often called *blue shampoo* because of its color) are available for you to use to clean small areas of your dog's coat in a pinch.

Simply use a sponge or paper towels to wet, apply the no-rinse shampoo, and scrub the affected area clean. Then you can use your comb or slicker brush to puff-up the hair so it dries (or use a doggie blow-dryer).

Keep a Rubber Basin Handy for Quick Cleanups

If you don't already have a portable rubber sink or basin (like the kind people use to use while doing dishes by hand), buy one! It's perfect for doing messy jobs like spot cleanings and clippings, and it localizes the mess and reduces the need for cleanup.

Having a rubber basin around is good when you have to clean off your dog's paws, for example. You can pour blue shampoo or water and some regular doggie shampoo in it and stick your dog's feet in, washing them one at a time — if need be. For small dogs, the rubber sink also serves as an emergency wash basin.

You can put a small dog in the basin when you're clipping his coat. Doing so helps contain and capture the falling hair as it comes off. If your dog is larger, you can use your rubber basin as a catch-all as you groom your dog from one section to the next.

The basin also makes a handy-dandy catch-all for storing all of your quick cleanup supplies.

Grind Rather Than Clip Your Dog's Nails

So your dog hates nail clippers. One solution that a breeder suggests is using a nail grinder (similar to a Dremel rotary tool) on your dog's toenails. (I don't know why some dogs prefer grinding to clipping, they just do.) A bonus is that you don't have to file rough edges.

Two caveats:

- Beware that you can grind too much. A friend who is a veterinarian told me how a client overused her grinder and ground her dog's nails too far, eventually causing a serious infection. She ground the nails into the quick, and the grinder cauterized the bleeding nails, so the owner wasn't alerted to the problem. The infection passed from the grinder into the nails and into the dog's bloodstream. Regardless of how you trim your dog's nails, always be mindful of where the quick is.

- Grinders can get caught in your dog's hair and rip it out. Tools made especially for grinding dog's nails are available. These grinders automatically stop when they get caught in the dog's hair — before they rip it out.

Brush Regularly to Keep Fido's Breath Fresh and Teeth Clean

If your dog has bad breath and hasn't eaten anything rancid (like poop), you need to schedule an appointment with the veterinarian, because bad breath is a sign of more serious problems, including gingivitis or a bad tooth. In some cases, it's a sign of a more serious disease, like cancer.

In any event, you need to brush your dog's teeth at least once a week (preferably every day) and give him good toys made to clean his teeth — always. My dogs like hard rubber and nylon toys that have nubs or grooves on them for teeth cleaning. You can add a bit of doggie toothpaste to help keep them clean between brushings.

Employ Snoods and Hoods to Keep Clean

Many long-haired dogs experience problems with keeping their beautiful coats clean. Pet and show dog owners have come up with a solution called a snood. A *snood* is a type of wrap-around cloth that keeps the dog's ears and hair from getting dirty. You can purchase or make your own snoods by sewing together some stretch fabric to fit around your dog's neck.

If you're concerned about your dog's legs getting icky with under brush or piddle, you can either sew some simple leg protectors that wrap around your dog's hind legs or find some inexpensive stretch socks and snip the toes out of them so you can slide them over your dog's legs. You obviously must gauge the size of the sock to your dog's legs. You can buy leg cuffs like these at pet supply stores; they prevent male dogs from wetting on themselves and cover Poodle *bracelets,* the unclipped fur around that breed's feet.

You can also prevent long hair from dragging along the ground when your pooch goes outside for a potty or play break. Simply wrap a towel or cloth loosely around your dog's waist and clip the ends of the towel together with a potato chip bag clip (found where kitchen supplies are sold). Use the small bag clips and be careful not to catch any of the dog's hair or skin in them.

Keep Your Pooch in a Pet Cut

Although you should never be in a hurry while clipping your dog's coat, you may be looking for the best way to tidy up his fur coat without much hassle. Use the pet cut that I describe in Chapter 7 for occasionally cleaning up or trimming your dog's coat between major clippings.

Before you do that, however, invest in some snap-on guide combs for your clippers. Using guide combs is an easy way to make sure you have an even cut without much muss or fuss. Choose the hair length you want, snap the guide onto your clippers, and you're off!

Add Beautiful Shine to Your Dog's Coat

Is your dog's coat dull and drab? If you have a dog with a short coat, you can perk it up with an oil-based coat conditioner. Sometimes lanolin or mink oil works well. Spread a small amount in your palms and rub them together before rubbing your hands all over your dog's coat. Then, finish up with a hound glove, which is a grooming mitt for short-coated dogs (see Chapter 3).

If your dog's coat is long, spray the conditioner liberally throughout the hair and then comb or brush it through the coat.

Use common sense when applying conditioner. Be sure to use a conditioner that's made for your dog's coat, and check the package for recommendations on its use. There is such a thing as too much, particularly with regard to spray conditioners. You can overspray and cause a big mess, because it can streak or stain clothing or furnishings if your dog likes to rub up against them.

Enjoy a Refreshing Blast

Sometimes your dog doesn't, well, smell like a rose. When you can't bathe him, or company is due to arrive any minute, you can make him smell good anyway by using any one of the doggie scents sold at pet supply stores. Bodifier and coat dressing often work in a pinch, too. This quick fix for a smelly dog won't get your dog clean, but it will make him a little nicer to be around.

Always follow label directions. Don't spray in the face or near the eyes of your dog. When applying any products to your dog's face (if the product is safe for that purpose), first spray it on a cloth and then gently wipe around your dog's head, avoiding the eyes, nose, and mouth. ***Note:*** Scents, bodifiers, and coat dressing will do nothing for skunk odor. Check out Chapter 15 for how to get rid of that funky problem.

Perform a Quick Hair Pickup

After you clean your dog, you may wonder how to clean up all that dog hair. Have no fear; pet-hair pickups can help you. Try using the rollers equipped with two-sided tape rather than the ones that you have to rinse to clean and reactivate. My own experience has been that the rinse-and-use rollers lose their stickiness after a while, so it's better to go with the more reliable peel-off, tape-type rollers.

Substitute in a Pinch

What happens if you don't have the right shampoo and conditioner for your kind of dog? Can you substitute other kinds?

In a pinch, yes. You don't want to use other shampoos and conditioners that aren't meant for dogs too often because they also don't have the proper pH-balance for their coats. You can occasionally substitute the following:

- ✔ Human shampoo for dog shampoo.

- ✔ Human conditioner for dog conditioner.

- ✔ Plain Ivory or Dawn hand-dishwashing soap for dog shampoo.

   Don't use any other dishwashing soap except plain Ivory or Dawn hand-dishwashing soap on your dog's coat, and when you do, use it sparingly.

- ✔ A blow-dryer intended for human hair as long as it has a "no-heat" setting, which can be used as a substitute for a dog blow-dryer.

Chapter 22

Ten Best Ways to Make Grooming a Pleasant Experience

In This Chapter

▶ Making grooming easy for you

▶ Grooming your dog in comfort

▶ Settling into an enjoyable time for dog and groomer alike

*Y*ou may not believe it, but I'm here to tell you that grooming can be a fun time for you *and* your dog. You have plenty of tricks at your disposal, so in this chapter, I explain some of them and show you how you can make grooming fun and enjoyable (or at least tolerable) for you and your dog.

Getting into a Grooming Routine

Everyone complains about being in a rut. But some ruts actually can be good, especially when it comes to grooming. You see, dogs love routine, and when it comes to discovering what to expect from their owners, they're masters at it. That should tell you right away that today you need to start a grooming routine. Every day at the same time, plan to do a grooming task, such as brushing out your dog's coat, brushing his teeth, clipping his nails — whatever needs to be done.

Your grooming tasks don't have to be major productions, like a full brush out, unless, of course, that's what's scheduled in your routine. Maybe you only need to clean your dog's ears or brush his teeth. Whatever the case, if you establish a daily grooming routine, your dog will come to expect something every day at that time, and if you make those sessions fun (see the suggestions later in this chapter), your dog actually will enjoy them, too.

Pick up a white-board calendar and mark the grooming task you're going to do each day. That's right, schedule those tasks, so you know exactly what you'll be doing and when. Then just do it. Here's a sample week from my grooming calendar that you can use as a model:

- ✔ Monday — Brush out Mishka
- ✔ Tuesday — Brush Mishka's teeth
- ✔ Wednesday — Clean Mishka's ears
- ✔ Thursday — Brush out Mishka
- ✔ Friday — Clip Mishka's toenails
- ✔ Saturday — Brush Mishka's teeth
- ✔ Sunday — Choose a task that needs to be performed

Depending on whether you have a hairless dog or one who needs to be clipped or stripped, your schedule is likely to be different than my sample calendar. If, for example, you have a corded breed (or a breed with doggie dreadlocks such as the Komondor or Puli), one of your daily tasks will be separating the cords rather than brushing. Similarly, if you have a dog who is *blowing coat,* or shedding, every day may be a brush-out day.

Be sure to keep a log of your grooming activities (a diary) every day, so you always know not only what you did that day, but also how your dog behaved and how much work you were able to do. Chapter 1 provides a sample diary to get you started.

Starting Out Small and Building Up

Rome wasn't built in a day, or so the saying goes. Most dogs (and owners) are resistant to grooming, because it takes so darn long. Instead of putting you and your dog through a marathon grooming session, try starting out small.

Maybe your dog hates having his toenails trimmed. Try this: Trim toenails on only one paw today and maybe brush your dog a bit, and then tomorrow, do the next paw and brush him a bit more. As your dog becomes more tolerant of grooming, you can try doing two paws or adding more brushing. Otherwise, the longer you take, the more nervous your dog will become and the worse the struggle.

Taking Your Time While Grooming

One reason some dogs hate grooming is the way their owners handle them. Do you just start grabbing your dog and running a brush or comb through his fur, grumbling all the while that you just don't have time to do this? Think about it. If you rush through grooming, your dog will look at it as a time when you're hurried and possibly upset. Dogs pick up on your emotions pretty well. If you're in a hurry to get done, the dog's going to be in a hurry to get the heck out of there.

Here's another more important reason to take your time while grooming your dog: When you get in a hurry, you make mistakes, and some mistakes can be downright dangerous for your dog — like being in a hurry with clippers or with scissors. Any time you cause pain to your dog (such as clipping a toenail too short and cutting a quick), you solidify his attitude about not wanting to be groomed in whatever way you caused him pain.

Choose a time to groom your dog when you're not in a rush — preferably later in the day when you're done with work or school, a time when you don't have any real commitments. Choosing a time later in the day also is good because that's when your dog is a bit tired out and less likely to struggle with you.

Using the Right Equipment

Use the right tools for the job. (Yes, I'm using up all my clichés in this chapter!) Your grooming sessions will go much easier and smoother when you use the right equipment — not the worthless junk that someone gave to you as a hand-me-down. Although you can use any equipment that still is in good condition as long as it works with your particular dog, you should never use any equipment that just won't get the job done.

For example, you don't want to use a pin brush or a hound glove on long-coated or double-coated dogs, because they're not intended for use with dogs that have those kinds of coats.

Oddly enough most owners insist on not getting a grooming table. Yes, the cost of a grooming table can be somewhat daunting — but so is the cost of visits to the doctor or chiropractor when you've wrenched your back from bending over too much. Do yourself a favor and get one.

Having all the right equipment in the world won't help one iota unless what you're using is within reach. Make sure your equipment is ready to go and within reach of the grooming area before you start grooming.

Controlling the Situation at All Times

Prior planning prevents poor performance. In the case of grooming, that means you need to be in control of your dog at all times during the grooming session. You don't want to chase your dog all around the house while trying to brush him or give him a bath.

That means crating your dog when you're unable to watch him and keeping him still with aids like a tub noose when you're washing him or a head noose when you're grooming him on the grooming table.

Restraining a dog for safety's sake

If you're fearful of being bitten during certain procedures, sometimes a quick muzzle, groomer's muzzle, or veterinarian's muzzle is the safest thing for you to use with your dog. I don't necessarily recommend muzzling your dog, but if you have no choice other than being bitten, you may have to use one. Chapter 17 explains how to muzzle your dog.

If your dog continues to show aggressive tendencies, have her examined by a veterinarian to determine whether a health issue is at the root of the problem. If not, you can consult a dog behaviorist or trainer to evaluate your dog. You can find behaviorists and trainers who can help you at the Association of Pet Dog Trainers (APDT) at www.apdt.com.

Never leave a dog unattended in a noose at any time. Your dog can be strangled if left alone in one of them.

Check out Chapter 4 for more information about showing your dog how to accept grooming.

Sparing Yourself the Agony: Ergonomics

Does your back hurt when you wash or brush your dog? Are your hands aching when you comb? *Ergonomics* is a fancy word that came into fashion in the 1980s when scientists in the workplace discovered that certain positions while sitting or standing and doing work are less prone to repetitive injury than others. Likewise, those same scientists discovered certain shapes for tools that fit better in your hands and cause less fatigue than others.

If you suffer from carpal tunnel, thoracic outlet, arthritis, fibromyalgia, back pain, or any other condition that severely affects your hands or back, consider buying tools that are ergonomically designed. Although they may be a bit more expensive, they're well worth it.

If you suffer from back pain (or do not want to suffer from back pain in the future), consider these items:

- **A raised groomer's tub:** Yes, a raised tub can be pretty expensive, but then how expensive is a bad back?

- **Grooming steps or ramps:** Steps or a ramp not only help get your dog to and from the tub or grooming table, they keep you from having to lift your dog into and onto them.

✔ **Nonslip cushion mat:** If you have hard floors, try putting a nonslip cushion mat on the floor where you walk or stand. Doing so helps with leg, hip, and back fatigue.

✔ **A grooming table:** Yes, I've belabored this point. I'll stop now, but be sure to see Chapter 3.

Making Your Dog Comfortable

Do you like going to the dentist? Unless your dentist is one of those who can guarantee a painless visit, the answer is probably, "No." Why? Well, besides the possibility of having your teeth drilled, chances are you aren't comfortable going to the dentist. When you groom your dog, he often isn't comfortable with what you're doing and probably is thinking, *"You're going to comb around my WHAT?"* or *"Don't you dare get near my paws with that clippie thing!"* The upshot: Make your dog as comfortable as possible during each grooming session.

Temperature is important when performing any type of grooming procedure. Being too cold or too warm makes any dog upset. Be sure the temperature is just right for the air in the room *and* the water in the tub. Although *you* may find a hot bath relaxing, your pooch won't; it's too hot. Pour a tepid bath (just warm to the touch). Dogs don't like cold showers, either.

So, the trick is to make your dog as comfortable as possible with the procedures and with where he sits and lies.

To make grooming a pleasant experience, try:

✔ Picking up some inexpensive rubber-backed rugs (nonskid, made for bathrooms) at a bath store or even the local discount department store. Appearance doesn't matter because you're going to lay them on your grooming table and in your dog's crate. (Okay, maybe it does matter.)

✔ Giving your dog toys while he waits for you or even while you're grooming him. Some dogs will even chew on those soft, plush toys while they're being groomed. The toy helps ease his fears quite a bit.

✔ Caring for your dog's needs before, after, and while grooming him. Your dog may be thirsty, hungry, or need to relieve himself. Nothing is worse than waiting for someone to finish working on you when you have to pee.

✔ Keeping bath temperatures tepid and keepng the room temperatures slightly warmer than usual while bathing your dog. Keep him warm and away from drafts, especially in cooler weather.

✔ Keeping your dog cool in the summer. Dogs can overheat easily.

Showing Your Dog that Grooming Is Fun

After reading that headline you're probably thinking, "Yeah, right. How can a dog enjoy grooming?" Well, believe it or not, many dogs do enjoy it. They enjoy the attention they get from their owners and love being fussed over.

Dogs that love grooming aren't born that way; they're made. They've been brought up being groomed regularly and taught that grooming is a special time with their owners.

You can try the following to make your grooming more fun:

- ✔ Starting your grooming session after a vigorous play session — when your dog is a bit tired.

- ✔ Giving your dog plenty of pets and praise and a treat or two while you're working on him.

- ✔ Avoiding anything that may cause pain. It takes only one painful experience to make him change his mind about grooming.

- ✔ Giving him plenty of praise and perhaps a special treat or toy when you're done with grooming your dog.

Procrastination = Grooming Nightmare

Maintaining a well-groomed coat is easier than trying to groom out a tangled mess — any professional groomer will tell you that. Keep your dog's coat well groomed (make a grooming schedule like the one suggested in the earlier section on "Getting into a Grooming Routine"), and you'll never have a grooming nightmare. Even if you have a schedule that has you grooming your dog once or twice a week, that's better than not doing it at all.

If you've been procrastinating, the best thing is to have a professional groomer take care of the problem first so your dog has a coat you can maintain.

Don't Worry, Be Happy: Keeping It Upbeat

Lastly, keep your grooming sessions positive and upbeat. Being angry and grumpy makes for an unhappy dog and only frustrates you. Never groom your dog while angry or frustrated.

If you can't be upbeat while grooming, skip the grooming session for today and try tomorrow or just do a quick brush over or quick exam. Then give your dog a treat for being so good and curl up on the couch with him with some ice cream and watch your favorite movie. I guarantee doing so will improve your outlook and make for a better grooming session tomorrow.

Appendix

Grooming Resources

So you're in the market for some supplies with which to start grooming your dog. This Appendix is the right place to look. It provides you with lists of Web sites where you can find information about grooming in general (and grooming education and certification specifically) and about where to find grooming products at good prices. If that isn't enough, I also provide you with a list of books you can check out for additional information.

Web Sites

You can check out the Web sites that I list in the sections that follow regardless of whether you merely want only to groom your own dog or you're leaning toward turning pro and using your skills to groom other folks' best friends.

Grooming your own dog

If you're looking for information about grooming your own dog or finding someone to do it for you, be sure to check these two Web sites:

- **Petgroomer.com (www.petgroomer.com):** Petgroomer.com is a great Internet resource guide for folks whose focus mainly is on grooming their own dogs.
- **Find A Groomer Directory (www.findagroomer.com):** This site helps you locate a groomer in your area via the Internet.

Grooming for yourself and others

Even if you're only grooming your own dog, you can find some really cool pointers from Web sites aimed at professional groomers. Nevertheless, the sites in the list that follows focus on providing groomers who already are working professionally or the ones who are looking to turn pro:

- **Intergroom (`www.intergroom.com`):** This annual international confer-
  ence for groomers features educational opportunities and seminars, a
  trade show, and certification information and opportunities.

  Intergroom, Inc.
  c/o Christine DeFilippo
  76 Carol Drive
  Dedham, MA, USA 02026
  Phone: 781-326-3376
  E-mail: `intergroom@msn.com`

- **National Dog Groomers Association of America (NDGAA —
  `www.nationaldoggroomers.com`):** NDGAA is a national association
  founded in 1969 for specifically for dog groomers. It provides educational and certification opportunities.

  NDGAA
  P.O. Box 101
  Clark, PA 16113
  Phone: 724-962-2711
  E-mail: `ndga@nationaldoggroomers.com`

- **International Society of Canine Cosmetologists (ISCC — `www.
  petstylist.com`):** ISCC offers opportunities for education and
  certification.

  ISCC
  18710 Kelly Blvd.
  Dallas, TX 75287
  Phone: 972-414-9715
  E-mail: `iscc@petstylist.com`

- **International Pet Groomers (IPG — `www.ipgcmg.org`):** IPG offers
  opportunities for education and certification.

  IPG
  c/o Judy Kurpiel, CMG
  IPG President
  120 Turner Avenue
  Elk Grove Village, IL 60007
  Phone: 847-758-1938
  E-mail: `jkurpiel@ipgcmg.org`

Grooming Supplies

Need grooming supplies? A bunch of suppliers and manufacturers — retail
and wholesale, mail-order and Internet — are out there at your beck and call,
ready to provide for your every grooming need regardless of your status as a
groomer, whether an amateur or a professional. Check out these suppliers:

- **Petedge (www.petedge.com):** Petedge is a wholesale distributor and manufacturer of groomer and other pet supplies. Supplies can be ordered either over the Internet or by mail-order.

  Petedge
  P. O. Box 128
  Topsfield, MA 01983
  Phone: 978-887-2368
  Toll-free: 800-627-2232

- **Groomer's Choice Pet Products (www.groomerschoice.com):** Order your groomer supplies through Groomer's Choice Pet Products either by mail-order or over the Internet.

  Groomer's Choice
  2205 E. 39th Street N, Suite 300
  Sioux Falls, SD 57104
  Phone: 605-334-3886
  Toll-free: 888-364-6242

- **GroomStar (www.groomstar.com):** Grooming supply purchases from GroomStar can be made either by mail-order or over the Internet.

  GroomStar
  2222 Academy Place
  Colorado Springs, CO 80909
  Phone: 719-570-1113
  Toll-free: 866-570-1113

- **The Shampoo Lady (www.theshampoolady.com):** The Shampoo Lady sells shampoos and other grooming supplies at wholesale prices

  The Shampoo Lady
  9616 NE 227th Avenue
  Vancouver, WA 98682
  Phone: 360-944-7477
  Toll-free: 877-476-6673

- **American Pet Pro (www.americanpetpro.com):** American Pet Pro offers grooming supplies over the Internet and by mail-order.

  American Pet Pro
  2313 American Avenue
  Hayward, CA 94545
  Phone: 510-732-2781
  Toll-free: 800-543-9480

- **Groomtech (www.groomtech.com):** Groomtech is a groomer's supply house with mail-order and Internet access.

  Groomtech
  555 Saturn Blvd., #436
  San Diego, CA 92154
  Phone: 800-898-4766
  Toll-free: 800-898-4766

- **J-B Wholesale Pet Supplies (`www.jbpet.com`):** J-B Wholesale offers discount pet supplies by mail-order or through the Internet.

  J-B Wholesale Pet Supplies
  5 Raritan Road
  Oakland, NJ 07436
  Phone: 800-526-0388

- **KV Vet Supply (`www.kvvet.com`):** KV Vet Supply provides discount pet and veterinary supplies, offering convenient mail-order and Internet ordering options.

  KV Vet
  3190 N Road
  PO Box 245
  David City, NE 68632
  Phone: 402-367-6047
  Toll-free: 800-423-8211

- **Petsupplies4less.com (`www.petsupplies4less.com`):** Discount pet supplies are available by mail-order or through the Internet from Petsupplies4less.com.

  Petsupplies4less.com
  713 4th Street
  Fairbury, NE 68352
  Toll-free: 877-813-PETS (877-813-7387)

- **UPCO (`www.upco.com`):** Founded in 1952, UPCO is a discount pet supply company. You can place orders through UPCO via mail-order or the Internet.

  UPCO
  3705 Pear Street
  P.O. Box 969
  St. Joseph, MO 64502
  Phone: 816-233-8800
  Toll-free: 800-254-8726

- **Jeffers Pet and Equine Supplies (`www.jefferspet.com`):** Founded in 1975, Jeffers is a privately owned catalog and eCommerce animal health supply retailer.

  Jeffers
  P.O. Box 100
  Dothan, AL 36302
  Phone: 334-793-6257
  Toll-free: 800-JEFFERS (800-533-3377)

Grooming and Dog-Related Magazines

Whether you want to subscribe or just pick up a copy at your local news-stand, here are some great dog-related magazines that can help you keep up to date with all of the innovations in grooming:

- ✔ *AKC Gazette* (`www.akc.org/pubs/index.cfm`): This magazine is published by the AKC and covers all sorts of topics on purebred dogs.

  AKC Gazette
  51 Madison Ave.
  New York, NY 10010
  Phone: 800-533-7323

- ✔ *Dog Fancy* (`www.dogfancy.com`): This magazine's articles cater to the pet owner (both purebred and mixed breed).

  Dog Fancy
  P.O. Box 53264
  Boulder, CO 80322-3264

- ✔ *Dog World* (`www.dogworldmag.com`): This magazine caters to both pet and show dog owners. It includes good health and grooming articles.

  Dog World
  P.O. Box 56240
  Boulder, CO 80323-6240

- ✔ *Groom and Board:* This magazine focuses on the professional groomer.

  HH Backer and Associates
  200 South Michigan Avenue, Suite 840
  Chicago, IL 60604
  Phone: 312-663-4040
  E-mail: `grmbrd@aol.com`

- ✔ *Groomer to Groomer* (`www.groomertogroomer.com`): This is another groomer magazine aimed toward the professional.

  Barkleigh Productions, Inc.
  6 State Road 113
  Mechanicsburg, PA 17050
  Phone: 717-691-3388

Other Useful Reference Books

As if *Dog Grooming For Dummies* isn't enough, here are some other books that can help answer any questions you may have about grooming in general or specifically:

- *All-Breed Dog Grooming* (TFH Publications, 1987): This grooming reference covers different breeds.

- *Bring Me Home: Dogs Make Great Pets* by yours truly Margaret H. Bonham (Howell Book House, 2005): This book includes tons of useful information about getting and owning a dog, if I do say so myself.

- *Canine Terminology* by Harold R. Spira (Dogwise Publishing, 2001): This book does a great job of defining the dog.

- *Don't Shoot the Dog! The New Art of Teaching and Training* by Karen Pryor (Bantam Doubleday Dell, 1999): This is a good clicker training book.

- *K-9 Structure and Terminology* by Edward M. Gilbert, Jr., and Thelma R. Brown (Howell Book House, 1995): This book also helps define the dog.

- *Poodle Clipping and Grooming: The International Reference* by Shirlee Kalstone (Howell Book House, 2000): You got it – this is a great poodle clipping reference book.

- *The Complete Dog Book: Official Publication of The American Kennel Club,* 19th edition (Howell Book House, 1997): The book on AKC dog breeds.

- *The Complete Idiot's Guide to Dog Health and Nutrition* by yours truly Margaret H. Bonham and James M. Wingert (Alpha Books, 2001): An excellent reference on canine health and nutrition.

- *The Dog Owner's Home Veterinary Handbook,* 3rd edition, by James M. Giffin, MD, and Liisa D. Carlson, DVM, (Howell Book House, 2000): An excellent reference on dog health.

- *The Dog Repair Book* by Ruth B. James, DVM, (Alpine Press, 1990): Another excellent reference on dog health.

- *The Dry Dog Food Reference* by Howard D. Coffman (Pig Dog Press, 1995): This reference is hard to find and slightly outdated, but you can order it from the publisher if you're interested in the ingredients and nutritional content of dry dog food.

- *The Merck Veterinary Manual,* 8th edition, (Merck and Co, Inc., 1991): This is an excellent resource on dog health.

- *Ultimate Dog Grooming* by Eileen Geeson (Firefly Books, 2004): Another nice book on dog grooming.

Index

• K •

Notes

Notes

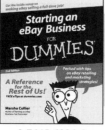

SPORTS, FITNESS, PARENTING, RELIGION & SPIRITUALITY

0-7645-5146-9

0-7645-5418-2

Also available:

- Adoption For Dummies
  0-7645-5488-3
- Basketball For Dummies
  0-7645-5248-1
- The Bible For Dummies
  0-7645-5296-1
- Buddhism For Dummies
  0-7645-5359-3
- Catholicism For Dummies
  0-7645-5391-7
- Hockey For Dummies
  0-7645-5228-7

- Judaism For Dummies
  0-7645-5299-6
- Martial Arts For Dummies
  0-7645-5358-5
- Pilates For Dummies
  0-7645-5397-6
- Religion For Dummies
  0-7645-5264-3
- Teaching Kids to Read For Dummies
  0-7645-4043-2
- Weight Training For Dummies
  0-7645-5168-X
- Yoga For Dummies
  0-7645-5117-5

TRAVEL

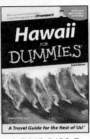

0-7645-5438-7

0-7645-5453-0

Also available:

- Alaska For Dummies
  0-7645-1761-9
- Arizona For Dummies
  0-7645-6938-4
- Cancún and the Yucatán For Dummies
  0-7645-2437-2
- Cruise Vacations For Dummies
  0-7645-6941-4
- Europe For Dummies
  0-7645-5456-5
- Ireland For Dummies
  0-7645-5455-7

- Las Vegas For Dummies
  0-7645-5448-4
- London For Dummies
  0-7645-4277-X
- New York City For Dummies
  0-7645-6945-7
- Paris For Dummies
  0-7645-5494-8
- RV Vacations For Dummies
  0-7645-5443-3
- Walt Disney World & Orlando For Dumm
  0-7645-6943-0

GRAPHICS, DESIGN & WEB DEVELOPMENT

0-7645-4345-8

0-7645-5589-8

Also available:

- Adobe Acrobat 6 PDF For Dummies
  0-7645-3760-1
- Building a Web Site For Dummies
  0-7645-7144-3
- Dreamweaver MX 2004 For Dummies
  0-7645-4342-3
- FrontPage 2003 For Dummies
  0-7645-3882-9
- HTML 4 For Dummies
  0-7645-1995-6
- Illustrator cs For Dummies
  0-7645-4084-X

- Macromedia Flash MX 2004 For Dumm
  0-7645-4358-X
- Photoshop 7 All-in-One Desk
  Reference For Dummies
  0-7645-1667-1
- Photoshop cs Timesaving Techniqu
  For Dummies
  0-7645-6782-9
- PHP 5 For Dummies
  0-7645-4166-8
- PowerPoint 2003 For Dummies
  0-7645-3908-6
- QuarkXPress 6 For Dummies
  0-7645-2593-X

NETWORKING, SECURITY, PROGRAMMING & DATABASES

0-7645-6852-3

0-7645-5784-X

Also available:

- A+ Certification For Dummies
  0-7645-4187-0
- Access 2003 All-in-One Desk
  Reference For Dummies
  0-7645-3988-4
- Beginning Programming For Dummies
  0-7645-4997-9
- C For Dummies
  0-7645-7068-4
- Firewalls For Dummies
  0-7645-4048-3
- Home Networking For Dummies
  0-7645-42796

- Network Security For Dummies
  0-7645-1679-5
- Networking For Dummies
  0-7645-1677-9
- TCP/IP For Dummies
  0-7645-1760-0
- VBA For Dummies
  0-7645-3989-2
- Wireless All In-One Desk Reference
  For Dummies
  0-7645-7496-5
- Wireless Home Networking For Dumm
  0-7645-3910-8

0-7645-6820-5 *†   0-7645-2566-2

Also available:

Alzheimer's For Dummies
0-7645-3899-3

Asthma For Dummies
0-7645-4233-8

Controlling Cholesterol For Dummies
0-7645-5440-9

Depression For Dummies
0-7645-3900-0

Dieting For Dummies
0-7645-4149-8

Fertility For Dummies
0-7645-2549-2

Fibromyalgia For Dummies
0-7645-5441-7

Improving Your Memory For Dummies
0-7645-5435-2

Pregnancy For Dummies †
0-7645-4483-7

Quitting Smoking For Dummies
0-7645-2629-4

Relationships For Dummies
0-7645-5384-4

Thyroid For Dummies
0-7645-5385-2

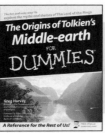

0-7645-5194-9   0-7645-4186-2

Also available:

Algebra For Dummies
0-7645-5325-9

British History For Dummies
0-7645-7021-8

Calculus For Dummies
0-7645-2498-4

English Grammar For Dummies
0-7645-5322-4

Forensics For Dummies
0-7645-5580-4

The GMAT For Dummies
0-7645-5251-1

Inglés Para Dummies
0-7645-5427-1

Italian For Dummies
0-7645-5196-5

Latin For Dummies
0-7645-5431-X

Lewis & Clark For Dummies
0-7645-2545-X

Research Papers For Dummies
0-7645-5426-3

The SAT I For Dummies
0-7645-7193-1

Science Fair Projects For Dummies
0-7645-5460-3

U.S. History For Dummies
0-7645-5249-X

Get smart @ dummies.com®

- **Find a full list of Dummies titles**
- **Look into loads of FREE on-site articles**
- **Sign up for FREE eTips e-mailed to you weekly**
- **See what other products carry the Dummies name**
- **Shop directly from the Dummies bookstore**
- **Enter to win new prizes every month!**

arate Canadian edition also available
arate U.K. edition also available

le wherever books are sold. For more information or to order direct: U.S. customers visit www.dummies.com or call 1-877-762-2974.
stomers visit www.wileyeurope.com or call 0800 243407. Canadian customers visit www.wiley.ca or call 1-800-567-4797.